comfort food fix

Ellie Krieger

Ellie Krieger

comfort food fix

Feel-Good Favorites Made Healthy

PHOTOGRAPHY BY QUENTIN BACON

WILEY

John Wiley & Sons, Inc.

Library of Congress Cataloging-in-Publication Data
Krieger, Ellie.
  Comfort food fix : feel-good favorites made healthy / Ellie
Krieger ; photography by Quentin Bacon.
     p. cm.
  Includes index.
  ISBN 978-0-470-60309-3 (cloth)
1. Comfort food. 2. Cookbooks. I. Title.
  TX714.K748 2011
  641.3--dc22
                                    2010046384

Printed in China
10 9 8 7 6 5 4 3 2 1

FOR THOM AND ISABELLA

120 213

TABLE OF **CONTENTS**

8 ACKNOWLEDGMENTS

10 INTRODUCTION

16 CHAPTER 1: BREAKFAST, BRUNCH, AND BAKERY

50 CHAPTER 2: SNACK AND STARTERS

92 CHAPTER 3: SOUPS AND SANDWICHES

126 CHAPTER 4: MEAT MAIN DISHES

158 CHAPTER 5: POULTRY MAIN DISHES

182 CHAPTER 6: SEAFOOD MAIN DISHES

202 CHAPTER 7: VEGETARIAN MAIN DISHES

218 CHAPTER 8: SIDES AND SALADS

254 CHAPTER 9: DESSERTS

298 INDEX

ACKNOWLEDGMENTS

Many talented people have put their extraordinary passion, skill and hard work into this book. I am grateful to have the opportunity to recognize them here.

THANK YOU

- Thom and Isabella, for being my heart's center and my most dedicated tasters
- Mom and Dad, Fran Wilder and Howard Krieger, for giving me comfort in countless ways and teaching me that if I put my mind to it, I can do anything.
- Robert Flutie and Hilary Polk Williams, for managing the big picture skillfully and creatively while also keeping track of the smallest details.
- Jane Dystel and Miriam Goderich, literary agents, and Marc Szafran, Esq., for your guidance, expertise, and support.
- Justin Schwartz, editor extraordinaire. You said it and I agree: "We make a great team."
- Adeena Sussman, for being wholeheartedly involved in this book and lending your talent to so many of the recipes from concept to development to styling.
- Chefs Molly Rundberg and Karen Ferries, RD, for your hard work, good company, and educated palates.
- Dani Koch MacKinnon, MS RD, for the precision and professionalism you brought to each and every nutrition analysis and comparison.
- Quentin Bacon photographer; Lori Powell food stylist; and Natasha Louise King, prop stylist, for stunning photos that truly capture the food's lusciousness and comfort factor. Lori, thanks also for your creative help with a number of the recipes themselves.
- Suzanne Katz, make-up artist, and Nicole Gulotta and Isabel Butel, wardrobe stylists, for helping me look my very best.
- Janell Vantrease and Jaclyn Rutigliano, publicists, for your flair, enthusiasm, organization, and persistence.
- All the folks at John Wiley and Sons who have dedicated so much to this book.
- Food Network, for all your support.

INTRODUCTION

Comfort food is the food that makes us feel good—satisfied, calm, cared for, and carefree. It's food that fills us up emotionally and physically, connecting us back to our first eating experiences that soothed hunger pangs and put us cozily in the arms of our caregiver. Finding comfort in food is a basic human experience.

But what you think of as comfort food is as unique as you are. If your heritage is Italian, risotto and lasagna might hit the spot for you, whereas if you're from down South, it is more likely grits and banana pudding. Chocolate chip cookies might stir warm, fuzzy memories of cooking with your grandma, or you might yearn for the apple crisp you had every year after your family's apple-picking outing. For some it's the "happy hour" wings and nachos that take the edge off a stressful day; for others it's creamy potato salad and coleslaw that bring them back to happy childhood moments.

What comforts you is shaped by your individual memories, experiences, and food traditions. It also depends on whether you are a man or woman. Studies show women tend to go for fuss-free, sweet snacks like cookies and chocolate while men like to be pampered with homemade soups and pasta dishes. There is chemistry involved too—foods rich in carbohydrates can trigger compounds in your brain that have a calming effect. No matter what you yearn for, you will find it here, where over 150 recipes cover every corner of the comfort food realm. In this book, you are sure to find your familiar feel-good favorites, as well as discover some delicious new ones.

Food is one of the most glorious and joyful parts of life and it should make you feel good, but not just while you are eating it. I believe food should provide well-being for the long term too. Unfortunately, while many typical comfort foods taste good, they leave us overstuffed and uncomfortable; and because they are laden with calories, sodium, and saturated fat, over time, they could make us feel quite awful, contributing to health issues like overweight, diabetes, and heart disease.

Happily, the dishes in this book are edible proof that you don't have to choose between your favorite foods and your well-being. That's because each recipe here is fixed, or redesigned, so it hits just the right comfort spot, giving you your "fix" without the unhealthy downsides. I don't rely on artificial ingredients and additives to achieve this, as many make-over cookbooks do. Rather, I use all-natural, real foods, employ a few simple techniques and swap-outs (see The 15 Fix Factors, following) and I follow my tried-and-true "Usually-Sometimes-Rarely" food philosophy.

By amplifying the healthiest "Usually" ingredients—fruit, vegetables, whole grains, low-fat dairy, nuts, seeds, beans, and healthy oils—and strategically using "Sometimes" foods like white flour or dark chocolate and even "Rarely" foods like cream, butter, and bacon, I am able to create recipes with all the full-flavored appeal you yearn for, but in a more balanced, healthier way. With these recipes, in addition to the immediate pleasure of taste, you get the lasting sense of well-being, knowing the food you and your loved ones are enjoying could contribute to a full, happy life down the road. Now that's what I call comforting.

ABOUT THE NUTRITION FACTS AND COMPARISONS

I don't cook with a calculator at hand to get a certain nutrient profile from a recipe. Rather, I set out to make a delicious dish with all the familiar tastes and textures you expect, using the principles laid out in my "Usually-Sometimes-Rarely" food philosophy. Incredibly, when I do so, the numbers tend to work out on their own. While I prefer to focus on the balance and quality of the food, numbers can be a helpful guide, so I have included the nutrition facts for each recipe, with the amount of calories, fat, protein, carbohydrate, fiber, cholesterol, and sodium in each serving. Since some fats are beneficial and others detrimental, I further break down fat into saturated (bad fat), monounsaturated, and polyunsaturated (good fats).

I have also listed good and excellent sources of essential nutrients in each recipe. To qualify as a good source, a serving must contain at least 10% of the Daily Value (the standard daily recommended intake) and to be called an excellent source it needs to provide at least 20% of the Daily Value. I encourage you not to get hung up on these values, but factor them in when planning your meals and let them serve as a reminder that vitamins and minerals are not just found in powders and pills as so many marketers would have us believe. They are bountifully present in delicious, wholesome foods.

Keep in mind that the nutrition information excludes optional ingredients or anything added to taste, and if there is a choice of ingredients, like "nonfat or low-fat yogurt," I always use the first option listed for the analysis.

FAT MATH

If you have an eye for numbers you might wonder why the breakdown of the individual types of fat (mono, poly, and sat) listed in my nutrition data usually add up to less than the total fat. For example, one recipe lists the fat content like this: Total Fat 11g (Mono 5g, Poly 2g, Sat 1g). The answer requires a little "Chemistry 101," so bear with me. I'll make it easy.

All fat molecules are made of three chains, called fatty acids, which are connected to a base. Picture a chain link fence where the poles holding it up are the base and the chain links are the fatty acids. There are different types of fatty acid chains– monounsaturated, polyunsaturated, and saturated —which give the fat its defining characteristics.

So here's where the numbers come in: the total fat is a measure of the entire "fence" (the poles and the chain links) whereas the mono, poly, and sat fat only pertain to the chain links. Also, there are trace amounts of naturally occurring trans fat (another kind of link) in many foods that is not reflected in my analysis. Plus, all the numbers are rounded to the nearest tenth, so that affects the total, too, however slightly. In all, that's why the mono, poly, and sat fats usually add up to less than the total fat.

To help put the nutrition breakdown in perspective, here are some daily total numbers to shoot for based on a 2,000-calorie diet (the maintenance calorie level for most moderately active women):

Total Fat: 65 g
(Saturated fat: 20 g or less, Monounsaturated fat: 25 g,
    Polyunsaturated fat: 20 g)
Protein: 90 g
Carbohydrate: 275 g
Fiber: 28 g or more
Cholesterol: 300 mg or less
Sodium: 2,300 mg or less

Regarding portion size, since everyone has different appetites and different caloric needs, there will always be a range of how many people a given recipe serves. But in order to do the nutrition analysis I had to pick one number, so I chose to base the serving sizes on amounts that would satisfy most moderately active women. If you are serving a group of high school football players, you are training for a marathon, or you are not as active as you'd like to be, adjust the portions accordingly.

You will notice that for each recipe there is a before and after comparison of calories, saturated fat, sodium, fiber, and cholesterol. I think you will be as startled as I was to see the huge differences a few small changes to a typical preparation can make. What those numbers don't reveal is that the "fixed" or "after" recipes are also considerably richer in nutrients and health-protecting antioxidants as well. Unless otherwise noted, the "before" recipe is analyzed from a common analogous recipe found on a popular Web site or in a classic cookbook. And I equalized the servings so the comparison you see reflects the same portion sizes, except in recipes where a serving is a whole item like a sandwich or a muffin. In those cases I compared them item for item.

THE 15 FIX FACTORS

1. Get Creamy, (Nearly) Creamlessly

Low-fat milk thickened with flour or cornstarch, along with canned evaporated milk, which is simply milk that has been cooked down to release some of its water, are ideal for velvety cream sauces, soups, and puddings. Sometimes I finish the dish with a little real cream, but just a touch. For salad dressings, dips, and dessert toppings, I cut half the mayo or whipped cream in a typical recipe with regular or Greek-style nonfat yogurt to get a rich, creamy base more healthfully. A small amount of reduced-fat sour cream also amps up the creamy factor beautifully with less fat but no artificial ingredients.

2. Go Halfsies

Substituting all egg whites in an egg dish robs it of its sunny yellow richness, and using only whole-wheat flour in brownies and cookies makes them too heavy and "healthy" tasting. Same goes for other substitutions. That's why I split the difference for most of my fixes. By using half whole eggs and half egg whites, or half whole-grain and half all-purpose flour, and so on, you get the taste and texture you yearn for while still improving the nutrition profile.

3. Un-Fry

You can achieve that craveable crispy texture that makes foods like fried chips, cutlets, and fish fingers so good by lightly breading if necessary, then tossing or spraying with oil and baking until crispy brown. For some dishes, like crab cakes, go for maximum crispiness by cooking them in a large nonstick skillet, which allows you to use just a tablespoon of oil.

4. Boost Veggies and Beans

Adding extra beans and veggies to dishes helps cut back on high-cal starches and meat without skimping on portions. It also provides volumes of important nutrients, color, taste, and texture. That's why I stir ribbons of zucchini into my fettuccine Alfredo, and add mushrooms to my meatloaf and beans to my beef tacos.

5. Bake Better

For tender, moist, lighter muffins and quickbreads, fruit and vegetable purees like applesauce, pumpkin puree, or carrot puree can substitute for up to half the fat typically used. Yogurt or almond butter work well to replace some of the butter in brownies and cookies.

6. Oil Well

I use antioxidant-rich extra-virgin olive oil for most dishes, but it doesn't take high heat well and its fruity flavor isn't right for every dish, so I use neutral-tasting canola oil for stir-fries and baking. Although these oils are healthy, all fat has about the same number of calories—120 per tablespoon—so use it sparingly. It just takes two teaspoons of oil to cook one onion—which is how so many recipes start—so measure it out instead of glug-glugging it in. And always keep some oil spray handy for oven frying and prepping baking pans.

7. Go Lo-So

The best way to rein in sodium is to start with good flavor by focusing on the freshest high-quality ingredients. When using canned staples like tomatoes, broth, or beans, buy no-salt-added or low-sodium, then season the dish generously with healthful ingredients like fresh herbs, citrus, aromatics like garlic and onions, and ground spices. Add salty ingredients like olives, capers, and cheese sparingly, and then just enough salt to bring all the flavors together in the end.

8. Be a Cheese Wiz

When it comes to cheeses like cheddar, Parmesan, and blue, I always use the real thing for full flavor and meltability. I just use less—which dramatically cuts fat, calories, and sodium—and I use it strategically. My rule: get the best quality and go for the most flavorful variety. So I always grate my own Parmesan and use extra-sharp cheddar instead of mild. And I put the cheese on top of the dish where you can see it all. This way has more mouthwatering visual impact than if you were to fold it in.

9. Sweeten Smartly

Whenever possible I use unrefined sweeteners like honey, maple syrup, and molasses. They give your blood sugar a more gentle rise than refined sugar does and they have some antioxidants and minerals to offer. Even so, they are all basically still high-calorie "added sugars," so I use them sparingly.

10. Add Whole Grain

Simply using whole-grain pasta, brown rice, or whole-grain bread instead of their refined white counterparts dramatically boosts the fiber, antioxidants, and minerals in a dish. Plus since they are digested more slowly, whole grains make you feel fuller longer. For baking I use whole-wheat pastry flour, which is extra-soft and tender so it provides whole-grain goodness but keeps things light and mild tasting.

11. Think CTP (Cut-Trim-Portion)

There's no need to give up red meat to eat healthy—meat is the center point of so many fabulous comfort foods. The key is to do it right: 1) Get the leanest cut. As a rule, cuts with the word "loin" or "round" in the name are leanest. Buy ground meat that's 90% lean or higher. 2) Trim the meat of all visible fat before cooking. 3) Cook sensible portions, 3 to 4 ounces, cooked, per person.

12. Keep it Real

Sometimes a little of the real thing goes a long way. That's why I would rather use two slices of real bacon in my BLT than four slices of turkey or tofu "bacon." And I believe there is no acceptable substitute for real dairy, full-fat whipped cream. I use these and other "Rarely" ingredients in minimum amounts for maximum impact.

13. Use a Bit of Butter

For most recipes I am able to substitute healthy oil or other ingredients for butter without sacrificing taste or texture, but for some, a bit of butter is necessary. Cookies, pie crusts, and mashed potatoes for example, all need a little butter to get their respective crumbly, flaky, or rich texture. But just a few tablespoons cover a whole batch of cookies or pie dough, and all you need is one tablespoon for really creamy mashed potatoes.

14. Cook to Keep Nutrients and Lose Fat

It's not only the ingredients you choose, but the way you cook them that makes a difference. I recommend steaming or microwaving vegetables instead of boiling them to preserve the water-soluble vitamins (like B vitamins and vitamin C), which leach out when immersed in liquid. Also, since the skin of produce has so many nutrients, I keep the skins on my potatoes, apples, cucumbers, and others whenever possible. And just as I cook to keep the nutrients, I also cook to eliminate fat by broiling or boiling higher-fat meats like chicken wings or lamb shank to render and discard the fat.

15. Repro-Portion

Most of us have grown accustomed to much bigger servings of food than we need. It doesn't matter how healthy the food, it's not good to eat too much of it. The servings I have noted for each recipe here are ample to satisfy most moderately active women. Once you adjust to your individual needs, get a grip on portions by measuring out your servings the first few times. This will give you a reference point for what a sensible amount really is.

chapter one

BREAKFAST, BRUNCH, AND BAKERY

Nothing helps ease the transition from cozy covers and PJs like a cinnamon-scented quick bread, berry-bursting muffin, maple-drizzled pancakes, or flaky-crusted quiche. Whichever you choose to make, the recipes here will surely help you face the day with a smile.

CORNED BEEF HASH AND EGGS

1½ pounds russet potatoes, cut into ¼-inch cubes

2 tablespoons olive oil

1 small onion, diced

2 green bell peppers, diced

6 ounces cooked corned beef (request thick-cut from your deli counter), cut into very small dice

½ teaspoon freshly ground black pepper

4 large eggs

Hot pepper sauce, such as Tabasco, for serving

This satisfying meat-and-potatoes breakfast is hearty without being heavy. The aromatic bed of potatoes, onions, peppers, and lip-smacking corned beef is cooked to crispy-brown perfection, then crowned with an egg just begging to be cut into. Finely dicing the corned beef and using one egg per person means there's meaty indulgence in every bite without overdoing it.

Place the potatoes in a large steamer basket fitted over a pot of boiling water. Cover and steam until the potatoes are tender, about 6 minutes. When the potatoes are cooked, reserve ½ cup of the steaming water.

Meanwhile, heat the oil in a large skillet over medium-high heat. Add the onion and bell peppers and cook, stirring, until the edges are browned, about 10 minutes. Reduce the heat to medium, add the potatoes, corned beef, and black pepper, and cook for an additional 10 minutes, stirring once after 5 minutes. Add the reserved potato cooking water and cook, not stirring, until the liquid is evaporated, the mixture is slightly moistened, and the bottom has developed a nice brown crust, about 10 minutes more.

Poach the eggs or cook them sunny-side up in a nonstick skillet. Divide the hash among four plates and top each serving with an egg. Serve with hot pepper sauce.

Makes 4 servings

SERVING SIZE 1 cup hash and 1 egg
PER SERVING Calories 330; Total Fat 13 g (Sat Fat 3.5 g, Mono Fat 6.8 g, Poly Fat 1.5 g); Protein 18 g; Carb 36 g; Fiber 4 g; Cholesterol 235 mg; Sodium 380 mg
EXCELLENT SOURCE OF Iron, Phosphorus, Potassium, Protein, Selenium, Vitamin B6, Vitamin C
GOOD SOURCE OF Copper, Fiber, Folate, Iodine, Magnesium, Manganese, Molybdenum, Niacin, Pantothenic Acid, Riboflavin, Thiamin, Vitamin B12, Vitamin K

BEFORE		AFTER	
470 cal.	Sat. Fat 13g, Chol. 505mg Fiber 3g, Sodium 960mg	Sat. Fat 3.5g, Chol. 235mg Fiber 4g, Sodium 380mg	**330 cal.**

QUICHE LORRAINE WITH SPINACH

FOR THE CRUST:

½ cup all-purpose flour

½ cup whole-wheat pastry flour or regular whole-wheat flour

¼ teaspoon baking powder

⅛ teaspoon salt

3 tablespoons cold unsalted butter, cut into pieces

3 tablespoons Neufchâtel cheese (reduced-fat cream cheese)

3 tablespoons ice-cold water

Nonstick cooking spray

FOR THE FILLING:

2 teaspoons olive oil

1 small onion, thinly sliced

4 cups shredded fresh baby spinach leaves

1¼ cups cold low-fat (1%) milk

3 tablespoons all-purpose flour

3 large eggs

2 large egg whites

3 ounces shredded Swiss cheese

3 ounces cooked smoked ham, diced

1 teaspoon mustard powder

¼ teaspoon salt

¼ teaspoon freshly ground black pepper

Eggs, ham, and cheese are always a tasty trio, but they are at their absolute best together in this classic, savory custard baked in a flaky pastry crust. Using a modest amount of butter in the crust and low-fat milk for the filling lightens the pie while retaining that decadent quality. The spinach adds a bonus burst of color, flavor, and nutrients.

To make the dough, place the flours, baking powder, and salt in a food processor and pulse to combine. Add the butter and cream cheese and pulse about 12 times, until the mixture resembles coarse meal. Add the cold water and pulse, 3 to 5 times more, just until a dough is formed. Shape the dough into a flat disk, wrap it in wax paper, and chill at least 1 hour and up to 2 days in advance.

When ready to bake, preheat the oven to 400°F and spray a 9-inch pie plate with cooking spray.

Lightly flour a work surface and roll the dough out to an 11-inch circle. Drape the dough over the rolling pin and transfer to the prepared pie plate. Press the dough lightly into the pie plate, and tuck the edges under and crimp. Pierce the dough all over with a fork. Cover the edges of the dough with foil and bake for 10 minutes, until the dough browns slightly. Remove from the oven and allow to cool. Reduce the oven temperature to 350°F.

continued on page 20

	BEFORE	AFTER	
420 cal.	Sat. Fat 19g, Chol. 225mg Fiber 1g, Sodium 260mg	Sat. Fat 9g, Chol. 145mg Fiber 2g, Sodium 430mg	**310 cal.**

continued from page 19

To make the filling, heat the oil in a large skillet over medium-high heat. Add the onion and cook, stirring occasionally, until translucent, about 4 minutes. Add the spinach and cook, stirring occasionally, until the spinach has wilted, its water has released, and the mixture is mostly dry, about 5 minutes. Remove from the heat and allow to cool.

In a large bowl, whisk together the milk and flour until the flour is dissolved. Add the eggs and egg whites and whisk to incorporate. Stir in the spinach-onion mixture, cheese, ham, mustard powder, salt, and black pepper.

Place the prepared pie crust on a baking sheet. Pour the filling into the crust and bake until a knife inserted in the middle comes out clean, about 50 minutes. Allow to cool for 5 minutes before cutting into 6 wedges and serving.

Makes 6 servings

SERVING SIZE ⅙ quiche
PER SERVING Calories 310; Total Fat 17 g (Sat Fat 9 g, Mono Fat 5.4 g, Poly Fat 1.2 g); Protein 17 g; Carb 25 g; Fiber 2 g; Cholesterol 145 mg; Sodium 430 mg
EXCELLENT SOURCE OF Calcium, Folate, Iodine, Manganese, Phosphorus, Protein, Riboflavin, Selenium, Vitamin A, Vitamin K
GOOD SOURCE OF Iron, Magnesium, Molybdenum, Niacin, Potassium, Thiamin, Vitamin B12, Vitamin C, Vitamin D, Zinc

CORN BREAD WITH SWEET CORN KERNELS

Nonstick cooking spray
½ cup all-purpose flour
½ cup whole-wheat pastry
   flour or whole-wheat flour
1 cup yellow cornmeal
1½ teaspoons baking powder
¾ teaspoon salt
1 large egg
1 large egg white
1¼ cups low-fat buttermilk
3 tablespoons honey
3 tablespoons canola oil
1 cup fresh or frozen
   (thawed) corn kernels

I am happy to eat this scrumptious corn bread any time of day or night—for breakfast, with my afternoon tea, at a holiday (or everyday) dinner—even as a midnight snack (guilty as charged!). It has a perfect, subtle sweetness, it strikes the ideal crumbly-moist balance, and the whole grain and nuggets of sweet corn give it a delightfully hearty texture.

Move the oven rack to the center of the oven and preheat to 350°F. Lightly spray a 9×5-inch loaf pan with cooking spray.

In a large bowl, whisk together the flours, cornmeal, baking powder, and salt. In another large bowl, whisk together the egg, egg white, buttermilk, honey, and oil. Add the wet ingredients to the dry ingredients, mixing just enough to combine them. Stir in the corn.

Pour the batter into the prepared pan. Bake until the top is golden brown and a wooden skewer inserted into the center comes out with crumbs, about 45 minutes. Allow to cool in the pan for 15 minutes, then transfer the bread to a wire rack to cool completely before slicing.

Makes 8 servings

SERVING SIZE one 1-inch-thick slice
PER SERVING Calories 220; Total Fat 7 g (Sat Fat 1 g, Mono Fat 3.9 g, Poly Fat 2 g); Protein 6 g; Carb 36 g; Fiber 3 g; Cholesterol 30 mg; Sodium 370 mg
EXCELLENT SOURCE OF Manganese, Selenium
GOOD SOURCE OF Calcium, Fiber, Iodine, Magnesium, Molybdenum, Phosphorus, Protein, Riboflavin, Thiamin

BEFORE		AFTER	
330 cal.	Sat. Fat 9g, Chol. 90mg Fiber 1g, Sodium 390mg	Sat. Fat 1g, Chol. 30mg Fiber 3g, Sodium 370mg	**220 cal.**

MUSHROOM, ONION, AND GRUYÈRE QUICHE WITH OAT CRUST

FOR THE CRUST:

¾ cup old-fashioned rolled oats

½ cup all-purpose flour

¼ teaspoon salt

3 tablespoons cold unsalted butter, cut into small pieces

3 tablespoons cold low-fat buttermilk

Nonstick cooking spray

FOR THE FILLING:

4 teaspoons olive oil

1 medium onion, thinly sliced into half-moons

4 ounces mixed mushrooms, such as cremini, oyster, shiitake, coarsely chopped

½ teaspoon salt

¼ teaspoon freshly ground black pepper

¼ teaspoon dry mustard

1 tablespoon chopped fresh thyme, or 1 teaspoon dried

1½ cups cold low-fat (1%) milk

3 tablespoons all-purpose flour

3 large eggs

2 large egg whites

¾ cup grated Gruyère cheese (2 ounces)

Each of the deeply flavorful ingredients in this recipe—from the rustic rolled oats in the crust to the earthy mix of mushrooms, caramelized onions, thyme, and toasty Gruyère in the filling—builds on each other for an unforgettable, full-bodied taste experience.

To make the crust, place the oats, flour, and salt in a food processor and pulse to combine. Add the butter and pulse about 12 times, until the mixture has a pebbly coarse texture. Add the buttermilk and pulse 3 to 5 times more to combine. Shape the dough into a flat disk, wrap it in a large piece of wax paper, and chill at least 1 hour and up to 2 days in advance.

When ready to bake, preheat the oven to 400°F and spray a 9-inch pie plate with cooking spray.

Open the wax paper so the dough sits on top of it. Place another large piece of wax paper on top of the dough. Roll the dough out, between the wax paper sheets, to an 11-inch circle. Remove the top sheet of wax paper. Transfer the crust, still on the other piece of wax paper, to the pie dish, then remove the wax paper from the top. Press the crust gently into the dish. Bake for 9 minutes, remove from the oven, and allow to cool. Reduce the oven temperature to 350°F.

To make the filling, heat 2 teaspoons of the oil in a large nonstick

continued on page 24

	BEFORE	AFTER	
530 cal.	Sat. Fat 22g, Chol. 205mg Fiber 1g, Sodium 440mg	Sat. Fat 7g, Chol. 135mg Fiber 2g, Sodium 410mg	**290 cal.**

continued from page 23

pan over medium heat. Add the onion and cook, stirring occasionally, until softened, about 6 minutes. Reduce the heat to medium low, cover, and cook, stirring occasionally, until the onion is golden brown and caramelized, about 20 minutes more. Transfer the onion to a bowl. Add the remaining 2 teaspoons oil to the pan and heat over medium-high heat. Add the mushrooms and cook, stirring occasionally, until they have released their water and begun to brown, about 6 minutes. Add the onion back to the pan and stir in the salt, black pepper, mustard, and thyme.

In a medium bowl, whisk together the milk and flour until the flour is dissolved. Add the eggs and egg whites and whisk until well combined.

Sprinkle the cheese into the pie crust. Top with the mushroom-onion mixture. Pour the egg mixture on top. Bake until a knife inserted in the middle comes out clean, 45 to 50 minutes. Allow to cool for 5 minutes before cutting into 6 wedges and serving.

Makes 6 servings

SERVING SIZE 1 wedge
PER SERVING Calories 290; Total Fat 16 g (Sat Fat 7 g, Mono Fat 5.8 g, Poly Fat 1.2 g); Protein 14 g; Carb 24 g; Fiber 2 g; Cholesterol 135 mg; Sodium 410 mg
EXCELLENT SOURCE OF Calcium, Iodine, Molybdenum, Phosphorus, Protein, Riboflavin, Selenium
GOOD SOURCE OF Folate, Iron, Pantothenic Acid, Thiamin, Vitamin A, Vitamin B12, Vitamin D

MANGO-STUFFED CHALLAH FRENCH TOAST

¼ cup whipped cream cheese

¼ cup part-skim ricotta cheese

¼ cup finely diced mango

1 tablespoon honey

Pinch ground cinnamon

¾ cup low-fat (1%) milk

2 large eggs

1 large egg white

1 teaspoon vanilla extract

Four 1-inch-thick slices challah bread, preferably whole wheat (6 ounces)

Nonstick cooking spray

¼ cup maple syrup

"Ambrosial" is the first word that comes to mind when you take a bite of this luxurious French toast. The juicy mango mingled with warm, creamy filling and tucked into soft, golden, crisped bread is an alluring incentive to get out of bed in the morning.

In a small bowl, combine the cream cheese, ricotta cheese, mango, honey, and cinnamon. In a shallow dish, whisk together the milk, eggs, egg white, and vanilla until well incorporated.

Carefully slice a pocket into each piece of the bread, making sure not to cut all the way through and to leave the top and bottom intact. As evenly and gently as possible, spread 2 tablespoons of the mango filling into each pocket.

Spray a cast-iron or nonstick skillet with cooking spray and preheat over medium heat. Dip each piece of stuffed bread into the milk-egg mixture to coat well, about 10 seconds per side. Place the stuffed bread in the skillet and cook, turning once, until golden brown, about 3 minutes per side. Serve drizzled with maple syrup.

Makes 4 servings

SERVING SIZE 1 piece of French toast and 1 tablespoon maple syrup
PER SERVING Calories 320; Total Fat 10 g (Sat Fat 4.5 g, Mono Fat 3.3 g, Poly Fat 1 g); Protein 12 g; Carb 44 g; Fiber 2 g; Cholesterol 145 mg; Sodium 330 mg
EXCELLENT SOURCE OF Fiber, Iodine, Manganese, Protein, Riboflavin, Selenium
GOOD SOURCE OF Calcium, Folate, Phosphorus, Niacin, Thiamin, Vitamin A, Vitamin B12, Zinc

BEFORE	AFTER
470 cal. Sat. Fat 12g, Chol. 185mg Fiber 1g, Sodium 380mg	Sat. Fat 4.5g, Chol. 145mg Fiber 2g, Sodium 330mg **320 cal.**

CRISPY FRENCH TOAST FINGERS

1 cup sliced almonds

3 cups cornflakes

½ teaspoon ground cinnamon

½ teaspoon ground nutmeg

¼ teaspoon salt

2 large eggs

¾ cup low-fat (1%) milk

1 tablespoon pure maple syrup

1 teaspoon vanilla extract

Nonstick cooking spray

4 large slices firm whole-grain bread (6 ounces), each piece cut crosswise to make 5 fingers each

1 recipe Blueberry Maple Sauce (recipe follows) or maple syrup for serving, optional

Crisp and nutty outside, tenderly eggy inside, and wafting with cinnamon and vanilla, these fun French toast fingers are a natural for dipping into a sweet, syrupy sauce. They're perfect for kids—or anyone who wants to feel like one again.

In a food processor, pulse the almonds until coarsely ground. Add the cornflakes, cinnamon, nutmeg, and salt and pulse until the cornflakes resemble the texture of oats. Transfer the cornflake mixture to a shallow bowl.

In a medium bowl, whisk together the eggs, milk, maple syrup, and vanilla until well combined.

Spray a large nonstick skillet or griddle with cooking spray and preheat over medium heat. Working with one piece at a time, dip the bread into the egg mixture until completely moistened and coated but not falling apart, about 30 seconds each. Coat each slice of bread

continued on page 28

	BEFORE	AFTER	
430 cal.	Sat. Fat 9g, Chol. 110mg Fiber 5g, Sodium 580mg	Sat. Fat 2g, Chol. 80mg Fiber 6g, Sodium 520mg	**340 cal.**

continued from page 26

in the cornflake mixture, gently pressing it onto the bread. Place each slice of bread in the skillet and cook over medium-low heat, turning once, until the outside is golden brown and the center is warm, about 6 minutes total.

Serve with Blueberry Maple Sauce (page 29) or pure maple syrup on the side for dipping, if desired.

Makes 4 servings

SERVING SIZE 5 pieces
PER SERVING Calories 340; Total Fat 13 g (Sat Fat 2 g, Mono Fat 6.8 g, Poly Fat 3.3 g); Protein 14 g; Carb 43 g; Fiber 6 g; Cholesterol 80 mg; Sodium 520 mg
EXCELLENT SOURCE OF Fiber, Folate, Iron, Magnesium, Manganese, Niacin, Phosphorus, Protein, Riboflavin, Selenium, Thiamin, Vitamin B6, Vitamin B12
GOOD SOURCE OF Calcium, Copper, Iodine, Molybdenum, Vitamin A, Vitamin D, Zinc

BLUEBERRY MAPLE SAUCE

2 cups fresh or frozen (unsweetened) blueberries (10 ounces)

1 tablespoon pure maple syrup, plus more to taste

1 tablespoon orange juice

A touch of maple syrup brings out the natural sweetness of the blueberries in this delightful fruit sauce. Try it on French toast, waffles, pancakes, over ice cream or angel food cake, or as a drizzle for fresh fruit.

In a medium saucepan, combine the blueberries, maple syrup, and orange juice. Bring the mixture to a gentle boil. Reduce the heat to medium low and simmer, stirring occasionally, for 2 minutes. Transfer the mixture to a blender, or use an immersion blender, and blend until almost smooth. Add more maple syrup to taste depending on the sweetness of the fruit. The sauce may be made up to 4 days ahead of using and stored in the refrigerator in an airtight container.

Makes 4 servings

SERVING SIZE ¼ cup
PER SERVING Calories 50; Total Fat 0 g (Sat Fat 0 g, Mono Fat 0 g, Poly Fat 0 g); Protein 0 g; Carb 13 g; Fiber 3 g; Cholesterol 0 mg; Sodium 0 mg
EXCELLENT SOURCE OF Manganese
GOOD SOURCE OF Fiber

BEFORE*	AFTER
210 cal.	Sat. Fat 0g, Chol. 0mg / Fiber 0g, Sodium 120mg	Sat. Fat 0g, Chol. 0mg / Fiber 3g, Sodium 0mg	50 cal.

*compared to blueberry-flavored breakfast syrup

BUTTERMILK WAFFLES

¾ cup all-purpose flour
¾ cup whole-wheat pastry flour or whole-wheat flour
2 tablespoons toasted wheat germ
1¼ teaspoons baking powder
½ teaspoon baking soda
¼ teaspoon salt
1½ cups low-fat buttermilk
1 tablespoon canola oil
1 tablespoon honey
1 large egg
½ teaspoon vanilla extract
  Nonstick cooking spray
1 recipe Chunky Strawberry Topping (recipe follows) or confectioners' sugar for garnish, optional

These waffles give you all of the cozy comfort and crisp, light taste you yearn for, but with so much more to feel good about, thanks to their fiber-rich whole wheat and healthy oil. They are equally decadent served simply dusted with confectioners' sugar or smothered in Chunky Strawberry Topping.

Preheat a waffle iron.

In a large bowl, whisk together the flours, wheat germ, baking powder, baking soda, and salt. In another large bowl, whisk together the buttermilk, oil, honey, egg, and vanilla. Stir the wet ingredients into the dry ingredients, mixing just enough to combine them.

Spray the waffle iron with cooking spray. Ladle enough of the batter to cover three-fourths of the surface of the waffle iron (a heaping ½ cup for a 6-inch waffle iron), close it, and cook until golden brown, 3 to 5 minutes. Repeat with the remaining batter. Serve with the Chunky Strawberry Topping or a dusting of confectioners' sugar, if desired.

Makes 4 servings

SERVING SIZE one 6-inch Belgian-style waffle
PER SERVING Calories 280; Total Fat 6 g (Sat Fat 1g, Mono Fat 3 g, Poly Fat 1.7 g); Protein 11g; Carb 45 g; Fiber 4 g; Cholesterol 50 mg; Sodium 570 mg
EXCELLENT SOURCE OF Calcium, Iodine, Manganese, Phosphorus, Protein, Riboflavin, Selenium, Thiamin
GOOD SOURCE OF Fiber, Folate, Iron, Magnesium, Niacin, Zinc

	BEFORE	AFTER	
350 cal.	Sat. Fat 11g, Chol. 150mg Fiber 1g, Sodium 840mg	Sat. Fat 1.5g, Chol. 50mg Fiber 4g, Sodium 560mg	**340 cal.**

CHUNKY STRAWBERRY TOPPING

2 cups fresh or frozen
  (unsweetened)
  strawberries, stems
  removed (10 ounces)

2 tablespoons pure maple
  syrup, plus more to taste

2 teaspoons freshly squeezed
  lemon juice

Just a little warming, plus a touch of lemon juice and maple syrup, call out the sweet-tart essence of this favorite fruit, transforming it into a luxurious, yet homey topping. Make extra so you can enjoy some with a dollop of yogurt later.

In a medium saucepan, stir together the strawberries, maple syrup, and lemon juice and bring to a gentle boil. Reduce the heat to medium low and simmer until the liquid has thickened slightly, about 5 minutes. Flavor with additional maple syrup, depending on the sweetness of the fruit. The topping will keep up to 4 days in the refrigerator stored in an airtight container.

Makes 4 servings

SERVING SIZE ¼ cup
PER SERVING Calories 50; Total Fat 0 g (Sat Fat 0 g, Mono Fat 0 g, Poly Fat 0 g); Protein 0 g; Carb 13 g; Fiber 1 g; Cholesterol 0 mg; Sodium 0 mg
EXCELLENT SOURCE OF Manganese, Vitamin C
GOOD SOURCE OF N/A

	BEFORE	AFTER	
100 cal.	Sat. Fat 2g, Chol. 10mg Fiber 1g, Sodium 20mg	Sat. Fat 0g, Chol. 0mg Fiber 1g, Sodium 0mg	**50 cal.**

THREE BEARS PORRIDGE

2 tablespoons whole natural almonds

2 tablespoons unsalted pecan halves

1 tablespoon unsalted sunflower seeds

3 cups water

¼ teaspoon salt, optional

2 cups old-fashioned rolled oats

½ cup low-fat (1%) milk

1⅓ cups mixed fresh berries, such as blueberries, raspberries, blackberries (halved if large), and strawberries (hulled and quartered)

4 teaspoons honey, plus more to taste

After reading the classic fairy tale together, my daughter and I were so intrigued by how bears prepare their cereal (with berries, nuts, and honey) that we decided to try it ourselves. It turns out those bears are onto something. This breakfast is truly just right. Ripe juicy berries and crunchy toasted nuts mean it has plenty of fiber and protein to keep you satisfied all morning, and making it with low-fat milk keeps it optimally healthy.

Place the almonds and pecans in a small dry skillet and cook over medium-high heat, stirring frequently, until nearly toasted, about 2 minutes. Add the sunflower seeds and continue to cook, stirring, until the nuts and seeds are fragrant and lightly browned, 1 to 2 minutes more. Allow to cool, then chop coarsely.

Bring the water and salt, if using, to a boil in a medium saucepan. Stir in the oats, reduce the heat to medium, and cook until the oats are nearly tender, about 4 minutes. Add the milk, return to a simmer, then reduce the heat to medium low and cook until thickened and the oats are tender, 1 to 2 minutes more.

Distribute the oatmeal among 4 bowls. Top each with ⅓ cup berries and 1½ tablespoons nuts, and drizzle with 1 teaspoon honey.

Makes 4 servings

SERVING SIZE ¾ cup oatmeal, ⅓ cup berries, 1½ tablespoons nuts, and 1 teaspoon honey
PER SERVING Calories 420; Total Fat 11 g (Sat Fat 1.5 g, Mono Fat 4.7 g, Poly Fat 4 g); Protein 16 g; Carb 66 g; Fiber 11 g; Cholesterol 0 mg; Sodium 170 mg
EXCELLENT SOURCE OF Copper, Fiber, Iron, Magnesium, Manganese, Molybdenum, Phosphorus, Protein, Thiamin, Vitamin C, Zinc
GOOD SOURCE OF Calcium, Folate, Pantothenic Acid, Potassium, Riboflavin

BEFORE		AFTER	
440 cal.	Sat. Fat 4.5g, Chol. 15mg Fiber 11g, Sodium 170mg	Sat. Fat 1.5g, Chol. 0mg Fiber 11g, Sodium 170mg	**420 cal.**

CITRUS SALAD WITH CHERRIES

2 pink grapefruits
4 large navel oranges
½ cup fresh or frozen
   (unsweetened, thawed, and
   drained) sweet cherries,
   pitted and halved
1 tablespoon honey

When I was a child, my grandma and grandpa always had a jar of store-bought citrus salad in the fridge that I would devour at breakfast whenever I slept over. When I eat this one, even with its upgrade to honey-sweetened, fresh-cut fruit, it brings me right back to their humble little kitchen table.

Cut the top and bottom off of a grapefruit, then set the fruit on its end and, following the curve of the fruit with the knife, cut off all of the rind and pith. Over a large bowl to catch the juice, use a paring knife to remove each segment from the fruit, letting the segments drop into the bowl. Discard the remaining membrane. Repeat with the remaining grapefruit and the oranges. Gently stir in the cherries and honey. The salad will keep for up to a week in an airtight container in the refrigerator.

Makes 6 servings

SERVING SIZE ⅔ cup
PER SERVING Calories 100; Total Fat 0 g (Sat Fat 0 g, Mono Fat 0 g, Poly Fat 0 g); Protein 2 g; Carb 25 g; Fiber 4 g; Cholesterol 0 mg; Sodium 0 mg
EXCELLENT SOURCE OF Vitamin A, Vitamin C
GOOD SOURCE OF Fiber, Folate

BEFORE*	AFTER
120 cal.	100 cal.
Sat. Fat 0g, Chol. 0mg	Sat. Fat 0g, Chol. 0mg
Fiber 1g, Sodium 30mg	Fiber 4g, Sodium 0mg

*compared to jarred citrus salad

BETTER BLUEBERRY MUFFINS

Nonstick cooking spray
1 cup all-purpose flour
1 cup whole-grain pastry flour or whole-wheat flour
2 teaspoons baking powder
¼ teaspoon baking soda
½ teaspoon salt
¾ cup sugar
¼ cup canola oil
2 large eggs
1 cup natural unsweetened applesauce
½ cup plain low-fat yogurt
¼ cup nonfat milk
1 teaspoon vanilla extract
1½ teaspoons finely grated lemon zest
1½ cups fresh or frozen (unsweetened and unthawed) blueberries

With a store-bought muffin weighing in at around (gasp!) five hundred calories, simply making your own is a fix in itself, whatever recipe you choose. But this muffin is the best of the best—tender, cakey, and studded with barely bursting berries. The secret ingredient is applesauce, which, by locking in moisture, allows you to use less fat.

Preheat the oven to 400°F. Coat a 12-cup muffin pan with cooking spray.

In a medium bowl, whisk together the flours, baking powder, baking soda, and salt.

In a large bowl, beat together the sugar, oil, and eggs, until the mixture is light yellow and slightly frothy. Whisk in the applesauce, yogurt, milk, vanilla, and lemon zest. Stir the dry ingredients into the wet, mixing just enough to combine them. Do not overmix. Gently stir in the blueberries.

Pour the batter into the prepared muffin pan. Tap the pan on the counter a few times to remove any air bubbles. Bake until a wooden toothpick inserted into the center of one of the muffins comes out clean, about 20 minutes.

continued on page 36

	BEFORE	AFTER	
240 cal.	Sat. Fat 5g, Chol. 40mg Fiber 1g, Sodium 230mg	Sat. Fat 1g, Chol. 35mg Fiber 3g, Sodium 230mg	**200 cal.**

continued from page 35

Allow to cool on a wire rack for 15 minutes. Run a knife around them to loosen and unmold. Enjoy warm or let cool completely before storing in an airtight container in the refrigerator for up to 3 days or wrap individually and freeze for up to 3 months.

Makes 12 servings

SERVING SIZE 1 muffin
PER SERVING Calories 200; Total Fat 6 g (Sat Fat 1 g, Mono Fat 3.3 g, Poly Fat 1.6 g); Protein 4 g; Carb 34 g; Fiber 3 g; Cholesterol 35 mg; Sodium 230 mg
EXCELLENT SOURCE OF Manganese
GOOD SOURCE OF Fiber, Selenium

BANANA-WALNUT MULTIGRAIN PANCAKES

½ cup walnut pieces

½ cup all-purpose flour

½ cup whole-grain pastry flour or whole-wheat flour

¼ cup cornmeal

¼ cup quick-cooking oats

2 tablespoons toasted wheat germ

1½ teaspoons baking powder

½ teaspoon baking soda

⅛ teaspoon salt

2 large eggs

1¼ cups nonfat milk

½ cup plain nonfat yogurt

1 tablespoon honey

½ teaspoon vanilla extract

Nonstick cooking spray

2 ripe firm medium bananas, sliced

⅓ cup pure maple syrup, for serving

"These are the best pancakes I've ever had" was all I needed to hear from my friend to know I achieved pancake perfection. By combining white and whole-grain flours, cornmeal, oats, and wheat germ, you get a hearty texture and rich flavor without losing the light fluffiness you expect. And thanks to the yogurt, they are tender and moist without a drop of butter.

Toast the walnuts in a dry skillet over medium-high heat, stirring frequently, until fragrant, about 2 minutes. Allow to cool, then chop coarsely.

In a large bowl, whisk together the flours, cornmeal, oats, wheat germ, baking powder, baking soda, and salt. In a medium bowl, beat together the eggs, milk, yogurt, honey, and vanilla.

Coat a large nonstick griddle or skillet with cooking spray and heat over medium-low heat. Stir the wet ingredients into the dry ingredients, mixing just enough to combine them. The batter will be somewhat lumpy. Gently stir in the bananas and walnuts.

continued on page 38

BEFORE		AFTER	
530 cal.	Sat. Fat 12g, Chol. 115mg Fiber 3g, Sodium 390mg	Sat. Fat 1.5g, Chol. 70mg Fiber 4g, Sodium 360mg	320 cal.

continued from page 37

Ladle ¼ cup of the batter onto the griddle. Flip the pancakes when they are golden brown on the bottom and bubbles are forming on top, 1½ to 2 minutes. Cook the other side until golden brown, about 1½ minutes more. Repeat with the remaining batter, keeping the prepared pancakes warm in a 200°F oven. Serve with maple syrup.

Makes 6 servings

SERVING SIZE 2 pancakes and 1 tablespoon syrup
PER SERVING Calories 320; Total Fat 9 g (Sat Fat 1.5 g, Mono Fat 1.7 g, Poly Fat 5.4 g); Protein 11 g; Carb 52 g; Fiber 4 g; Cholesterol 70 mg; Sodium 360 mg
EXCELLENT SOURCE OF Calcium, Iodine, Manganese, Phosphorus, Protein, Riboflavin, Selenium
GOOD SOURCE OF Copper, Fiber, Folate, Iron, Thiamin, Magnesium, Molybdenum, Niacin, Potassium, Vitamin B6, Zinc

APPLE COFFEE CAKE

½ medium Golden Delicious apple, cored and finely diced

Nonstick cooking spray

1 cup all-purpose flour

1 cup whole-wheat pastry flour or whole-wheat flour

1 teaspoon baking soda

¼ teaspoon salt

3 tablespoons granulated sugar

½ teaspoon ground cinnamon

½ cup chopped walnuts

⅔ cup packed light brown sugar

2 tablespoons unsalted butter, at room temperature

2 tablespoons canola oil

2 large eggs

1 teaspoon vanilla extract

1 cup nonfat plain yogurt

Moist, tender cake with a ribbon of soft, sweet apple chunks running through it and finished with a nutty brown-sugar topping is just the treat you crave with your coffee, and it's so much better for you.

Place the apple in a microwave-safe bowl, tightly cover with plastic wrap, and microwave on high until softened, about 90 seconds. Set aside.

Preheat the oven to 350°F. Spray an 8-inch square pan with cooking spray.

In a large bowl, whisk together the flours, baking soda, and salt. In a small bowl, stir together the granulated sugar, cinnamon, and walnuts. In a large bowl, beat the brown sugar, butter, and oil until well combined. If necessary, use the back of a spoon to press out any lumps in the brown sugar. Beat in the eggs until well combined. Beat in the vanilla and yogurt. Add the flour mixture in two batches, stirring until just combined after each addition.

continued on page 40

	BEFORE	AFTER	
310 cal.	Sat. Fat 6g, Chol. 50mg Fiber 1g, Sodium 190mg	Sat. Fat 2g, Chol. 40mg Fiber 2g, Sodium 190mg	**230 cal.**

continued from page 39

Pour half of the batter into the prepared pan and spread evenly. Sprinkle half of the nut mixture over the batter and top with the apples, gently pressing them into the batter. Spoon the rest of the batter into the pan, smoothing the top. Sprinkle the remaining nut mixture over the batter, pressing gently. Bake until a wooden skewer inserted into the center comes out clean, about 35 minutes. Allow to cool slightly before cutting the cake into 12 squares.

Makes 12 servings

SERVING SIZE 1 square
PER SERVING Calories 230; Total Fat 9 g (Sat Fat 2 g, Mono Fat 2.8 g, Poly Fat 3.3 g); Protein 6 g; Carb 34 g; Fiber 2 g; Cholesterol 40 mg; Sodium 190 mg
EXCELLENT SOURCE OF Manganese, Selenium
GOOD SOURCE OF Phosphorus, Protein, Riboflavin, Thiamin

BREAKFAST COOKIES

¾ cup whole-wheat pastry
flour or whole-wheat flour

½ cup all-purpose flour

½ teaspoon baking soda

1 teaspoon ground cinnamon

½ teaspoon ground nutmeg

¼ teaspoon salt

2 tablespoons unsalted
butter

¼ cup canola oil

¼ cup dark brown sugar

3 tablespoons granulated
sugar

1 large egg

¼ cup pureed strained
cooked carrots or 1 small
jar strained carrot baby
food

1 teaspoon vanilla extract

½ cup old-fashioned rolled
oats

½ cup bran cereal flakes

⅓ cup raisins

⅓ cup walnut pieces, lightly
toasted in a dry skillet for
2 minutes until fragrant,
chopped

It gives me great comfort just knowing I live in a world where it is OK to eat a cookie for breakfast. These chunky, satisfying, lightly sweetened treats are chock-full of energizing whole grains, nuts, and fruit. I even manage to squeeze in a veggie by adding naturally sweet, tenderizing carrot puree.

Move the oven rack to the center of the oven and preheat to 350°F.

In a medium bowl, whisk together the flours, baking soda, cinnamon, nutmeg, and salt. In a large bowl, beat together the butter, oil, brown sugar, and granulated sugar until the sugars are dissolved and the mixture becomes somewhat lighter in color. Add the egg, carrot puree, and vanilla and beat until well incorporated. Add the flour mixture and stir to combine. Add the oats, bran flakes, raisins, and walnuts and mix until incorporated. The dough will be slightly sticky and less cohesive than traditional cookie dough.

Line a baking sheet with parchment paper. Form a ball using 3 to 4 tablespoons of dough, and place it on the cookie sheet. Repeat with the remaining dough, leaving about 3 inches between the balls. Wet your hands and use your palm to flatten the balls to about ¼ inch thick. Bake until fragrant but still soft, about 12 minutes,. Allow to cool slightly in the pan, then transfer to a wire rack to cool completely.

Makes 12 servings

SERVING SIZE 1 cookie
PER SERVING Calories 190; Total Fat 9g (Sat Fat 2 g, Mono Fat 3.5 g, Poly Fat 3 g); Protein 3 g; Carb 23 g; Fiber 2 g; Cholesterol 25 mg; Sodium 120 mg
GOOD SOURCE OF Thiamin, Vitamin A

	BEFORE*	AFTER	
290 cal.	Sat. Fat 7g, Chol. 55mg Fiber 2g, Sodium 200mg	Sat. Fat 2g, Chol. 25mg Fiber 2g, Sodium 120mg	190 cal.

*compared to a fruit-and-nut muffin recipe

ZUCCHINI-WALNUT BREAD

Nonstick cooking spray
¾ cup whole-wheat pastry flour
¾ cup all-purpose flour
½ cup sugar
1 teaspoon ground cinnamon
1 teaspoon baking soda
½ teaspoon ground nutmeg
¼ teaspoon salt
⅓ cup canola oil
⅓ cup natural unsweetened applesauce
2 large eggs
1 small zucchini (6 ounces), coarsely grated (about 1¼ cups)
⅓ cup chopped walnuts

With its generous helping of warm spices, perfectly balanced sweetness, and rich walnut-studded texture, this bread turns a garden-variety vegetable into an extraordinary treat.

Preheat the oven to 350°F. Spray a 9×5-inch loaf pan with cooking spray.

In a large bowl, whisk together the flours, sugar, cinnamon, baking soda, nutmeg, and salt. In another large bowl, whisk together the oil, applesauce, and eggs. Stir in the zucchini. Stir the wet ingredients into the dry ingredients, mixing just enough to combine. Stir in the walnuts.

Pour the batter into the prepared loaf pan. Bake until a wooden skewer inserted into the center comes out clean, 50 to 60 minutes. Allow to cool for 15 minutes in the pan, then transfer the bread to a wire rack to cool completely before slicing.

Makes 8 servings

SERVING SIZE one 1-inch-thick slice
PER SERVING Calories 270; Total Fat 14 g (Sat Fat 1.5 g, Mono Fat 6.9 g, Poly Fat 5.3 g); Protein 5 g; Carb 33 g; Fiber 3 g; Cholesterol 55 mg; Sodium 250 mg
EXCELLENT SOURCE OF Manganese, Selenium
GOOD SOURCE OF Fiber, Folate, Phosphorus, Protein, Riboflavin, Thiamin, Vitamin K

BEFORE		AFTER	
370 cal.	Sat. Fat 6g, Chol. 70mg Fiber 1g, Sodium 310mg	Sat. Fat 1.5g, Chol. 55mg Fiber 3g, Sodium 250mg	**270 cal.**

PUMPKIN BREAD WITH CRANBERRIES

Nonstick cooking spray
¾ cup all-purpose flour
¾ cup whole-wheat pastry flour or whole-wheat flour
1 teaspoon baking soda
1 teaspoon ground cinnamon
½ teaspoon baking powder
½ teaspoon ground nutmeg
¼ teaspoon ground allspice
¼ teaspoon salt
1 cup canned pumpkin puree
⅔ cup honey
⅓ cup canola oil
2 large eggs
1 large egg white
1 cup fresh whole cranberries

This gloriously autumnal pumpkin bread, enhanced with bursts of crimson tart cranberries, is special enough to grace your holiday table but easy enough to make anytime.

Preheat the oven to 350°F. Spray a 9×5-inch loaf pan with cooking spray.

In a large bowl, whisk together the flours, baking soda, cinnamon, baking powder, nutmeg, allspice, and salt. In another large bowl, whisk together the pumpkin, honey, oil, eggs, and egg white until well combined. Stir the dry ingredients into the wet ingredients, mixing just enough to combine evenly. Gently stir in the cranberries.

Pour the batter into the prepared pan. Bake until the top is browned and a wooden skewer inserted into the center comes out clean, 50 to 60 minutes. Allow to cool in the pan for 15 minutes, then transfer the bread to a wire rack to cool completely before slicing.

Makes 8 servings

SERVING SIZE one 1-inch-thick slice
PER SERVING Calories 290; Total Fat 11 g (Sat Fat 1 g, Mono Fat 6.4 g, Poly Fat 3 g); Protein 5 g; Carb 45 g; Fiber 3 g; Cholesterol 55 mg; Sodium 290 mg
EXCELLENT SOURCE OF Magnesium, Selenium, Vitamin A
GOOD SOURCE OF Fiber, Iron, Niacin, Phosphorus, Protein, Riboflavin, Vitamin K

BEFORE	AFTER
360 cal. Sat. Fat 2.5g, Chol. 65mg Fiber 2g, Sodium 450mg	Sat. Fat 1g, Chol. 55mg Fiber 3g, Sodium 290mg **290 cal.**

HONEY WHOLE-WHEAT CINNAMON RAISIN BREAD

2 cups bread flour

2 cups whole-wheat flour

¼ cup nonfat dry milk

1¼ cups very warm water (120°F to 130°F)

1 large egg

3 tablespoons canola oil

3 tablespoons honey

1 teaspoon salt

1½ teaspoons instant dry yeast
   Nonstick cooking spray

¼ cup packed dark brown sugar

1 tablespoon plus 1 teaspoon ground cinnamon

½ cup golden raisins, soaked in boiling water for 30 minutes, drained, and patted dry

The simple process of making this bread is half the homey pleasure of it—from working with the soft yeasty dough to the incredible cinnamon-laced aroma during baking. It comes out of the oven beautifully golden brown with a stunning swirl of sweetness throughout. My main incentive to resist devouring all of it on the spot is that it makes for incredible French toast the next morning.

Place the flours, dry milk, water, egg, 2 tablespoons of the oil, honey, salt, and yeast into the bowl of a stand mixer. Using the dough hook attachment, mix on the lowest setting ("stir") for 3 minutes, then increase to the next highest setting ("2") and mix 5 minutes more. The dough should be soft and fairly sticky.

Place the dough in a bowl sprayed with cooking spray, cover tightly with plastic wrap, and let stand at room temperature until its size has nearly doubled, about 1½ hours.

Spray two 9×5×3-inch baking pans with cooking spray.

Transfer the dough to a well-floured work surface. Pick up one side of the dough, lifting about a third of the bulk and fold it across. With spread fingers, pat down on the dough to remove most of the trapped gases. Repeat with the remaining three sides of the dough.

Divide the dough in half and roll each half into a flat square, about

continued on page 48

	BEFORE	AFTER	
240 cal.	Sat. Fat 4g, Chol. 45mg Fiber 2g, Sodium 210mg	Sat. Fat 0g, Chol. 15mg Fiber 3g, Sodium 160mg	**190 cal.**

continued from page 46

8×8 inches. Brush each square with some of the remaining oil. Sprinkle 2 tablespoons sugar, 2 teaspoons cinnamon, and ¼ cup raisins over each square. Roll each square into a tight cylinder and place each one, seam side down, into one of the prepared pans. Cover tightly with plastic wrap and allow to sit at room temperature for 1½ hours, until the dough fills the pan and springs back slowly when touched.

After the dough has been sitting for about 1 hour, preheat the oven to 375°F. Uncover the pans and brush the tops of each loaf with oil. Bake until the bread is golden brown and the sides spring back when pressed, 25 to 30 minutes. Transfer the bread to a wire rack and allow to cool completely.

Makes 16 servings

SERVING SIZE 2 slices
PER SERVING Calories 190; Total Fat 3.5 g (Sat Fat 0 g, Mono Fat 1.9 g, Poly Fat 1 g); Protein 5 g; Carb 35 g; Fiber 3 g; Cholesterol 15 mg; Sodium 160 mg
EXCELLENT SOURCE OF Manganese, Selenium
GOOD SOURCE OF Folate, Iron, Niacin, Riboflavin, Thiamin

BANANA-PECAN BREAD

Nonstick cooking spray

⅓ cup pecan pieces

¾ cup all-purpose flour

1 cup whole-wheat pastry flour

¼ cup granulated sugar

¼ cup packed light brown sugar

1 teaspoon baking soda

½ teaspoon baking powder

¼ teaspoon salt

¼ cup canola oil

¼ cup plain nonfat yogurt

2 large eggs

1 teaspoon vanilla extract

3 very ripe, large bananas, peeled and mashed (about 1½ cups)

The not-so-secret ingredient in this decadent bread is the bananas themselves, which add moisture and natural sweetness, allowing you to use less fat and sugar without compromising taste. Buttery pecans provide toasty, crunchy contrast to the tender crumb.

Preheat the oven to 350°F. Spray a 9×5-inch loaf pan with cooking spray.

Spread the pecans on a baking sheet and toast in the oven until fragrant, about 8 minutes. Set aside to cool.

In a large bowl, whisk together the flours, sugars, baking soda, baking powder, and salt.

In a medium bowl, whisk together the oil, yogurt, eggs, and vanilla. Whisk in the bananas. Stir the wet ingredients into the dry ingredients, mixing just enough to combine them. Stir in the toasted pecans.

Pour the batter into the prepared pan. Bake until a wooden skewer inserted into the center comes out clean, 50 to 55 minutes. Allow to cool in the pan for 15 minutes, then transfer the bread to a wire rack to cool completely before slicing.

Makes 8 servings

SERVING SIZE one 1-inch-thick slice
PER SERVING Calories 300; Total Fat 12 g (Sat Fat 1.5 g, Mono Fat 6.8 g, Poly Fat 3.3g); Protein 6 g; Carb 44 g; Fiber 4 g; Cholesterol 55 mg; Sodium 290 mg
EXCELLENT SOURCE OF Manganese, Selenium
GOOD SOURCE OF Fiber, Folate, Magnesium, Niacin, Riboflavin, Thiamin, Phosphorus, Protein, Vitamin B6

BEFORE		AFTER	
500 cal.	Sat. Fat 12g, Chol. 115mg Fiber 3g, Sodium 430mg	Sat. Fat 1.5g, Chol. 55mg Fiber 4g, Sodium 290mg	**300 cal.**

chapter two

SNACKS AND STARTERS

Whether you crave a solo snack break or you want a crowd-pleasing party starter,
you'll find it here. From crunchy chips with creamy dips to feel-good finger foods, this
is happy hour food you can really celebrate.

ROASTED RED PEPPER HUMMUS

1 large roasted red pepper, drained and rinsed if jarred

1 clove garlic, minced

½ teaspoon salt, plus more to taste

One 15-ounce can chickpeas, preferably low-sodium, drained and rinsed

2 tablespoons tahini

3 tablespoons fresh lemon juice

2 tablespoons extra-virgin olive oil, plus 1 teaspoon for garnish

¼ teaspoon ground cumin

2 tablespoons water

I take comfort knowing my fridge is stocked with luscious healthy foods to enjoy at a moment's notice. Hummus is one of those go-to staples I am never without. I snack on it with veggies, serve it as a chip dip, spread it on sandwiches, and stuff it in a pita. Once you see how easy and delicious it is to make yourself, you will never go back to store bought. Here, the roasted red peppers add a subtle sweet and colorful twist. Try serving this with Lemon-Dill Pita Chips (page 57).

Finely chop 1 tablespoon of the roasted red pepper and reserve for a garnish. Coarsely chop the remaining roasted red pepper.

Using the broad side of a knife blade, mash together the garlic and the ½ teaspoon salt to form a paste. Place the garlic paste, chickpeas, tahini, lemon juice, 2 tablespoons of the oil, the cumin, the water, and the roasted red pepper into a food processor and process until smooth. Season with additional salt to taste.

Place the hummus into a serving bowl and garnish with the reserved red pepper. Drizzle the remaining 1 teaspoon oil over the top. Hummus will keep for about 1 week in an airtight container in the refrigerator.

Makes 8 servings

SERVING SIZE ¼ cup
PER SERVING Calories 150; Total Fat 7 g (Sat Fat 1 g, Mono Fat 3.9 g, Poly Fat 1.9 g); Protein 6 g; Carb 17 g; Fiber 4 g; Cholesterol 0 mg; Sodium 180 mg
EXCELLENT SOURCE OF Folate, Manganese, Molybdenum, Vitamin C
GOOD SOURCE OF Copper, Iron, Fiber, Protein

	BEFORE*	AFTER	
205 cal.	Sat. Fat 1g, Chol. 0mg Fiber 3g, Sodium 330mg	Sat. Fat 1g, Chol. 0mg Fiber 4g, Sodium 180mg	150 cal.

*compared to store-bought

FIVE-LAYER MEXICAN DIP

2 teaspoons olive oil

1 medium onion, diced

2 cloves garlic, minced

One 15-ounce can black beans, preferably low-sodium, drained and rinsed

1½ teaspoons minced chipotle pepper from seeded canned chipotle peppers in adobo sauce

4 tablespoons fresh lime juice

1 tablespoon water

½ teaspoon salt, plus more to taste

¼ teaspoon ground cumin

2 cups corn kernels (one 10-ounce box frozen corn)

¼ cup fresh cilantro leaves, chopped

Salt and freshly ground black pepper to taste

2 ripe avocados

4 medium tomatoes, seeded and diced (about 2 cups)

¼ cup thinly sliced scallion

1 tablespoon finely diced and seeded jalapeño pepper, optional

¾ cup shredded extra-sharp cheddar cheese

Serving this dip is like having a mariachi band at the party. It's vibrant, fun, and gets everyone in a festive mood. It is satisfyingly rich, thanks to buttery avocado and creamy bean dip, but its lime-spiked, colorful freshness is a welcome update. Try serving this with Chili Tortilla Chips (recipe follows).

Heat the oil in a skillet over medium-high heat. Add the onion and cook, stirring, until softened, about 3 minutes. Add the garlic and cook, stirring, about 2 minutes more.

Place half the onion mixture, the black beans, chipotle, 2 tablespoons of the lime juice, the water, salt, and cumin in a food processor and puree until smooth. Set aside.

Add the corn to the skillet with the remaining onion mixture and cook over medium-high heat, stirring, about 3 minutes. Remove from

	BEFORE	AFTER	
280 cal.	Sat. Fat 7g, Chol. 25mg. Fiber 3g, Sodium 1130mg	Sat. Fat 2g, Chol. 10mg Fiber 5g, Sodium 230mg	**150 cal.**

the heat and stir in the cilantro and salt and black pepper.

Pit and peel the avocados, then in a small bowl, mash the avocados with the remaining 2 tablespoons lime juice. In a medium bowl, toss together the tomatoes, scallion, and jalapeño, if using. Season with salt and black pepper to taste.

Spread the black bean dip into the bottom of an 8-inch square glass baking dish or serving dish. Top with the corn mixture, spreading it out to form a single layer over the beans. Spread the avocado in a single layer over the top, then the tomatoes. Top with the cheese. Serve with baked tortilla chips.

Makes 12 servings

SERVING SIZE ½ cup
PER SERVING Calories 150; Total Fat 8 g (Sat Fat 2 g, Mono Fat 4 g, Poly Fat 0.8 g); Protein 5 g; Carb 17 g; Fiber 5 g; Cholesterol 10 mg; Sodium 230 mg
EXCELLENT SOURCE OF Fiber, Vitamin C
GOOD SOURCE OF Folate, Potassium, Protein, Vitamin K

CHILI TORTILLA CHIPS

2 tablespoons olive oil
2 teaspoons chili powder
½ teaspoon ground coriander
½ teaspoon ground cumin
½ teaspoon garlic powder
½ teaspoon salt
Pinch cayenne pepper
Twelve 6-inch corn tortillas,
each cut into 6 wedges

Sometimes I make these chips just to have the homey aroma of roasted corn fill my kitchen. But it's their shattering crunch and deep corn flavor that makes you think: this is what tortilla chips are supposed to taste like. The spices give them a zesty kick, but they are scrumptious with just a sprinkle of salt too. Plain or spiced, they are the best possible scoop for the Five-Layer Mexican Dip (page 54).

Preheat the oven to 350°F.

In a large bowl, combine the oil, chili powder, coriander, cumin, garlic powder, salt, and cayenne pepper. Add the tortilla wedges and toss to coat evenly. Spread in a single layer on two baking sheets and bake until crisp, 20 to 25 minutes.

Makes 12 servings

SERVING SIZE 6 wedges
PER SERVING Calories 80; Total Fat 3 g (Sat Fat 0 g, Mono Fat 1.8 g, Poly Fat 0.6 g); Protein 1 g; Carb 11 g; Fiber 2 g; Cholesterol 0 mg; Sodium 110 mg
EXCELLENT SOURCE OF N/A
GOOD SOURCE OF N/A

	BEFORE*	AFTER	
140 cal.	Sat. Fat 1g, Chol. 0mg Fiber 1g, Sodium 160mg	Sat. Fat 0g, Chol. 0mg Fiber 2g, Sodium 110mg	**80 cal.**

*compared to fried packaged tortilla chips

LEMON-DILL PITA CHIPS

4 whole-wheat pita pockets
(about 6 inches in diameter)

2 tablespoons plus
2 teaspoons extra-virgin
olive oil

1 tablespoon finely grated
lemon zest

1 tablespoon fresh lemon
juice

1 tablespoon dried dill weed

¼ teaspoon salt

This recipe takes the humble pita chip to new heights with a bright twist of lemon and a touch of earthy dill. Dipped in the creamy Roasted Red Pepper Hummus (page 53), they are a true Mediterranean delight.

Preheat the oven to 350°F.

Slice each pita in half into 2 rounds. Then cut each round into 8 wedges.

In a large bowl, whisk together the oil, lemon zest, lemon juice, dill, and salt. Add the pita wedges and toss gently to coat evenly.

Spread the pita wedges in a single layer onto two baking sheets and bake until crisped and golden brown, about 15 minutes. The chips will crisp further as they cool on the sheets. Store the pita chips at room temperature for up to 3 days.

Makes 8 servings

SERVING SIZE 8 wedges
PER SERVING Calories 130; Total Fat 5 g (Sat Fat 0.5 g, Mono Fat 3.4 g, Poly Fat 0.8 g); Protein 3 g; Carb 18 g; Fiber 3 g; Cholesterol 0 mg; Sodium 240 mg
EXCELLENT SOURCE OF Manganese, Selenium
GOOD SOURCE OF Fiber

BEFORE*	AFTER
140 cal. Sat. Fat 0.5g, Chol. 0mg / Fiber 2g, Sodium 270mg	Sat. Fat 0.5g, Chol. 0mg / Fiber 3g, Sodium 240mg **130 cal.**

*compared to packaged multigrain pita chips

SMOKED PAPRIKA POTATO CHIPS

Nonstick cooking spray
2 large russet potatoes
   (about 1¼ pounds total),
   unpeeled
1 tablespoon olive oil
2 teaspoons sweet Spanish
   smoked paprika
½ teaspoon salt

If you don't already have a mandoline slicer, it is worth getting one just to be able to make these chips. Their deep potato flavor is a revelation and they make for a crunchy indulgence you can feel good about. The smoked paprika gives them a depth of flavor that elevates them to another level, but they are also delicious simply salted. Either way, these chips pair perfectly with the Triple Onion Dip (recipe follows).

Preheat the oven to 400°F. Spray two baking sheets with cooking spray.

Slice the potatoes using a mandoline into very thin (1/16-inch) rounds. Rinse the potatoes well under cold water, then spread them on paper towels. Dry them completely using more paper towels.

In a large bowl, whisk together the oil, paprika, and salt. Add the potatoes and toss to coat evenly.

Spread the potatoes in a single layer onto the prepared baking sheets. Bake until the potatoes are crisp and browned and release easily from the baking tray, 12 to 30 minutes. Since small variations in slice thickness can make a big difference in cooking time, check the trays after 12 minutes and every 5 minutes thereafter to remove any chips that are already done, then return the rest to the oven if necessary. The chips will crisp further as they cool. Once cool, store in a paper bag for up to 3 days.

Makes 6 servings

SERVING SIZE about 10 chips
PER SERVING Calories 120; Total Fat 2.5 g (Sat Fat 0 g, Mono Fat 1.7 g, Poly Fat 0.3 g); Protein 3 g; Carb 23 g; Fiber 2 g; Cholesterol 0 mg; Sodium 200 mg
EXCELLENT SOURCE OF Vitamin B6
GOOD SOURCE OF Potassium, Vitamin C

	BEFORE*	AFTER	
150 cal.	Sat. Fat 1g, Chol. 0mg Fiber 1g, Sodium 200mg	Sat. Fat 0g, Chol. 0mg Fiber 2g, Sodium 200mg	**120 cal.**

*compared to fried packaged potato chips

TRIPLE ONION DIP

2 teaspoons olive oil

1 small onion, minced

2 scallions, thinly sliced, green and white parts separated

1¼ cups plain Greek-style nonfat yogurt

¼ cup mayonnaise

¾ teaspoon garlic powder

¾ teaspoon onion powder

½ teaspoon salt, plus more to taste

¼ teaspoon freshly ground black pepper

My friends swear this mouthwatering dip is even more flavorful and addictive than the classic. I must say I agree. I also love that it's nearly as easy to make as opening a spice packet, and it gets its thick creaminess from healthy yogurt. Try serving this with Smoked Paprika Potato Chips (page 58).

Heat the oil in a medium nonstick skillet over medium heat. Add the onion and scallion whites and cook, stirring often, until golden brown and soft, about 10 minutes. Allow to cool completely.

In a large bowl, stir together the onion mixture, yogurt, mayonnaise, garlic powder, onion powder, salt, black pepper, and scallion greens to incorporate. Chill for 1 hour to let the flavors meld. Serve with baked potato chips.

Makes 6 servings

SERVING SIZE ¼ cup
PER SERVING Calories 90; Total Fat 5 g (Sat Fat 0.5 g, Mono Fat 2 g, Poly Fat 2 g); Protein 5 g; Carb 6 g; Fiber 0 g; Cholesterol 5 mg; Sodium 280 mg
EXCELLENT SOURCE OF Vitamin K

	BEFORE	AFTER	
180 cal.	Sat. Fat 6g, Chol. 30mg Fiber 1g, Sodium 380mg	Sat. Fat 0.5g, Chol. 5mg Fiber 1g, Sodium 280mg	**90 cal.**

ROSEMARY PIZZA-DOUGH DIPPERS

1 **pound whole-wheat pizza dough**

1 **tablespoon olive oil**

1 **tablespoon finely chopped fresh rosemary leaves**

¼ **teaspoon coarse sea salt**

You can find whole-wheat pizza dough in the freezer section of many grocery stores these days. It's fun to cook with and the whole grain means it has lots more fiber and antioxidants. Thinking outside the pizza box, I use it for my Broccoli and Cheese Calzones (page 211) and these playful little dippers, which come out warm from the oven, golden brown, wafting of rosemary, ready to be devoured like a little dinner roll, or dipped in Cheesy Pizza Dip (recipe follows).

Preheat the oven to 450°F. Line two baking sheets with parchment paper.

On a lightly floured work surface, using a rolling pin, roll the dough into a large circle about 16 inches in diameter. Using a 2½-inch biscuit cutter, cut out circles of dough and place them on the baking trays. After cutting out as many rounds as possible, reroll the scraps into another circle about the same thickness as the previous one, cut out more rounds, and place them on the tray. You should wind up with about 30 rounds in all.

Brush each round with olive oil, then sprinkle with the rosemary and salt. Bake until golden brown and crisp on the outside, about 10 minutes.

Makes 8 servings

SERVING SIZE 3 to 4 dippers
PER SERVING Calories 140; Total Fat 3.5 g (Sat Fat 0.5 g, Mono Fat 2.5 g, Poly Fat 0 g); Protein 4 g; Carb 24 g; Fiber 3 g; Cholesterol 0 mg; Sodium 370 mg
GOOD SOURCE OF Fiber

	BEFORE*	AFTER	
150 cal.	Sat. Fat 0.5g, Chol. 0mg Fiber 0g, Sodium 400mg	Sat. Fat 0.5g, Chol. 0mg Fiber 3g, Sodium 370mg	**140 cal.**

*compared to regular foccacia bread

CHEESY PIZZA DIP

2 cups Quick Marinara Sauce
(recipe follows)

½ cup part-skim ricotta
cheese

⅓ cup shredded part-skim
mozzarella cheese

2 tablespoons freshly grated
Parmesan cheese

4 large or 6 small whole basil
leaves

What could be more comforting than dipping bread into a bubbling hot dish of savory marinara sauce laden with melted cheese? For me those warm fuzzies are enhanced knowing it is good for you too.

Preheat the oven to 450°F.

Pour the sauce into a 10-inch ovenproof skillet. Heat the sauce over medium-high heat to warm through, about 4 minutes.

Remove the pan from the heat and spoon the ricotta cheese in 4 large dollops onto the sauce, tucking each dollop slightly into the sauce with the spoon. Sprinkle the mozzarella, then the Parmesan over the top. Top with the basil leaves.

Bake until the sauce is bubbling and the cheese is melted, 3 to 4 minutes. Serve warm, directly from the skillet, with slices of whole-wheat Italian bread or Rosemary Pizza-Dough Dippers (page 61).

Makes 8 servings

SERVING SIZE about ¼ cup
PER SERVING Calories 70; Total Fat 3.5 g (Sat Fat 1.5 g, Mono Fat 2 g, Poly Fat 0 g); Protein 4 g; Carb 4 g; Fiber 1g; Cholesterol 10 mg; Sodium 170 mg
EXCELLENT SOURCE OF Vitamin C
GOOD SOURCE OF Calcium, Vitamin A

BEFORE	AFTER	
100 cal. Sat. Fat 3.5g, Chol. 20mg	Sat. Fat 1.5g, Chol. 10mg	
Fiber 1g, Sodium 410mg	Fiber 1g, Sodium 170mg **70 cal.**	

QUICK MARINARA SAUCE

1 tablespoon olive oil

1 small onion, finely chopped

4 cloves garlic, minced

One 28-ounce can crushed
tomatoes (preferably no-
salt-added)

1 teaspoon dried basil

Pinch crushed red pepper
flakes

½ teaspoon salt (if using no-
salt-added tomatoes), or to
taste

Freshly ground black
pepper to taste

A good marinara is a comfort food staple, especially if pasta, pizza, and Parmesan dishes rank high on your feel-good list. This versatile tomato sauce gives you maximum flavor fast so you won't be tempted to resort to the high-sodium jarred stuff. When you make it yourself, you know you are getting the best ingredients, and you control the salt.

Heat the oil in a large, deep skillet over medium-high heat. Add the onion and cook, stirring occasionally, until tender and translucent, about 5 minutes. Add the garlic and cook, stirring, for 1 minute. Add the tomatoes, basil, and red pepper flakes and bring to a boil. Reduce the heat to medium low and simmer for 15 minutes. Season with salt and black pepper.

Makes 6 servings

SERVING SIZE ½ cup
PER SERVING Calories 60; Total Fat 2.5 g (Sat Fat 0 g, Mono Fat 2 g, Poly Fat 0.5 g); Protein 1 g; Carb 8 g; Fiber 2 g; Cholesterol 0 mg; Sodium 210 mg
EXCELLENT SOURCE OF Vitamin C
GOOD SOURCE OF Vitamin A

	BEFORE*	AFTER	
90 cal.	Sat. Fat 0.5g, Chol. 0mg Fiber 2g, Sodium 580mg	Sat. Fat 0g, Chol. 0mg Fiber 2g, Sodium 210mg	**60 cal.**

*compared to jarred marinara sauce

SESAME WHOLE-WHEAT SOFT PRETZELS

Nonstick cooking spray

1 packet instant yeast
  (2¼ teaspoons)

3 tablespoons honey

1½ cups warm water (110°F to
  115°F)

2¼ cups whole-wheat flour

2½ cups all-purpose flour

2 teaspoons salt

2 tablespoons canola oil

1 tablespoon unsalted butter,
  melted

1 large egg

1 teaspoon water

3 tablespoons sesame seeds

1½ teaspoons coarse salt

Soft pretzels remind me of childhood outings in New York City with my dad when he would promise we could "eat under the umbrella"—the street vendor's umbrella, that is. I brought those warm memories home where I make these pretzels with my daughter. I just downsized them a bit so the portion is smarter, used whole-grain flour, and added a sprinkle of sesame seeds so you need less salt. These pretzels couldn't be more kid-friendly. The dough doesn't require rising, so you get that instant gratification and it is easy to work with so children can have fun making different shapes—knots, braids, hearts, twists. It even freezes well so you can make it in advance. Try serving this with the Honey-Mustard Dip (recipe follows).

Preheat the oven to 425°F. Spray two baking sheets with cooking spray.

In the bowl of a stand mixer, using a spoon, stir together the yeast, honey, and warm water until the yeast is dissolved. Let the yeast mixture sit until it begins to foam, 5 or 6 minutes.

Meanwhile, in a large bowl, whisk together the flours and salt to combine. Add the flour mixture, oil, and butter to the yeast mixture and mix on low speed with the paddle attachment just enough to combine them and a dough begins to form, 10 to 15 seconds. Switch to a dough hook and mix on low to medium speed until the dough is smooth but still pliable, about 2 to 3 minutes.

Remove the dough from the bowl and divide into 6 equal parts (about 6 ounces each). Divide each part into three 2-ounce balls. Using

	BEFORE*	AFTER	
400 cal.	Sat. Fat 3.5g, Chol. 10mg Fiber 3g, Sodium 990mg	Sat. Fat 0.5g, Chol. 10mg Fiber 3g, Sodium 420mg	**160 cal.**

*compared to a store-bought soft pretzel

your hands, roll each ball out until it is about 14 inches long, then twist into the shape of a pretzel.

In a small bowl, beat together the egg and the water. On a plate, combine the sesame seeds and coarse salt. Brush the top of each pretzel generously with the egg wash, dip into the sesame-salt mixture, then place on the prepared baking sheets. Bake until a golden crust is formed but the pretzels are still soft inside, 18 to 20 minutes. Serve with the Honey-Mustard Dip (page 66) if desired.

Makes 18 pretzels

SERVING SIZE 1 pretzel
PER SERVING Calories 160; Total Fat 3.5 g (Sat Fat 0.5 g, Mono Fat 1.5 g, Poly Fat 1 g); Protein 4 g; Carb 28 g; Fiber 3 g; Cholesterol 10 mg; Sodium 420 mg
EXCELLENT SOURCE OF Manganese, Selenium
GOOD SOURCE OF Fiber, Folate, Niacin, Thiamin

HONEY-MUSTARD DIP

¼ **cup grainy mustard**
¼ **cup Dijon mustard**
¼ **cup honey**

It's pretty eye-opening that many honey mustards on the market have high-fructose corn syrup, not honey, as one of the first ingredients. All it takes is a quick stir of real, antioxidant-rich honey and mustard to make your own tangy-sweet spread or dip. Here I use two kinds of mustard for a textural twist.

In a small bowl, stir together the mustards and honey to combine.

Makes 18 servings

SERVING SIZE 2 teaspoons
PER SERVING Calories 15; Total Fat 0 g (Sat Fat 0 g, Mono Fat 0 g, Poly Fat 0 g); Protein 0 g; Carb 4 g; Fiber 0 g; Cholesterol 0 mg; Sodium 85 mg
EXCELLENT SOURCE OF N/A
GOOD SOURCE OF N/A

	BEFORE*	AFTER	
20 cal.	Sat. Fat 0g, Chol. 0mg Fiber 0g, Sodium 85mg	Sat. Fat 0g, Chol. 0mg Fiber 0g, Sodium 85mg	**15 cal.**

*compared to store-bought

DEVILISH CRAB DIP

Nonstick cooking spray
1 tablespoon olive oil
1 medium onion, finely chopped
1 large rib celery, finely chopped
1 clove garlic, minced
½ cup Neufchâtel cheese (reduced-fat cream cheese; 4 ounces), at room temperature
½ cup reduced-fat sour cream
2 tablespoons fresh lemon juice
1 teaspoon Dijon mustard
¼ teaspoon salt
¼ teaspoon hot pepper sauce, like Tabasco
One 10-ounce package frozen chopped spinach, thawed
½ pound lump crabmeat, drained and picked over for shells and cartilage
1 scallion, green part only, chopped

This dreamy, creamy, warm dip is loaded with succulent crab and has the perfect spicy kick. The addition of chopped spinach gives it a touch of beautiful color and a nutritional boost. It is so delicious it will certainly be devoured before it has a chance to cool.

Move the oven rack to the center of the oven and preheat the oven to 375°F. Spray a 1-quart shallow baking dish or 9-inch pie plate with cooking spray.

Heat the oil in a medium skillet over medium-low heat. Add the onion and celery and cook, stirring occasionally, until softened, 3 to 5 minutes. Add the garlic and cook, stirring, for 1 minute. Remove from the heat and allow to cool.

Place the cream cheese, sour cream, lemon juice, mustard, salt, and hot pepper sauce in a food processor and process until smooth. Add the onion-celery mixture and pulse to combine. Transfer the mixture to the prepared baking dish.

Place the spinach into a strainer and press out as much liquid as you can. Stir the spinach into the cream cheese mixture, then gently fold in the crabmeat and scallion. Bake until heated through, 20 to 25 minutes. Serve hot with crackers and crudités.

Makes 12 servings

SERVING SIZE ¼ cup
PER SERVING Calories 80; Total Fat 5 g (Sat Fat 2 g, Mono Fat 1.7 g, Poly Fat 0.5 g); Protein 7 g; Carb 3 g; Fiber 1 g; Cholesterol 25 mg; Sodium 190 mg
EXCELLENT SOURCE OF Vitamin A, Vitamin K
GOOD SOURCE OF Folate, Protein

	BEFORE	AFTER	
140 cal.	Sat. Fat 8g, Chol. 50mg Fiber 0g, Sodium 300mg	Sat. Fat 2g, Chol. 25mg Fiber 1g, Sodium 190mg	**80 cal.**

STUFFED POTATO SKINS WITH AVOCADO CREAM

8 small russet potatoes, scrubbed and dried (about 2½ pounds)

4 teaspoons olive oil

¼ teaspoon salt

4 cups broccoli florets, coarsely chopped (about 8 ounces)

Olive oil cooking spray

3 pieces Canadian bacon, finely diced (about 3 ounces)

¾ cup grated extra-sharp cheddar cheese (about 3 ounces)

1 recipe Avocado Cream (recipe follows)

The crispy skin of a baked potato has been a favorite of mine since childhood. I always waited to eat mine so it could be the grand finale of my meal. How nice to know the skin is the healthiest part of the potato too. And what better way to make the most of it than to stuff it with mouthwatering melted cheddar cheese, fresh tender broccoli, smoky Canadian bacon, and cool avocado cream.

Preheat the oven to 450°F.

Pierce the potatoes all over with a fork and wrap in paper towels. Microwave on high until the potatoes are cooked through, 13 to 15 minutes. Remove from the microwave and cool until the potatoes are easy to handle. Slice the potatoes in half lengthwise. Using a spoon, scoop out all but ⅛ inch of the inside of the potato, leaving the skin intact. Reserve the scooped-out potatoes for another use.

Brush both the inside and outside of the potatoes with the oil and sprinkle with the salt. Place the potatoes, skin side down, on a baking sheet and bake until the skins are crisp and the edges are golden brown, about 20 minutes.

In the meantime, make the filling. Steam the broccoli until crisp-

BEFORE		AFTER	
350 cal.	Sat. Fat 11g, Chol. 80mg Fiber 2g, Sodium 560mg	Sat. Fat 3.5g, Chol. 20mg Fiber 5g, Sodium 350mg	**210 cal.**

tender, 3 to 4 minutes. Spray a nonstick pan with cooking spray and heat over medium-high heat. Add the Canadian bacon and cook until crisp, stirring often, 3 to 4 minutes.

Toss the broccoli with the cheese. Divide the filling equally among the potatoes. Lower the oven temperature to 400°F and return the potatoes to the oven until the cheese is melted, about 5 minutes. Spoon 1 heaping tablespoon of the Avocado Cream on top of the broccoli-filled potatoes and garnish with the scallion greens (from the Avocado Cream recipe) and 1 teaspoon of the crisped Canadian bacon bits.

Makes 8 servings

SERVING SIZE 2 potato halves and 2 rounded tablespoons avocado cream
PER SERVING Calories 210; Total Fat 11 g (Sat Fat 3.5 g, Mono Fat 5.6 g, Poly Fat 1 g); Protein 9 g; Carb 23 g; Fiber 5 g; Cholesterol 20 mg; Sodium 350 mg
EXCELLENT SOURCE OF Vitamin A, Vitamin B6, Vitamin C, Vitamin K
GOOD SOURCE OF Calcium, Copper, Folate, Fiber, Iron, Magnesium, Manganese, Niacin, Phosphorus, Potassium, Protein, Thiamin

AVOCADO CREAM

1 medium avocado
2 scallions, thinly sliced, white and green parts separated
2 tablespoons reduced-fat sour cream
2 tablespoons fresh lime juice
¼ cup fresh cilantro leaves
1 clove garlic
⅛ teaspoon salt, plus more to taste

I came up with this recipe as a topper for my stuffed potato skins, but I found myself using it for all sorts of dishes that might ordinarily beg for a dollop of sour cream. This way you get that cool creaminess plus vitamins, minerals, fiber, and fabulous flavor. Try it on regular baked potatoes, fish tacos, or chili. It's also nice as a veggie or chip dip.

Peel and pit the avocado, then combine the scallion whites, avocado, sour cream, lime juice, cilantro, garlic, and salt in a food processor and process on high until smooth, about 30 seconds. Stir in more salt, if needed, to taste. Serve garnished with the scallion greens. The avocado cream will last up to 2 days in an airtight container in the refrigerator.

Makes 8 servings

SERVING SIZE 2 rounded tablespoons
PER SERVING Calories 50; Total Fat 4 g (Sat Fat 1 g, Mono Fat 2.6 g, Poly Fat 0.5 g); Protein 1 g; Carb 3 g; Fiber 2 g; Cholesterol 0 mg; Sodium 40 mg
EXCELLENT SOURCE OF N/A
GOOD SOURCE OF Vitamin K

	BEFORE*	AFTER	
60 cal.	Sat. Fat 3.5g, Chol. 15mg Fiber 0g, Sodium 25mg	Sat. Fat 1g, Chol. 0mg Fiber 2g, Sodium 40mg	**50 cal.**

*compared to sour cream

CEREAL PARTY MIX

3 tablespoons olive oil

1 tablespoon plus 1 teaspoon Worcestershire sauce

½ teaspoon salt

½ teaspoon garlic powder

½ teaspoon ground cumin

½ teaspoon onion powder

¼ teaspoon cayenne pepper

3 cups whole-grain cereal squares, like Chex

1 cup cornflakes cereal

1 cup unsalted bite-size pretzels, preferably whole wheat

¼ cup whole natural almonds

¼ cup pumpkin seeds

1 whole-wheat pita bread, cut into 1-inch pieces

By swapping out the butter for olive oil and using whole-grain cereal, pretzels, and pita, I've turned the usual cereal party mix into a healthier snack without sacrificing that addictive savory, salty flavor. I have also added a touch of simple sophistication by using whole almonds and pumpkin seeds instead of the run-of-the-mill can of mixed nuts.

Preheat the oven to 250°F.

In a small bowl, whisk together the oil, Worcestershire sauce, salt, garlic powder, cumin, onion powder, and cayenne pepper. In a large bowl, mix together the cereals, pretzels, almonds, pumpkin seeds, and pita bread. Drizzle with the spice mixture and toss to coat evenly. Spread onto a baking sheet and bake for 1 hour, stirring every 20 minutes.

Makes 14 servings

SERVING SIZE about ½ cup
PER SERVING Calories 130; Total Fat 6 g (Sat Fat 1 g, Mono Fat 3.3 Poly Fat 1.2); Protein 3 g; Carb 18 g; Fiber 2 g; Cholesterol 0 mg; Sodium 260 mg
EXCELLENT SOURCE OF Folate, Iron, Manganese
GOOD SOURCE OF Niacin, Riboflavin, Thiamin, Vitamin B6

BEFORE	AFTER
Sat. Fat 2.5g, Chol. 10mg	Sat. Fat 1g, Chol. 0mg
Fiber 1g, Sodium 260mg	Fiber 2g, Sodium 260mg
140 cal.	130 cal.

BAKED JALAPEÑO POPPERS

Olive oil cooking spray
⅓ cup whipped cream cheese
⅓ cup part-skim ricotta cheese
½ cup packed grated Monterey Jack cheese (2 ounces)
2 tablespoons minced fresh parsley leaves
12 medium fresh jalapeño peppers, halved lengthwise, seeded, and deveined
¼ cup all-purpose flour
½ teaspoon salt
¼ teaspoon freshly ground black pepper
1 large egg
2 tablespoons water
1 cup Light-and-Crisp Whole-Wheat Bread Crumbs (recipe follows)
2 teaspoons smoked paprika
1 teaspoon garlic powder
Pinch cayenne pepper

These tempting bites are crisp and flavorful outside and luxurious inside, with the spicy jalapeños calmed by the creamy melted-cheese stuffing and a fresh sprinkle of parsley. They're total satisfaction without a deep fryer in sight.

Preheat the oven to 350°F. Spray a baking sheet with cooking spray.

In a small bowl, stir together the cheeses and parsley. Fill each jalapeño half with 2 teaspoons of the cheese mixture.

On a plate, combine the flour, ¼ teaspoon of the salt, and ⅛ teaspoon of the black pepper. In a small bowl, beat together the egg and the water to combine. On another plate, combine the bread crumbs, the remaining ¼ teaspoon salt, the remaining ⅛ teaspoon black pepper, the paprika, garlic powder, and cayenne pepper.

Dip each jalapeño half in the flour, shaking off the excess, then in the egg wash, and finally in the bread crumb mixture, shaking off the excess.

Place the coated jalapeños, cut side up, onto the prepared baking sheet and spray lightly to coat with cooking spray. Bake until golden brown and crisp and the cheese has melted, about 30 minutes.

Makes 6 servings

SERVING SIZE 4 poppers
PER SERVING Calories 110; Total Fat 9 g (Sat Fat 3.5g, Mono Fat 1.8 g, Poly Fat 0.5 g); Protein 6 g; Carb 8g; Fiber 2 g; Cholesterol 45 mg; Sodium 270 mg
EXCELLENT SOURCE OF Vitamin K
GOOD SOURCE OF Calcium, Manganese, Phosphorus, Protein, Riboflavin, Selenium, Vitamin A, Vitamin C

	BEFORE	AFTER	
210 cal.	Sat. Fat 6g, Chol. 55mg Fiber 1g, Sodium 290mg	Sat. Fat 3.5g, Chol. 45mg Fiber 2g, Sodium 270mg	**110 cal.**

LIGHT-AND-CRISP WHOLE-WHEAT BREAD CRUMBS

4 slices whole-wheat sandwich bread (about 1 ounce each)

Homemade bread crumbs are one of those "chef's secrets"—an important but often overlooked detail that can make a dish. These easy-to-make crumbs are flaky, mild, and versatile—they don't have that heavy whole-wheat taste and dense texture that most store-bought brands have. Since bread crumbs are a comfort-food cornerstone used in everything from cutlet coatings to casserole toppings, it's key to have the best.

Preheat the oven to 350°F.

Place the bread in a food processor and process until fine crumbs form, 25 to 30 seconds. Place the crumbs on a baking sheet, spreading them evenly. Bake until golden brown, about 12 minutes. Store the bread crumbs in an airtight container for up to 2 weeks.

Makes 1⅓ cups bread crumbs or 4 servings

SERVING SIZE ⅓ cup bread crumbs
PER SERVING Calories 70; Total Fat 1 g (Sat Fat 0 g, Mono Fat 0.5 g, Poly Fat 0.2 g); Protein 4 g; Carb 12 g; Fiber 2 g; Cholesterol 0 mg; Sodium 130 mg
EXCELLENT SOURCE OF Manganese
GOOD SOURCE OF Selenium

BEFORE*		AFTER	
110 cal.	Sat. Fat 0.5g, Chol. 0mg Fiber 1g, Sodium 220mg	Sat. Fat 0g, Chol. 0mg Fiber 2g, Sodium 130mg	**70 cal.**

*compared to regular (not whole-grain) store-bought bread crumbs

LOADED NACHOS

Eight 6-inch corn tortillas, each cut into 6 wedges

2 tablespoons olive oil

½ teaspoon salt

1 small onion, chopped

2 cloves garlic, minced

1 teaspoon ground coriander

½ teaspoon ground cumin

One 15-ounce can pinto beans, preferably low-sodium, drained and rinsed

¾ cup low-sodium chicken broth

Freshly ground black pepper to taste

2 jalapeño peppers, seeded and finely diced (¼ cup)

2 medium ripe tomatoes, seeded and diced

¾ cup packed finely shredded Monterey Jack cheese (3 ounces)

⅓ cup reduced-fat sour cream

2 teaspoons fresh lime juice

2 tablespoons chopped fresh cilantro leaves

Whenever I have nachos I am instantly transported back to college with my good friends, laughing it up and toasting over a beer. These nachos are so much better than the ones from back then—loaded with juicy tomatoes, just-made "refried" beans, fresh cilantro, the perfect amount of Jack cheese, and topped with a limey sour cream drizzle. Nowadays when I whip up this recipe, my friends (many of the same ones from college) and I share the food and laughter with our kids. But of course, we keep the beer for ourselves.

Preheat the oven to 350°F.

Place the tortilla wedges into a large bowl. Drizzle with 1 tablespoon of the oil and sprinkle with ¼ teaspoon of the salt. Toss to coat. Spread in a single layer on two baking sheets and bake until crisp, 20 to 25 minutes.

Heat the remaining 1 tablespoon oil in a medium skillet over medium-high heat. Add the onion and cook until softened, about 3 minutes. Add the garlic, coriander, and cumin and cook 30 seconds more. Stir in the beans and chicken broth and cook until the beans are warmed through, about 4 minutes. Mash the beans coarsely with the

	BEFORE	AFTER	
710 cal.	Sat. Fat 25g, Chol. 120mg Fiber 9g, Sodium 840mg	Sat. Fat 5g, Chol. 15mg Fiber 9g, Sodium 300mg	**320 cal.**

back of a wooden spoon or a potato masher. Season with the remaining ¼ teaspoon salt and black pepper.

Increase the oven temperature to 400°F. Spread half the chips out in a large shallow baking dish. Spoon half of the beans onto the chips, then sprinkle on half the jalapeños and half the tomatoes. Repeat with the remaining chips, beans, jalapeños, and tomatoes. Sprinkle with the cheese. Bake until warmed through and the cheese is melted, about 5 minutes.

In a small bowl, stir together the sour cream and lime juice to combine. When the nachos are ready, drizzle with the lime sour cream and sprinkle the cilantro over the top.

Makes 6 servings

SERVING SIZE 8 loaded chips
PER SERVING Calories 320; Total Fat 12 g (Sat Fat 5 g, Mono Fat 5.5 g, Poly Fat 1.3 g); Protein 14 g; Carb 40 g; Fiber 9 g; Cholesterol 15 mg; Sodium 300 mg
EXCELLENT SOURCE OF Calcium, Fiber, Folate, Manganese, Molybdenum, Phosphorus, Protein
GOOD SOURCE OF Copper, Iron, Magnesium, Potassium, Riboflavin, Selenium, Thiamin, Vitamin A, Vitamin B6, Vitamin C, Vitamin K, Zinc

BROILED BUFFALO WINGS

2 pounds chicken wings, split at the joint

¼ cup cayenne pepper sauce, preferably Frank's Red Hot, plus more for serving

1 tablespoon fresh lemon juice

3 tablespoons low-sodium chicken broth

3 large ribs celery, cut into sticks

1 recipe Blue Cheese Dip (recipe follows)

I knew I was onto something when my husband, one of the world's most critical, and perhaps most experienced, Buffalo wing eaters, reviewed these as "Excellent wings!" That's just the response I was going for and it is especially meaningful when you see how their numbers stack up against the ones he's used to eating. The secret to keeping them crispy and flavorful without the saturated fat and calories is to par-boil, then broil the chicken instead of frying it, and use a touch of oil and broth in the tongue-tingling sauce in place of the usual load of butter.

Preheat the broiler.

Place the wings in a large pot and fill the pot with water to cover by about 2 inches. Bring to a boil, then continue to boil for 10 minutes. Drain.

Meanwhile, in a small bowl, combine the cayenne pepper sauce, lemon juice, and broth. Reserve.

Transfer the wings to a broiler pan and broil 5 to 6 inches from the flame, until the skin begins to blister and brown, 5 to 6 minutes. Turn the wings over and broil 4 to 5 minutes more.

Transfer the wings to a baking sheet, drizzle with the reserved sauce, and toss well to coat. Place the baking sheet under the broiler for 1 minute to heat the wings and sauce together.

Serve with extra hot sauce on the side, celery sticks, and the blue cheese dip.

Makes 4 servings

SERVING SIZE 4 to 5 pieces, 2 tablespoons dip, and 4 to 5 celery sticks
PER SERVING Calories 240; Total Fat 12 g (Sat Fat 4 g, Mono Fat 3.6 g, Poly Fat 3 g); Protein 27 g; Carb 4 g; Fiber 1 g; Cholesterol 95 mg; Sodium 710 mg
EXCELLENT SOURCE OF Niacin, Phosphorus, Protein, Selenium, Vitamin B6, Vitamin C, Vitamin K
GOOD SOURCE OF Calcium, Pantothenic Acid, Potassium, Riboflavin, Vitamin A, Zinc

BEFORE	AFTER
770 cal. Sat. Fat 15g, Chol. 195mg Fiber 1g, Sodium 2560mg	Sat. Fat 4g, Chol. 95mg Fiber 1g, Sodium 710mg **240 cal.**

BLUE CHEESE DIP

¼ cup plain Greek-style nonfat yogurt

2 tablespoons mayonnaise

1 teaspoon white wine vinegar

⅓ cup crumbled blue cheese (1½ ounces)

Why settle for a blue cheese dip where you practically need a search party to find the few bits of cheese swimming around in the mayo? Especially when you can have this one, chock-full of pungent blue cheese—thick, tangy, decadent, and so much better for you.

In a small bowl, stir together the yogurt, mayonnaise, vinegar, and blue cheese. Mash any very large chunks of blue cheese with the back of a spoon to integrate it into the dip.

Make the dip up to 3 days ahead and store in an airtight container in the refrigerator. Allow to come to room temperature before serving.

Makes 4 servings

SERVING SIZE 2 tablespoons
PER SERVING Calories 70; Total Fat 6 g (Sat Fat 2.5 g, Mono Fat 1.5 g, Poly Fat 1.41 g); Protein 4 g; Carb 3; Fiber 0 g; Cholesterol 10 mg; Sodium 210 mg
EXCELLENT SOURCE OF N/A
GOOD SOURCE OF N/A

BEFORE
220 cal. Sat. Fat 4.5g, Chol. 15mg
Fiber 0g, Sodium 470mg

AFTER
Sat. Fat 2.5g, Chol. 10mg
Fiber 0g, Sodium 210mg **70 cal.**

PAPER BAG POPCORN

¼ cup popcorn kernels

½ teaspoon peanut or canola oil

¼ teaspoon salt, plus more to taste

1 paper lunch bag

Warning: This recipe will make you feel silly for having spent five times the money on microwave bags of popcorn all these years. All you really need is a paper bag and some corn kernels. You control the seasonings, and skip all the artificial flavors and preservatives. I like mine best lightly salted, but popcorn is also delicious with a sprinkle of Cajun or Chesapeake seasoning. Either way, it makes movie night even more fun.

In a small bowl, toss together the popcorn kernels, oil, and salt. Transfer the mixture to the paper bag and fold the bag over three or four times to close. Place the bag in the microwave on top of a plate, and cook on high until the kernels stop popping, about 2 minutes. Season with additional salt, if desired.

Makes 2 servings

SERVING SIZE about 3 cups
PER SERVING Calories 100; Total Fat 2 g (Sat Fat 0g, Mono Fat 0.8 g, Poly Fat 1g) ; Protein 3 g; Carb 18 g; Fiber 3 g; Cholesterol 0 mg; Sodium 290 mg
EXCELLENT SOURCE OF N/A
GOOD SOURCE OF Fiber, Manganese

	BEFORE*	AFTER	
170 cal.	Sat. Fat 6g, Chol. 0mg Fiber 3g, Sodium 380mg	Sat. Fat 0g, Chol. 0mg Fiber 3g, Sodium 290mg	**100 cal.**

* compared to regular microwave popcorn

SWEDISH MEATBALLS

Nonstick cooking spray
1 slice whole-wheat bread
3 tablespoons low-fat (1%) milk
3 tablespoons canola oil
1 small onion, finely diced (about 1 cup)
1 pound lean ground beef (90% lean or higher)
1 large egg, lightly beaten
¾ teaspoon ground nutmeg
¾ teaspoon salt
¼ teaspoon ground allspice
¼ teaspoon freshly ground black pepper
3 tablespoons all-purpose flour
2 cups low-sodium beef broth
½ cup reduced-fat sour cream
2 tablespoons chopped fresh parsley leaves

These heavenly meatballs are melt-in-your-mouth tender, soft, and light. The nutmeg gives them a gentle sweetness that mingles beautifully with a sour cream–enhanced beef broth. By using whole-wheat bread, lean beef, and broiling instead of frying, I give them an extra halo.

Preheat the broiler. Spray a baking sheet with cooking spray.

Place the bread in a food processor and process until fine crumbs form. Transfer the crumbs to a bowl and sprinkle evenly with the milk.

Heat 1 tablespoon of the oil in a nonstick skillet over medium heat. Add the onion and cook, stirring, until softened, about 5 minutes. Remove from the heat. Allow to cool slightly, 3 to 5 minutes.

In a large bowl, mix together the moistened bread crumbs, onion, beef, egg, nutmeg, ½ teaspoon salt, allspice, and black pepper to incorporate.

Form the mixture into ½-inch balls and place them on the prepared

	BEFORE	AFTER	
460 cal.	Sat. Fat 16g, Chol. 180mg Fiber 1g, Sodium 950mg	Sat. Fat 4g, Chol. 70mg Fiber 1g, Sodium 310mg	**220 cal.**

baking sheet. Broil about 5 inches from the flame, until browned and cooked through, 6 to 7 minutes.

Heat the remaining 2 tablespoons oil in a medium saucepan over medium-high heat. Sprinkle in the flour and whisk until the mixture is light brown and thickened, 2 to 3 minutes. Add the beef broth and stir to incorporate. Bring to a boil, reduce the heat to medium low, and simmer until thickened, about 5 minutes. Stir in the sour cream and the remaining ¼ teaspoon salt. Add the meatballs and cook over medium-low heat until heated through, about 5 minutes more. Serve garnished with parsley.

Makes 8 servings

SERVING SIZE 5 meatballs and 3 tablespoons sauce
PER SERVING Calories 220; Total Fat 14 g (Sat Fat 4 g, Mono Fat 7 g, Poly Fat 2 g); Protein 15 g; Carb 6 g; Fiber 1 g; Cholesterol 70 mg; Sodium 310 mg
EXCELLENT SOURCE OF Protein, Niacin, Vitamin B12, Vitamin K, Zinc
GOOD SOURCE OF Iron, Phosphorus, Riboflavin, Selenium, Vitamin B6

STUFFED MUSHROOMS

16 white button mushrooms
  (12 ounces)
2 tablespoons olive oil
¼ cup minced shallot
2 cloves garlic, minced
1 cup Light-and-Crisp Whole-
  Wheat Bread Crumbs
  (page 73)
3 sun-dried tomatoes,
  reconstituted in hot water if
  very dry, finely minced
2 tablespoons chopped fresh
  oregano, or 2 teaspoons
  dried
¼ teaspoon salt
¼ teaspoon freshly ground
  black pepper
¼ teaspoon crushed red
  pepper flakes
¼ cup freshly grated
  Parmesan cheese

These mushrooms owe their mouthwatering sensibility to umami—the fifth taste that, loosely translated from Japanese, means "deliciousness." Sun-dried tomatoes, aged cheese, and the mushrooms themselves are all umami heavy hitters. Together they make for edible proof that you don't need lots of fat for flavor.

Preheat the oven to 350°F.

Wipe the mushrooms with a damp paper towel. Carefully remove the stems. Trim any tough ends from the stems and discard. Finely chop the remaining stems.

Heat 1 tablespoon of the oil in a medium nonstick skillet over medium heat. Add the shallot and cook, stirring occasionally, until translucent, about 3 minutes. Add the garlic and cook for 30 seconds. Add the chopped mushroom stems and cook until they release their liquid, 4 to 5 minutes. Add the bread crumbs, sun-dried tomatoes, oregano, salt, black pepper, and red pepper flakes and stir until well combined. Remove from the heat and stir in the cheese.

	BEFORE	AFTER	
360 cal.	Sat. Fat 18g, Chol. 88mg Fiber 1g, Sodium 350mg	Sat. Fat 2g, Chol. 5mg Fiber 4g, Sodium 340mg	200 cal.

Brush the mushroom caps with the remaining 1 tablespoon olive oil, then stuff each cap with about 1 tablespoon of the filling. Place the stuffed mushrooms on a baking sheet and bake until the bread crumbs are browned, 20 to 25 minutes. Serve immediately.

Makes 4 servings

SERVING SIZE 4 mushrooms
PER SERVING Calories 200; Total Fat 10 g (Sat Fat 2 g, Mono Fat 5.7 g, Poly Fat 1.17 g); Protein 10 g; Carb 21 g; Fiber 4 g; Cholesterol 5 mg; Sodium 340 mg
EXCELLENT SOURCE OF Manganese, Niacin, Riboflavin, Selenium
GOOD SOURCE OF Calcium, Copper, Fiber, Iron, Magnesium, Pantothenic Acid, Phosphorus, Potassium, Protein, Thiamin, Vitamin A, Vitamin B6, Vitamin C, Vitamin K

SHRIMP SPRING ROLLS

2 tablespoons canola oil

2 slices Canadian bacon, finely diced (1 ounce)

1 tablespoon grated fresh ginger

3 cloves garlic, minced

3 scallions, thinly sliced

1 pound raw shrimp, peeled, deveined, and finely chopped

1½ cups finely shredded green cabbage

1 medium carrot, shredded

¼ cup fresh cilantro leaves, chopped

1 teaspoon toasted sesame oil

1 tablespoon reduced-sodium soy sauce

1 tablespoon rice vinegar

½ teaspoon crushed red pepper flakes

1 large egg white

2 teaspoons water

14 square spring-roll or egg-roll wrappers

Egg rolls dipped in duck sauce bring me back to festive childhood meals in Chinatown, where I spent half the time practicing to use my chopsticks. At least I could pick up the egg roll with my fingers! As an adult, on the rare occasions I have ordered them, I have been turned off with how greasy they are. This recipe brings all the best lip-smacking taste memories to the table—a crisped shell encasing mounds of fragrant, savory shrimp and shredded vegetables—totally grease-free. Try serving it with Apricot-Ginger Dipping Sauce (recipe follows).

Preheat the oven to 425°F.

Heat 1 tablespoon of the oil in a large nonstick skillet over medium-high heat. Add the Canadian bacon and cook until crisped, 2 to 3 minutes. Add the ginger, garlic, and scallions and cook, stirring, until fragrant, about 1 minute. Add the shrimp and cook until the shrimp has just turned pink but is not quite done, about 2 minutes. Allow to cool slightly.

In a large bowl, toss together the bacon-shrimp mixture, cabbage, carrot, cilantro, sesame oil, soy sauce, vinegar, and red pepper flakes. In a small bowl, beat together the egg white and the water.

Mound about ⅓ cup of the filling onto the lower third of a wrapper, leaving a 1-inch border on each side. Brush the egg wash along the edges of each border, then fold the sides up over the filling. Then fold

continued on page 86

	BEFORE	AFTER	
240 cal.	Sat. Fat 1.5 g, Chol. 90mg Fiber 2g, Sodium 1210 mg	Sat. Fat 0g, Chol. 55mg Fiber 1g, Sodium 310mg	**160 cal.**

continued from page 84

the bottom over the filling and roll up tightly, burrito style, to enclose the filling.

Using a skewer or toothpick, poke several holes all around each spring roll. Lightly brush the rolls all around with the remaining 1 tablespoon oil, then place the rolls on a rack sitting on a baking tray. Bake for 15 minutes, turn the rolls over, and bake until golden brown and crisped, 10 to 15 minutes more. Allow to cool for 5 minutes before serving. The spring rolls will continue to crisp as they cool.

Makes 14 servings

SERVING SIZE 1 roll
PER SERVING Calories 160; Total Fat 3.5 g (Sat Fat 0 g, Mono Fat 1.6 g, Poly Fat 1.1 g); Protein 11 g; Carb 20 g; Fiber 1 g; Cholesterol 55 mg; Sodium 310 mg
EXCELLENT SOURCE OF Protein, Selenium
GOOD SOURCE OF Iron, Manganese, Niacin, Phosphorus, Thiamin, Vitamin A, Vitamin C, Vitamin K

APRICOT-GINGER DIPPING SAUCE

½ cup all-fruit apricot jam
¼ cup rice vinegar
2 tablespoons water
1 teaspoon finely grated
  fresh ginger

You might want to double the recipe when you make this "duck sauce" to go with the Shrimp Spring Rolls because it is delicious spread on grilled chicken or pork, as a glaze for cooked carrots, or, by golly, even served with duck.

In a small bowl, mix together the jam, vinegar, water, and ginger to combine. Make the dip up to a week ahead and store in an airtight container in the refrigerator.

Makes 14 servings

SERVING SIZE 1 tablespoon
PER SERVING Calories 30; Total Fat 0 g (Sat Fat 0 g, Mono Fat 0 g, Poly Fat 0 g); Protein 0 g; Carb 7 g; Fiber 0 g; Cholesterol 0 mg; Sodium 0 mg
EXCELLENT SOURCE OF N/A
GOOD SOURCE OF N/A

BEFORE
40 cal.
Sat. Fat 0g, Chol. 0mg
Fiber 0g, Sodium 400mg

AFTER
Sat. Fat 0g, Chol. 0mg
Fiber 0g, Sodium 0mg
30 cal.

*compared to store-bought

DOGS IN BLANKETS

6 slices whole-wheat bread
1 tablespoon olive oil
18 cocktail-size chicken
  sausages or franks (about
  6 ounces)

I got the idea for this recipe and quickly dismissed it as too simple to work. But it was so easy that I just had to give it a whirl. When the first batch came out of the oven, golden brown and crisp on the outside, tender and warm inside, I was delighted. A little dip in deli mustard and they hit the spot perfectly for the party-food classic.

Preheat the oven to 400°F.

Cut the crusts off the bread, then, using a rolling pin, roll each piece of bread as flat as possible. Brush one side of each piece of bread with oil. Cut the bread into strips the same width as the sausages. Place a strip of bread, oil side down, onto a flat surface. Place a sausage on one end of the bread and roll it up. Place the roll, seam side down, onto a baking sheet. Repeat with the remaining sausages. Bake until the bread is crisp and browned and the sausage is warmed through, 18 to 20 minutes. Serve warm with mustard for dipping.

Makes 6 servings

SERVING SIZE 3 dogs in blankets
PER SERVING Calories 130; Total Fat 8 g (Sat Fat 1.5 g, Mono Fat 3.7 g, Poly Fat 1.5 g); Protein 7 g; Carb 9 g; Fiber 2 g; Cholesterol 25 mg; Sodium 340 mg
EXCELLENT SOURCE OF Manganese, Selenium
GOOD SOURCE OF Niacin, Protein

BEFORE*	AFTER
220 cal. Sat. Fat 6g, Chol. 25mg Fiber 0g, Sodium 490mg	Sat. Fat 1.5g, Chol. 25mg Fiber 2g, Sodium 340mg **130 cal.**

*compared to store-bought

PIMIENTO CHEESE

¾ cup plain Greek-style nonfat yogurt

¾ cup lightly packed shredded extra-sharp cheddar cheese (3 ounces)

One 3-ounce jar pimientos, drained and rinsed, or 1 large roasted red pepper, chopped

3 tablespoons mayonnaise

⅛ teaspoon cayenne pepper

This is one of those crowd-pleasing, home-style favorites that just seem to make the world a better place. My version has all the decadent, creamy, real-cheese flavor and gorgeous color of the classic, without all the mayo.

Place the yogurt in a fine-mesh strainer lined with a paper towel and set over a bowl. Place in the refrigerator and allow the yogurt to strain for at least 1 hour and up to 4. Discard the liquid that has drained into the bowl.

Place the thickened yogurt in a food processor. Add the cheese, pimientos, mayonnaise, and cayenne pepper and pulse until the mixture is well combined but there are still some visible pimiento bits. Transfer to a serving bowl and chill for at least 1 hour or overnight.

Makes 8 servings

SERVING SIZE 2 tablespoons
PER SERVING Calories 80; Total Fat 5 g (Sat Fat 2.5 g, Mono Fat 1.5 g, Poly Fat 1.1 g); Protein 5 g; Carb 3 g; Fiber 0 g; Cholesterol 15 mg; Sodium 115 mg
EXCELLENT SOURCE OF N/A
GOOD SOURCE OF Vitamin C

BEFORE

140 cal.

Sat. Fat 6g, Chol. 30mg
Fiber 0g, Sodium 300mg

AFTER

Sat. Fat 2.5g, Chol. 15mg
Fiber 0g, Sodium 115mg

80 cal.

"EVERYTHING" PARMESAN CRISPS

⅔ cup finely grated Parmesan cheese (2 ounces)
1 teaspoon all-purpose flour
2 teaspoons sesame seeds
1 teaspoon poppy seeds
1 teaspoon dried minced onion
½ teaspoon garlic powder

These easy, cheesy nibbles are a gigantic punch of Parmesan flavor in a light lacy crisp. They are perfect to serve with cocktails, for garnishing soup or salad, or just as an afternoon snack. I brought in an extra touch of fun by flavoring them with all of the seasonings of my favorite "everything" bagel.

Preheat the oven to 350°F. Line a baking sheet with parchment paper.

In a small bowl, combine the cheese, flour, seeds, onion, and garlic powder. Spoon heaping teaspoons of the mixture onto the prepared baking sheet, leaving 2 inches between each mound. Using your fingers, pat the mounds down, spreading them so each is about 2½ inches in diameter. Bake in the oven until they are golden brown, about 8 minutes. Allow to cool completely on the baking sheet before lifting them off carefully. Make the crisps up to 2 days ahead and store in an airtight container at room temperature.

Makes 8 servings

SERVING SIZE 2 crisps
PER SERVING Calories 40; Total Fat 2.5 g (Sat Fat 1.5 g, Mono Fat 0.76 g, Poly Fat 0.4. g); Protein 3 g; Carb 1 g; Fiber 0 g; Cholesterol 5 mg; Sodium 110 mg
EXCELLENT SOURCE OF N/A
GOOD SOURCE OF N/A

BEFORE*	AFTER
86 cal. Sat. Fat 2g, Chol. 10mg Fiber 0g, Sodium 190mg	Sat. Fat 1.5g, Chol. 5mg Fiber 0g, Sodium 110mg 40 cal.

*compared to store-bought cheese sticks

SOUPS AND SANDWICHES

Soup is like a bowlful of belly-warming love, with countless enticing variations that have the power to both soothe and satisfy. It partners perfectly with the sandwich—simple, hearty fulfillment you can hold in your hand.

BROCCOLI-CHEDDAR SOUP

2 teaspoons olive oil

1 medium onion, chopped

1 clove garlic, minced

½ teaspoon ground nutmeg

1 large head broccoli, florets and tender part of stems, chopped (about 6 cups)

3 cups low-sodium chicken broth

2 cups low-fat (1%) milk

2 tablespoons all-purpose flour

1¼ cups lightly packed shredded extra-sharp cheddar cheese (5 ounces)

½ teaspoon salt, plus more to taste

¼ teaspoon freshly ground black pepper, plus more to taste

You can't help but feel good eating broccoli and cheddar soup with its reassuringly familiar flavors and rich, indulgent texture. Happily, this recipe will leave you feeling good afterward too, energized and satisfied instead of overstuffed.

Heat the oil in a soup pot over medium heat. Add the onion and cook, stirring, until softened and translucent, about 4 minutes. Add the garlic and nutmeg and cook for 30 seconds. Add the broccoli and chicken broth and bring the mixture to a boil. Reduce the heat to medium low and cook until the broccoli is tender, about 5 minutes. Remove from the heat and allow to cool slightly, about 15 minutes.

Meanwhile, in a small saucepan, whisk together the milk and flour until the flour dissolves. Heat the mixture over medium-high heat, stirring constantly, and bring to a gentle boil. Reduce the heat to medium low and cook, stirring occasionally, until the mixture has thickened, about 3 minutes. Add one cup of the cheese and cook, stirring, until melted, 2 minutes more. Remove from the heat and cover to keep warm.

continued on page 96

	BEFORE	AFTER	
700 cal.	Sat. Fat 36g, Chol. 170mg Fiber 3g, Sodium 1440mg	Sat. Fat 9g, Chol. 45mg Fiber 4g, Sodium 660mg	**320 cal.**

continued from page 95

Working with about 1 cup at a time, puree the broccoli mixture in a blender until it is mostly smooth but still has some chunks, and then transfer it to another pot. (Alternatively, you can use an immersion blender.) Stir the cheese mixture into the broccoli puree, season with salt and black pepper to taste, and cook over medium-low heat until warmed through, 3 to 5 minutes more. Serve garnished with the remaining cheese.

Makes 4 servings

SERVING SIZE 1½ cups
PER SERVING Calories 320; Total Fat 17 g (Sat Fat 9 g, Mono Fat 5.8 g, Poly Fat 0.9 g);
Protein 21 g; Carb 23 g; Fiber 4 g; Cholesterol 45 mg; Sodium 660 mg
EXCELLENT SOURCE OF Calcium, Folate, Iodine, Phosphorus, Potassium, Protein, Riboflavin, Vitamin A, Vitamin C, Vitamin K
GOOD SOURCE OF Copper, Fiber, Iron, Magnesium, Manganese, Molybdenum, Pantothenic Acid, Selenium, Niacin, Thiamin, Vitamin B6, Vitamin B12, Vitamin D, Zinc

CHINESE CORN AND CRAB CHOWDER

6 ears sweet corn, or 4 cups frozen corn kernels, thawed

6 cups low-sodium chicken broth

1 tablespoon canola oil

2 scallions, finely sliced, white and green parts separated

1 tablespoon grated fresh ginger

2 tablespoons Chinese cooking wine or dry sherry

2 tablespoons cornstarch

2 tablespoons cold water

8 ounces lump crabmeat, drained and picked over for shells and cartilage

2 teaspoons rice vinegar

1 tablespoon low-sodium soy sauce

1 large egg, lightly beaten

½ teaspoon salt, plus more to taste

⅛ teaspoon ground white pepper, plus more to taste

In this soup the sweet, succulent corn-and-crab duo is given counterpoint by the light zing of ginger and a sprinkle of scallion greens. The soup is thickened with an easy corn puree and enriched with an egg stirred in at the end. Based on a classic Chinese recipe, it is a refreshingly lighter take on creamy chowder.

If using ears of corn, use a knife to remove the kernels, collecting any juices that are released. Discard the cobs. Place 2 cups of the corn kernels and 1 cup of the broth in a blender and puree until smooth.

Heat the oil in a soup pot over medium-high heat. Add the scallion whites and cook, stirring, for 1 minute. Stir in the ginger and add the remaining 5 cups broth, the remaining corn kernels with any juices, the pureed corn mixture, and the cooking wine and bring to a boil. Reduce the heat to medium low and simmer for 10 minutes.

In a small bowl, stir together the cornstarch and the water until the cornstarch is dissolved. Slowly add the mixture to the soup and cook over medium-high heat, stirring constantly, until the soup boils and thickens. Reduce the heat to medium low, add the crab, vinegar, and soy sauce, and cook until the crab is heated through, about 1 minute. Drizzle in the egg, stirring constantly, and cook for 1 minute more. Season with the salt and white pepper. Serve garnished with scallion greens.

Makes 4 servings

SERVING SIZE 2 cups
PER SERVING Calories 340; Total Fat 9 g (Sat Fat 1.5 g, Mono Fat 4.2 g, Poly Fat 2.5 g); Protein 26 g; Carb 45 g; Fiber 4 g; Cholesterol 105 mg; Sodium 840 mg
EXCELLENT SOURCE OF Copper, Folate, Niacin, Phosphorus, Potassium, Protein, Riboflavin, Selenium, Vitamin B6, Vitamin C, , Vitamin K, Zinc
GOOD SOURCE OF Fiber, Iron, Magnesium, Manganese, Thiamin, Vitamin B12

BEFORE*	AFTER
620 cal. Sat. Fat 19g, Chol. 140mg Fiber 5g, Sodium 1110mg	Sat. Fat 1.5g, Chol. 105mg Fiber 4g, Sodium 840mg **340 cal.**

*compared to a typical New England–style recipe

CREAMY TOMATO SOUP

1 tablespoon olive oil

1 small onion, chopped

2 cloves garlic, minced

Two 14.5-ounce cans no-salt-added diced tomatoes

2 tablespoons tomato paste

2 cups low-sodium chicken broth or vegetable broth

2 tablespoons heavy cream

2 teaspoons sugar

½ teaspoon salt

¼ teaspoon ground white pepper

1 tablespoon chopped fresh chives

This dish captures all the sweet tomato goodness you loved as a kid. A touch of cream is all it takes to give it that soothing, velvety richness.

Heat the oil in a large soup pot over medium heat. Add the onion and cook, stirring occasionally, until softened and translucent, about 4 minutes. Add the garlic and cook until fragrant, about 1 minute. Add the tomatoes, tomato paste, and chicken broth and bring to a boil. Reduce the heat to medium low and simmer, stirring occasionally, about 15 minutes. Remove from the heat and allow to cool slightly, about 15 minutes.

Working with about 1 cup at a time, puree the soup in a blender until smooth and then transfer the puree to another pot. (Alternatively, you can use an immersion blender.) Stir in the cream, sugar, salt, and white pepper. Serve garnished with the chives.

Makes 4 servings

SERVING SIZE 1½ cups
PER SERVING Calories 160; Total Fat 7 g (Sat Fat 2.5 g, Mono Fat 3.5 g, Poly Fat 0.8 g); Protein 5 g; Carb 14 g; Fiber 3 g; Cholesterol 10 mg; Sodium 420 mg
EXCELLENT SOURCE OF Vitamin A, Vitamin C
GOOD SOURCE OF Fiber, Protein, Iron

	BEFORE	AFTER	
240 cal.	Sat. Fat 11g, Chol. 70mg Fiber 3g, Sodium 860mg	Sat. Fat 2.5g, Chol. 10mg Fiber 3g, Sodium 420mg	**160 cal.**

CREAM OF MUSHROOM SOUP

1 tablespoon olive oil

1 small onion, chopped

2 cloves garlic, minced

10 ounces white button mushrooms, thinly sliced

2 large portobello mushroom caps, black gills removed, thinly sliced (about 10 ounces)

4 cups low-sodium beef broth

1½ teaspoons chopped fresh thyme

¼ cup dry sherry

1 teaspoon salt

¼ teaspoon freshly ground black pepper

3 tablespoons heavy cream

This recipe flips the usual mushroom soup formula (lots of cream, few mushrooms) on its head and achieves a hearty texture and full flavor with loads of meaty mushrooms and just enough cream to elevate them to luxurious.

Heat the oil in a soup pot over medium heat. Add the onion and cook, stirring occasionally, until softened and translucent, about 4 minutes. Add the garlic and cook until fragrant, about 1 minute. Add the mushrooms and cook until they release most of their liquid, 7 to 8 minutes. Remove ¼ cup of the cooked mushrooms and reserve.

Add the beef broth and thyme and bring to a boil. Reduce the heat to medium low and simmer for 10 minutes. Stir in the sherry, salt, and black pepper and cook an additional 3 minutes. Remove from the heat and allow to cool slightly, about 15 minutes.

Working with about 1 cup at a time, puree the soup in a blender until it is mostly smooth but still has some chunks, and then transfer it to another pot. (Alternatively, you can use an immersion blender.) Stir in the cream and warm through over medium heat. Serve garnished with the reserved mushrooms.

Makes 4 servings

SERVING SIZE 1½ cups
PER SERVING Calories 170; Total Fat 9 g (Sat Fat 3.5 g, Mono Fat 4 g, Poly Fat 1 g); Protein 9 g; Carb 12 g; Fiber 2 g; Cholesterol 15 mg; Sodium 850 mg
EXCELLENT SOURCE OF Copper, Niacin, Pantothenic Acid, Potassium, Riboflavin, Selenium
GOOD SOURCE OF Manganese, Phosphorus, Protein, Vitamin B6

BEFORE	AFTER
620 cal. Sat. Fat 38g, Chol. 220mg Fiber 1g, Sodium 1270mg	Sat. Fat 3.5g, Chol. 15mg Fiber 2g, Sodium 850mg **170 cal.**

NEW! NEW ENGLAND CLAM CHOWDER

1 tablespoon plus 1 teaspoon olive oil

4 slices Canadian bacon, diced (2 ounces)

1 large onion, chopped (about 2 cups)

6 ribs celery, diced (about 2 cups)

¾ teaspoon salt

½ teaspoon freshly ground black pepper

1 tablespoon finely chopped garlic (about 3 large cloves)

2 teaspoons chopped fresh thyme

1½ cups water

Two 1-pound containers frozen clams packed in their own juice, thawed, juice reserved

1¼ pounds russet potatoes, unpeeled, cut into ½-inch dice

1 bay leaf

2 cups cold low-fat (1%) milk

2 tablespoons heavy cream

3 tablespoons all-purpose flour

Hot pepper sauce, such as Tabasco, for serving

A big bowl of creamy clam chowder spiked with hot sauce and eaten on a dock off the coast of Maine is pretty much my idea of heaven. Whenever I make this soup it transports me right there. It has all the satisfaction of the classic—smoky pork, briny clams, and chunks of potato in a creamy base—but with a lighter new perspective.

Heat 1 teaspoon of the oil in a large soup pot over medium-high heat. Add the Canadian bacon and cook, stirring frequently, until crisp, 3 to 4 minutes. Transfer the bacon to a plate.

Add the remaining 1 tablespoon oil, the onion, celery, salt, and black pepper to the pot and cook over medium heat, stirring occasionally, until the vegetables have softened, about 6 minutes. Add the garlic and thyme and cook, stirring, for 1 minute more. Add the water, reserved clam juice (about 1½ cups), potatoes, and bay leaf and bring to a boil.

Partially cover the pot and simmer, stirring occasionally, until the

BEFORE	AFTER
470 cal. Sat. Fat 20g, Chol. 135mg Fiber 2g, Sodium 850mg	Sat. Fat 2.5g, Chol. 40mg Fiber 3g, Sodium 740mg 260 cal.

potatoes are tender, about 15 minutes. Whisk together the milk, cream, and flour until the flour is dissolved. Slowly add the mixture to the pot, stirring constantly. Continuing to stir, bring the soup to a simmer (do not boil). Reduce the heat to medium low and cook, stirring occasionally, until thickened, about 8 minutes. Add the clams and simmer for 2 minutes more. Discard the bay leaf.

Right before serving, stir in the bacon. Serve with the hot pepper sauce.

Makes 6 servings

SERVING SIZE about 1½ cups
PER SERVING Calories 260; Total Fat 8 g (Sat Fat 2.5 g, Mono Fat 3.4 g, Poly Fat 0.9 g); Protein 19 g; Carb 30 g; Fiber 3 g; Cholesterol 40 mg; Sodium 740 mg
EXCELLENT SOURCE OF Copper, Iron, Protein, Manganese, Niacin, Potassium, Phosphorus, Riboflavin, Selenium, Vitamin B6, Vitamin B12, Vitamin C, Vitamin K
GOOD SOURCE OF Calcium, Folate, Fiber, Iodine, Magnesium, Pantothenic Acid, Thiamin, Vitamin A, Vitamin D, Zinc

NAVY BEAN SOUP WITH HAM

1 pound dried navy beans
1 tablespoon olive oil
1 large onion, chopped
2 cloves garlic, minced
1 large carrot, diced
2 ribs celery, diced
1 tablespoon crumbled fresh sage
4 cups low-sodium beef broth
4 cups water
1 bay leaf
1 teaspoon salt
½ teaspoon freshly ground black pepper
4 ounces lean ham steak, cubed
¼ cup chopped fresh parsley leaves

My husband hails from Michigan where the winters are long and cold. But the genuine warmth of the people there and their home cooking keep you feeling cozy no matter the weather. This easy, but incredibly flavorful bean soup is my take on one of his childhood favorites. It has chunks of pork in every spoonful, just as he likes, but I've made it even healthier by using lean ham and less salt.

Pick over the beans and discard any stones. Soak the beans in cold water for at least 8 hours. Drain and rinse well.

Heat the oil in a soup pot over medium-high heat. Add the onion and cook, stirring, until soft and translucent, about 4 minutes. Add the garlic and cook for 30 seconds. Add the carrot, celery, and sage and cook, stirring, until the vegetables begin to soften, about 5 minutes. Add the beans, beef broth, water, bay leaf, salt, and black pepper and bring to a boil. Reduce the heat to medium low, cover, and cook until the beans have begun to soften, about 1 hour. Add the ham and cook, uncovered, until the beans are soft and the soup has thickened, about 30 minutes more. Serve garnished with the parsley.

Makes 8 servings

SERVING SIZE 1¾ cups
PER SERVING Calories 250; Total Fat 4 g (Sat Fat 1 g, Mono Fat 2 g, Poly Fat 1 g); Protein 16 g; Carb 38 g; Fiber 15 g; Cholesterol 5 mg; Sodium 530 mg
EXCELLENT SOURCE OF Folate, Fiber, Iron, Magnesium, Manganese, Phosphorus, Potassium, Protein, Thiamin, Vitamin A, Vitamin K
GOOD SOURCE OF Calcium, Copper, Niacin, Riboflavin, Vitamin B6, Vitamin C, Zinc

BEFORE	AFTER
300 cal. Sat. Fat 3g, Chol. 20mg Fiber 15g, Sodium 1160mg	Sat. Fat 1g, Chol. 5mg Fiber 15g, Sodium 530mg **250 cal.**

SIMPLY PERFECT SPLIT PEA SOUP

1 tablespoon olive oil
1 large onion, chopped
2 cloves garlic, minced
1 medium carrot, finely diced
2 ribs celery, finely diced
1¼ cups dried green split peas
8 cups low-sodium chicken broth or water
1 bay leaf
1 teaspoon salt
½ teaspoon freshly ground black pepper
Pumpernickel Croutons (recipe follows), optional

This soup is evidence of how a few simple ingredients simmered together, low and slow, can meld together into a complex, deeply satisfying meal in a bowl. Garlic-scented Pumpernickel Croutons (recipe follows) offer a crunchy contrast to the smooth soup.

Heat the oil in a soup pot over medium heat. Add the onion and cook, stirring, until soft and translucent, about 6 minutes. Add the garlic and cook for 1 minute. Add the carrot and celery and cook, stirring, until the vegetables begin to soften, about 5 minutes. Add the split peas, broth, bay leaf, salt, and black pepper and bring to a boil. Reduce the heat to medium low, cover, and simmer, stirring occasionally, until the split peas are tender, 1 to 1½ hours. Serve garnished with Pumpernickel Croutons, if desired.

Makes 6 servings

SERVING SIZE 1¾ cups
PER SERVING Calories 230; Total Fat 4.5 g (Sat Fat 1 g, Mono Fat 2.6 g, Poly Fat 0.9 g); Protein 17 g; Carb 33 g; Fiber 11 g; Cholesterol 0 mg; Sodium 510 mg
EXCELLENT SOURCE OF Copper, Folate, Fiber, Manganese, Niacin, Phosphorus, Potassium, Protein, Thiamin, Vitamin A
GOOD SOURCE OF Iron, Magnesium, Riboflavin, Vitamin K, Zinc

BEFORE	AFTER
240 cal. Sat. Fat 2g, Chol. 5mg Fiber 12g, Sodium 1840mg	Sat. Fat 1g, Chol. 0mg Fiber 11g, Sodium 510mg **230 cal.**

PUMPERNICKEL CROUTONS

2 teaspoons olive oil
½ teaspoon garlic powder
⅛ teaspoon salt
⅛ teaspoon freshly ground black pepper
Two ½-inch slices pumpernickel bread (4 ounces)

These croutons retain their crunch even as they soften slightly in a soup. They also add delicious excitement to salads. They're full flavored with less fat and calories because they are tossed in olive oil and baked, not pan-fried.

Preheat the oven to 325°F.

In a medium bowl, whisk together the oil, garlic powder, salt, and black pepper. Cut the bread into ½-inch cubes, add to the spice mixture, and toss to coat evenly. Spread the bread cubes in a single layer on a baking sheet and bake until crisp, 20 to 25 minutes, tossing two or three times. Allow to cool. Croutons keep up to 4 days in an airtight container.

Makes 6 servings

SERVING SIZE 2 heaping tablespoons
PER SERVING Calories 60; Total Fat 2 g (Sat Fat 0 g, Mono Fat 1.3 g, Poly Fat 0.4 g); Protein 2 g; Carb 9 g; Fiber 1 g; Cholesterol 0 mg; Sodium 180 mg
EXCELLENT SOURCE OF N/A
GOOD SOURCE OF Manganese

BEFORE*	AFTER
85 cal. Sat. Fat 1g, Chol. 0mg Fiber 1g, Sodium 190mg	Sat. Fat 0g, Chol. 0mg Fiber 1g, Sodium 180mg 60 cal.

*compared to store-bought croutons

TRIPLE ONION FRENCH ONION SOUP

2 small leeks (about ½ pound)

2 tablespoons olive oil

3 medium onions (about
1 pound), thinly sliced
(about 4 cups)

6 medium shallots (about
½ pound), thinly sliced
(1¾ cups)

2 tablespoons chopped fresh
thyme

1 fresh or dried bay leaf

1 tablespoon all-purpose
flour

½ cup dry sherry or white
wine

3 cups low-sodium beef broth

2 cups water

½ teaspoon salt

½ teaspoon freshly ground
black pepper

Four ¼-inch-thick slices
whole-wheat baguette

4 ounces Gruyère, Swiss, or
Emmental cheese, grated
(1 cup)

Three kinds of onions in this recipe—leeks, regular onions, and shallots—give the base a rich, multilayered flavor. They are caramelized to golden perfection in just a touch of healthy oil instead of lots of butter. That plus a satisfying, but not heavy-handed measure of full-flavored cheese, melted and bubbling, gives you the decadent experience you expect while keeping things in the healthy zone.

Cut the dark green tops from the leeks and discard or reserve for another use, such as stock. Halve the remaining tender pale green and white ends lengthwise and then cut them crosswise into thin slices. Transfer the sliced leeks to a bowl of cold water and toss them to allow the sand to drift to the bottom of the bowl. Lift the leeks out of the water with a slotted spoon and pat them dry with paper towels.

Heat the oil in a soup pot over medium-high heat. Add the leeks, onions, shallots, thyme, and bay leaf. Reduce the heat to medium low, cover, and cook, stirring occasionally, until the onions are golden, about 10 minutes. Remove the lid and cook, uncovered, stirring frequently,

continued on page 108

	BEFORE	AFTER	
710 cal.	Sat. Fat 17g, Chol. 80mg Fiber 5g, Sodium 2270mg	Sat. Fat 6g, Chol. 30mg Fiber 5g, Sodium 900mg	390 cal.

continued from page 106

until the onions turn a deep golden brown, about 10 minutes more. Sprinkle the flour over the onions and cook, stirring, for 1 minute. Stir in the sherry, increase the heat to medium, and cook until it is almost evaporated, about 2 minutes. Add the broth, water, salt, and black pepper and bring to a boil. Reduce the heat to medium and simmer, stirring occasionally, until reduced to about 6 cups, about 15 minutes.

Meanwhile preheat the oven to 350°F. Arrange the slices of bread in one layer on a baking sheet and toast, turning once, until golden on both sides, about 8 minutes.

Remove the bay leaf from the soup and divide the soup among four heatproof bowls, about 1½ cups of soup each. Top each bowl with a slice of bread, then sprinkle ¼ cup cheese over the top. Place the bowls on a baking sheet and bake until the cheese melts, about 4 minutes. Serve immediately.

Makes 4 servings

SERVING SIZE 1 bowl of soup
PER SERVING Calories 390; Total Fat 17 g (Sat Fat 6 g, Mono Fat 8 g, Poly Fat 1.5 g); Protein 16 g; Carb 42 g; Fiber 5g; Cholesterol 30 mg; Sodium 900 mg
EXCELLENT SOURCE OF Calcium, Manganese, Phosphorus, Protein, Vitamin A, Vitamin C, Vitamin K
GOOD SOURCE OF Copper, Folate, Fiber, Iron, Magnesium, Molybdenum, Niacin, Potassium, Riboflavin, Vitamin B6, Vitamin B12, Zinc

MINESTRONE SOUP

- 2 tablespoons olive oil
- 1 large onion, diced
- 4 cloves garlic, minced
- 2 ribs celery, diced (½ cup)
- 1 large carrot, peeled and diced
- 1 medium zucchini (about 8 ounces), diced
- 1 teaspoon dried oregano
- 1 teaspoon dried basil
- 1 teaspoon salt
- ½ teaspoon freshly ground black pepper
- One 28-ounce can no-salt-added diced tomatoes, with their juices
- One 14-ounce can crushed tomatoes, preferably no-salt-added
- 6 cups low-sodium vegetable or chicken broth (48 ounces)
- One 15-ounce can cannellini beans, preferably low-sodium, drained and rinsed
- ½ cup whole-grain elbow pasta
- ⅓ cup finely grated Parmesan cheese
- 2 tablespoons chopped fresh parsley leaves

Chock-full of veggies in a tomatoey broth, pretty much any minestrone you come across is going to be a reasonably good choice. But the real spoiler is sodium, which is off the charts in most typical recipes and prepared versions. This mouthwatering meal in a bowl is case in point that you don't need to lean on salt for flavor when you use lots of herbs like basil, oregano, and parsley and aromatics like garlic and onion.

Heat the oil in a large soup pot over medium-high heat. Add the onion and cook, stirring, until translucent, about 4 minutes. Add the garlic and cook for 30 seconds. Add the celery and carrot and cook, stirring, until the vegetables begin to soften, about 5 minutes. Add the zucchini, oregano, basil, salt, and black pepper and cook, stirring, for 2 minutes more.

Add the diced and crushed tomatoes and the vegetable broth and bring to a boil. Reduce the heat to medium low and simmer for 10 minutes. Add the beans and pasta, and cook until the pasta and vegetables are tender, 10 to 15 minutes. Serve garnished with the cheese and parsley.

Makes 6 servings

SERVING SIZE 2 cups soup, 1 tablespoon cheese, and 1 teaspoon parsley
PER SERVING Calories 240; Total Fat 7 g (Sat Fat 1.5 g, Mono Fat 3.7 g, Poly Fat 0.7 g); Protein 9 g; Carb 35 g; Fiber 7 g; Cholesterol 5 mg; Sodium 640 mg
EXCELLENT SOURCE OF Fiber, Iron, Manganese, Thiamin, Vitamin A, Vitamin C, Vitamin K
GOOD SOURCE OF Calcium, Copper, Magnesium, Phosphorus, Potassium, Protein, Riboflavin, Vitamin B6, Zinc

BEFORE	AFTER
280 cal. Sat. Fat 3g, Chol. 10mg Fiber 7g, Sodium 1650mg	Sat. Fat 1.5g, Chol. 5mg Fiber 7g, Sodium 730mg **240 cal.**

THREE-GENERATION
CHICKEN NOODLE SOUP

One 4-pound chicken, cut into 8 pieces

3 pounds chicken parts, such as wings, feet, backs, and necks

4 large carrots

5 stalks celery

2 large onions

14 cups cold water

2 teaspoons salt, plus more to taste

2 large sprigs fresh parsley

2 large sprigs fresh dill

1 medium parsnip

3 cups egg noodles (4½ ounces), preferably whole-wheat

This soup is so much more than just a recipe to me—it's my family's legacy—based on my grandma's recipe and passed down to me by my parents. Each generation has put its stamp on it, altering it slightly to make it uniquely theirs while keeping the integrity of grandma's. My take is to strain the stock of the boiled vegetables and incorporate fresh ones later so they are perfectly tender, not mushy. The result is real homemade flavor and healing power that you just can't package. I look forward to passing the torch to my daughter to see what she adds to the mix when she grows up.

Place the chicken into a very large stockpot. Coarsely chop 2 carrots, 2 celery stalks, and 1 onion and add them to the pot. Add the water and the 2 teaspoons salt and bring to a boil. Reduce the heat to medium low, partially cover the pot, and cook at a slow, steady simmer for 30 minutes.

Using a slotted spoon, remove the 2 chicken breasts, place them in a dish, cover, and refrigerate. Cook the soup for 1 hour more. Add the parsley and dill sprigs and cook for 30 minutes more.

Allow the broth to cool slightly, then strain it through a mesh strainer into another large pot, pressing down to extract as much of the liquid as possible. Discard the remaining vegetables and chicken. Place the broth in the refrigerator overnight or up to 2 days, then skim the hardened fat from the surface and discard.

	BEFORE	AFTER	
340 cal.	Sat. Fat 2.5g, Chol. 50mg Fiber 4g, Sodium 1230mg	Sat. Fat 1g, Chol. 40mg Fiber 4g, Sodium 680mg	200 cal.

Bring the stock to a boil. Dice the remaining 2 carrots, 3 celery stalks, 1 onion, and the parsnip and add to the stock. Return to a boil. Reduce the heat to medium low and simmer, partially covered, until the vegetables are tender, about 20 minutes. Meanwhile, remove the bone and skin from the reserved chicken breasts and dice the meat.

When the vegetables are done, add the noodles to the broth and cook until the noodles are tender, 6 minutes more. Add the diced chicken and allow it to warm through, about 1 minute more. Season with additional salt to taste.

Makes 8 servings

SERVING SIZE 2 cups
PER SERVING Calories 200; Total Fat 4.5 g (Sat Fat 1 g, Mono Fat 1.6 g, Poly Fat 1 g); Protein 18 g; Carb 24 g; Fiber 4 g; Cholesterol 40 mg; Sodium 680 mg
EXCELLENT SOURCE OF Manganese, Niacin, Protein, Vitamin A, Vitamin K
GOOD SOURCE OF Folate, Fiber, Magnesium, Phosphorus, Potassium, Selenium, Thiamin, Vitamin B6, Vitamin C

OPEN-FACE PHILLY CHEESE STEAK SANDWICHES

½ cup cold low-fat (1%) milk

1 tablespoon all-purpose flour

2 ounces extra-sharp cheddar cheese, finely shredded (½ cup, packed)

¾ teaspoon salt

2 tablespoons olive oil

1 pound boneless top loin steak, very thinly sliced

½ teaspoon freshly ground black pepper

1 large onion, very thinly sliced into half-moons

1 green bell pepper, thinly sliced

1 red bell pepper, thinly sliced

2 whole-grain Italian rolls (each about 6 inches long, 4 ounces each), halved lengthwise

Tender sliced steak dripping with real cheese sauce served on crusty bread may get your mouth watering but it doesn't exactly bring the word "healthy" to mind. You certainly won't think about health when you bite into this decadent sandwich; all you'll be thinking is how insanely good it tastes. But happily you'll know it's good for you too—moderate in saturated fat, with the goodness of whole grain and an excellent source of eighteen essential nutrients. The trick is to use lean meat, and serve it open-face to keep the portion smart.

To make the cheese sauce, place the milk and flour in a small saucepan and whisk until the flour is dissolved. Heat over medium-high heat, stirring constantly, and bring to a simmer. Lower the heat to medium low and continue to cook, stirring frequently, until thickened, about 2 minutes. Stir in the cheese and ¼ teaspoon salt and mix until the cheese melts. Simmer, stirring frequently, until the mixture is velvety and thick, about 2 minutes more. Remove from the heat and cover the surface of the sauce with foil to keep warm and prevent a skin from forming.

Heat 1 tablespoon of the oil in a large nonstick skillet over medium-high heat. Sprinkle the beef with ¼ teaspoon salt and ¼ teaspoon black pepper and cook until browned and just cooked through, 4 to 5 minutes.

BEFORE		AFTER	
1230 cal.	Sat. Fat 34g, Chol. 215mg Fiber 5g, Sodium 2190mg	Sat. Fat 6g, Chol. 65mg Fiber 7g, Sodium 880mg	**470 cal.**

Transfer to a plate and cover with foil to keep warm.

Heat the remaining 1 tablespoon oil in the pan over medium-high heat. Add the onion and bell pepper and cook until the edges are browned and the onion is tender, 12 to 14 minutes. Season with the remaining ¼ teaspoon salt and ¼ teaspoon black pepper.

Lightly toast the rolls. Place one half of each roll on a plate and top with one-quarter of the onion-pepper mixture, then one-quarter of the meat. Drizzle each sandwich with ¼ cup of the cheese sauce.

Makes 4 servings

SERVING SIZE 1 sandwich
PER SERVING Calories 470; Total Fat 19 g (Sat Fat 6 g, Mono Fat 8.9 g, Poly Fat 2.4 g); Protein 36 g; Carb 40 g; Fiber 7 g; Cholesterol 65 mg; Sodium 880 mg
EXCELLENT SOURCE OF Calcium, Fiber, Iron, Magnesium, Manganese, Niacin, Phosphorus, Potassium, Protein, Riboflavin, Selenium, Thiamin, Vitamin A, Vitamin B6, Vitamin B12, Vitamin C, Zinc
GOOD SOURCE OF Copper, Folate, Pantothenic Acid, Vitamin K

FRENCH BREAD PIZZA

One 8-ounce whole-grain French baguette (about 12 inches long)

1 cup Quick Marinara Sauce (page 63) or store-bought marinara sauce

2 cups lightly packed arugula leaves, coarsely chopped (about 2 ounces)

1 cup grated part-skim mozzarella cheese (4 ounces)

¼ cup freshly grated Parmesan cheese (¾ ounce)

I like an upscale artisanal pizza as much as the next person, but for real comfort I'll take my sauce and melted mozzarella home style. I've been making impromptu pizzas on everything from English muffins to mini bagels since I could reach the kitchen counter. These are by far my favorite, simple as can be yet somehow a little sophisticated too. Scooping out the bread is my way of getting a crispy crust without overdoing the bread and a sprinkle of peppery arugula is the perfect no-fuss vegetable topping.

Preheat the oven to 425°F. Line a baking sheet with foil.

Cut the bread in half lengthwise, then cut each half crosswise into 4 pieces. Scoop out the soft center of the bread and discard.

Place the bread, scooped side up, onto the prepared baking sheet. Spread 2 tablespoons of sauce on each piece. Top with the arugula, then the mozzarella and Parmesan cheeses. Bake until the bread is toasted and the cheese is melted and bubbling, about 12 minutes.

Makes 4 servings

SERVING SIZE 2 pieces
PER SERVING Calories 250; Total Fat 11 g (Sat Fat 4.5 g, Mono Fat 4.1 g, Poly Fat 0.7 g); Protein 16 g; Carb 23 g; Fiber 4 g; Cholesterol 20 mg; Sodium 540 mg
EXCELLENT SOURCE OF Calcium, Manganese, Phosphorus, Protein, Selenium, Vitamin C, Vitamin K
GOOD SOURCE OF Fiber, Magnesium, Niacin, Riboflavin, Thiamin, Vitamin A, Vitamin B12, Zinc

BEFORE	AFTER
460 cal. Sat. Fat 10g, Chol. 60mg Fiber 3g, Sodium 1010mg	Sat. Fat 4.5g, Chol. 20mg Fiber 4g, Sodium 540mg **250 cal.**

GRILLED SHRIMP PO' BOY

½ cup red wine vinegar

¼ cup sugar

½ small red onion, sliced (¾ cup)

½ cup plain Greek-style nonfat yogurt

3 tablespoons mayonnaise

3 tablespoons finely chopped cornichon or dill pickle

2 tablespoons fresh lemon juice

¼ cup chopped fresh chives

1 tablespoon chopped fresh tarragon

1¾ teaspoons Creole seasoning

Salt and freshly ground black pepper to taste

Nonstick cooking spray

1 pound large shrimp, peeled and deveined

4 teaspoons olive oil

One 8-ounce whole-wheat baguette (about 12 inches long)

1 cup shredded romaine lettuce

2 medium tomatoes, sliced

Calling it a sandwich doesn't do this down-home New Orleans classic justice. It's an exciting meal you can hold in your hands, with a combination of Creole-spiced grilled shrimp, cool creamy rémoulade sauce, and the tangy crunch of pickled onion, all piled onto toasted French bread and reflecting the soul and vibrancy of the great city that inspired it. Although it is most commonly made with fried shrimp, grilled also pleases purists and it certainly makes it better for you.

In a small saucepan, combine the vinegar and sugar and bring to a boil. Simmer over medium-low heat, stirring occasionally, until the sugar is dissolved, about 1 minute. Remove the pan from the heat and stir in the onion. Allow the mixture to cool completely at room temperature or in the refrigerator. Pickled onion will keep in an airtight container in the refrigerator for up to 2 weeks.

In a medium bowl, whisk together the yogurt, mayonnaise, cornichon, 1 tablespoon lemon juice, the chives, tarragon, and ¾ teaspoon Creole seasoning. Season with the salt and black pepper. The rémoulade sauce will keep in an airtight container in the refrigerator for up to 3 days.

Spray a nonstick grill pan with cooking spray and heat over medium-high heat or prepare a grill. Toss the shrimp with 2 teaspoons oil, the

	BEFORE	AFTER	
740 cal.	Sat. Fat 13g, Chol. 210mg Fiber 3g, Sodium 2860mg	Sat. Fat 2g, Chol. 175mg Fiber 4g, Sodium 790mg	**400 cal.**

remaining 1 teaspoon Creole seasoning, and the remaining 1 tablespoon lemon juice. Grill the shrimp until just cooked through, 2 to 3 minutes per side. Transfer the shrimp to a plate.

Cut the baguette in half lengthwise, then cut each half crosswise into 4 pieces. Scoop out the soft center of the bread and discard. Brush the cut sides of the baguette with the remaining 2 teaspoons olive oil. Grill the bread, cut sides down, until toasted, about 3 minutes.

Spread the grilled sides of each baguette piece with 1½ tablespoons of the rémoulade sauce. Fill 4 of the baguette pieces with about 6 grilled shrimp, a few slices of the pickled onion, ¼ cup lettuce, and 2 slices of tomato each, then top with the remaining baguette pieces.

Makes 4 servings

SERVING SIZE 1 sandwich
PER SERVING Calories 400; Total Fat 12 g (Sat Fat 2 g, Mono Fat 5.2 g, Poly Fat 3.5 g); Protein 32 g; Carb 40 g; Fiber 4 g; Cholesterol 175 mg; Sodium 790 mg
EXCELLENT SOURCE OF Copper, Iron, Magnesium, Manganese, Phosphorus, Protein, Selenium, Vitamin A, Vitamin B12, Vitamin C, Vitamin K
GOOD SOURCE OF Calcium, Fiber, Folate, Potassium, Niacin, Thiamin, Vitamin B6, Zinc

GARDEN TUNA MELT

Two 6-ounce cans or pouches light tuna in water, drained

2 cups lightly packed fresh baby spinach leaves, finely chopped (2 ounces)

1 medium red bell pepper, seeded and finely diced (about 1 cup)

1 medium carrot, shredded (about 1 cup)

¼ cup chopped fresh parsley leaves

3 tablespoons mayonnaise

1 tablespoon Dijon mustard

¼ teaspoon freshly ground black pepper

4 slices whole-wheat bread

4 thin slices extra-sharp cheddar cheese (2 ounces total)

A tuna melt used to be a diner favorite of mine until I discovered it can pack a day's worth of fat, calories, and sodium. Yikes! Making it at home from a regular recipe is considerably better, but I have made it better yet, keeping the creamy tuna salad and real melted cheddar while amping the flavor, color, and nutrition with crunchy garden vegetables and heaping it all on whole-wheat bread.

Preheat the oven to 325°F.

In a medium bowl, combine the tuna, spinach, bell pepper, carrot, parsley, mayonnaise, mustard, and black pepper. Place the bread on a baking sheet, divide the tuna mixture among the 4 pieces of bread, and top each with a slice of cheese.

Bake until the cheese melts and the edges of the bread are toasted, 6 to 8 minutes.

Makes 4 servings

SERVING SIZE 1 piece
PER SERVING Calories 290; Total Fat 10 g (Sat Fat 4 g, Mono Fat 2.9 g, Poly Fat 2.6 g); Protein 30 g; Carb 19 g; Fiber 3 g; Cholesterol 45 mg; Sodium 700 mg
EXCELLENT SOURCE OF Manganese, Niacin, Phosphorus, Protein, Selenium, Vitamin A, Vitamin B6, Vitamin B12, Vitamin C, Vitamin D, Vitamin K
GOOD SOURCE OF Calcium, Folate, Fiber, Iron, Magnesium, Potassium, Riboflavin, Thiamin, Zinc

BEFORE	AFTER
450 cal. Sat. Fat 9g, Chol. 55mg Fiber 2g, Sodium 1040mg	Sat. Fat 4g, Chol. 45mg Fiber 3g, Sodium 700mg **290 cal.**

GRILLED TURKEY REUBEN SANDWICHES

⅓ cup plain Greek-style nonfat yogurt

2 tablespoons ketchup

1 tablespoon mayonnaise

1 tablespoon finely chopped sweet or savory pickle

1 teaspoon white wine vinegar

¼ teaspoon freshly ground black pepper

8 slices pumpernickel bread

12 ounces cracked-pepper turkey breast, thinly sliced

1 cup sauerkraut, squeezed of excess liquid (about 4 ounces)

4 thin slices Swiss cheese (2 ounces total)

Olive oil cooking spray

Huge deli sandwiches are a way of life in New York City. I have the fondest memories of family meals at our local delicatessen where I'd inevitably fill up on pickles and coleslaw before the sandwich even arrived. I was always able to make two or three meals out of what was left of the sandwich I doggie-bagged. Nowadays I like to make my deli favorite, the Reuben, at home, where I include all the essentials—Russian dressing, sauerkraut, Swiss cheese, and dark pumpernickel bread—grilled so the sandwich is warm throughout and the cheese melts. Using cracked-pepper turkey gives it the same spicy-salty kick as pastrami without the fat, and keeping the portion sane makes it a much smarter sandwich. Serve it up with a frilly toothpick for the full deli effect.

In a small bowl, stir together the yogurt, ketchup, mayonnaise, pickle, vinegar, and black pepper. Spread 1 tablespoon of the dressing on each slice of bread. Divide the turkey among 4 of the slices, then top each with ¼ cup sauerkraut and 1 slice of cheese. Top each with another slice of bread, dressing side down.

Spray a medium cast-iron or nonstick skillet liberally with cooking spray and heat over medium-high heat. Place one sandwich in the skillet, spray the top with cooking spray, and weight down with another heavy skillet or a teakettle filled partially with water. Grill until the bread is toasted and the cheese is melted, 2 to 3 minutes per side. Repeat with the remaining sandwiches.

Makes 4 servings

SERVING SIZE 1 sandwich
PER SERVING Calories 280; Total Fat 7 g (Sat Fat 3 g, Mono Fat 1.7 g, Poly Fat 1.3 g); Protein 26 g; Carb 28 g; Fiber 3 g; Cholesterol 45 mg; Sodium 1350 mg
EXCELLENT SOURCE OF Manganese, Protein, Vitamin C
GOOD SOURCE OF Calcium, Fiber, Folate, Iron, Phosphorus, Riboflavin, Selenium

BEFORE	AFTER
760 cal. Sat. Fat 19g, Chol. 170mg Fiber 5g, Sodium 2650mg	Sat. Fat 3g, Chol. 45mg Fiber 3g, Sodium 1350mg **280 cal.**

CHIPOTLE BBQ "PULLED" PORK SLIDERS

6 large cloves garlic, minced (2 tablespoons)

1 teaspoon salt

2 tablespoons chili powder

1 tablespoon ground cumin

3½ tablespoons fresh lime juice

1 tablespoon plus 1 teaspoon olive oil

One 2½-pound center-cut pork loin, trimmed of all visible fat

1 medium onion, chopped

One 14-ounce can no-salt-added low-sodium tomato sauce

½ cup strong brewed coffee

⅓ cup cider vinegar

¼ cup unsulfured molasses

3 tablespoons tomato paste

1½ to 2 tablespoons finely minced canned chipotle chile in adobo sauce

½ cup chopped fresh cilantro leaves

24 slider rolls

1 medium red onion, halved lengthwise and each half cut into 8 slices

The lip-smacking flavor of these mini sandwiches with their tangy-sweet, smoky, spicy sauce is so memorable you are sure to catch yourself dreaming of them later. They are perfect for a party or game night when you want a crowd-pleaser that's fun to eat. Using lean pork loin keeps them healthy, and when cut into thin strips gives that "pulled" effect you get from much fattier cuts.

Preheat the oven to 350°F. Using the broad side of a knife blade, mash together the garlic and salt to form a paste. Transfer the paste to a small bowl and stir in the chili powder, cumin, 2 tablespoons lime juice, and 1 teaspoon oil. Set aside 2 tablespoons of the paste. Rub the remaining paste all over the pork.

Transfer the pork to a roasting pan and roast until an instant read meat thermometer inserted into the thickest part registers 155°F, 1 to 1¼ hours. Transfer the roast to a cutting board and allow it to rest for 15 minutes.

Meanwhile, heat the remaining 1 tablespoon oil in a large saucepan over medium heat. Add the chopped onion and cook, stirring, until soft and translucent, about 5 minutes. Add the reserved 2 tablespoons chili

continued on page 122

BEFORE		AFTER	
520 cal.	Sat. Fat 6g, Chol. 70mg Fiber 2g, Sodium 1030mg	Sat. Fat 3g, Chol. 55mg Fiber 3g, Sodium 560mg	**360 cal.**

continued from page 120

paste and cook, stirring, for 1 minute. Add the tomato sauce, coffee, vinegar, molasses, tomato paste, and chipotle and bring to a boil. Reduce the heat to medium low and simmer for 20 minutes. Stir in the cilantro and the remaining 1½ tablespoons lime juice.

Cut the pork into thin slices, then cut the slices into thin, shredded strips. Add the pork strips to the sauce and simmer for 5 minutes.

Split the buns, scoop out the bread to remove the soft inner portion, and discard. Place one slice of red onion on the bottom half of each bun, then pile on about ¼ cup of the pork mixture and cap with the bun tops.

Makes 12 servings

SERVING SIZE 2 sliders
PER SERVING Calories 360; Total Fat 10 g (Sat Fat 3 g, Mono Fat 4.2 g, Poly Fat 1.8 g); Protein 26 g; Carb 40 g; Fiber 3 g; Cholesterol 55 mg; Sodium 560 mg
EXCELLENT SOURCE OF Iron, Manganese, Niacin, Protein, Riboflavin, Selenium, Thiamin, Vitamin B6
GOOD SOURCE OF Calcium, Copper, Folate, Fiber, Magnesium, Phosphorus, Potassium, Vitamin C, Zinc

CREAMY CURRIED EGG SALAD SANDWICH

8 large eggs
¼ cup drained silken tofu
2 tablespoons mayonnaise
1 tablespoon yellow mustard
1½ teaspoons yellow curry powder
¼ teaspoon salt, plus more to taste
¼ teaspoon freshly ground black pepper
8 slices whole-wheat bread
1 large beefsteak tomato, cored and sliced
4 large leaves green-leaf lettuce

You don't need to let on that the secret ingredient in this ultra creamy egg salad is tofu (its silky smooth texture lets you use less mayo). Your family and guests will never guess it. All they will taste is a quintessential egg salad sandwich, spiked with curry to make things interesting and served in the classic all-American style—on toast with lettuce and tomato.

Place the eggs in a medium pot, cover with water, and bring to a boil. Reduce the heat to medium low and simmer for 9 minutes. Drain and rinse under cold water until the eggs are cool enough to handle, and then peel them. Discard 4 egg yolks, then finely chop the remaining eggs. Place the chopped eggs in a medium bowl.

In a small bowl, stir together the tofu, mayonnaise, mustard, curry powder, salt, and black pepper until well combined. Add the dressing to the eggs and toss gently to combine.

Toast the bread. Divide the egg salad among 4 slices of toast and top each with a tomato slice and a lettuce leaf. Top with the remaining toast.

Makes 4 servings

SERVING SIZE 1 sandwich
PER SERVING Calories 280; Total Fat 10 g (Sat Fat 2.5 g, Mono Fat 3.7 g, Poly Fat 2.8 g); Protein 19 g; Carb 29 g; Fiber 5 g; Cholesterol 215 mg; Sodium 640 mg
EXCELLENT SOURCE OF Fiber, Iodine, Manganese, Phosphorus, Protein, Riboflavin, Selenium, Vitamin A, Vitamin K
GOOD SOURCE OF Calcium, Copper, Folate, Iron, Magnesium, Molybdenum, Niacin, Pantothenic Acid, Potassium, Thiamin, Vitamin B6, Vitamin B12, Vitamin C, Zinc

BEFORE		AFTER	
390 cal.	Sat. Fat 4.5g, Chol. 430mg Fiber 2g, Sodium 1390mg	Sat. Fat 2.5g, Chol. 215mg Fiber 5g, Sodium 640mg	**280 cal.**

BLT WITH AVOCADO SPREAD

1 very ripe avocado

1 tablespoon fresh lemon juice

⅛ teaspoon salt

⅛ teaspoon freshly ground black pepper

8 slices bacon, preferably nitrate-free

8 slices whole-wheat bread

4 medium leaves romaine lettuce

2 ripe medium tomatoes, sliced

Let's be honest—to make a really good BLT, you need to use really good, real bacon. But a little goes a long way. Just two slices is all you need for the crisp, smoky baco-licious factor to shine through. Trading up the common slather of mayo for buttery avocado spread adds a rich, citrusy flavor dimension, not to mention fiber and valuable nutrients.

Peel and pit the avocado. In a small bowl, mash the avocado with the lemon juice, salt, and black pepper.

Heat a skillet over medium heat. Add the bacon and cook, turning two or three times, to the desired doneness, about 8 minutes for crispy. Drain on paper towels.

Toast the bread.

To make the sandwiches, spread 1 tablespoon of the avocado mixture on each slice of toast. Place 2 pieces of bacon on half the pieces of toast, then top with a folded lettuce leaf and 2 slices of tomato. Top with the remaining toast. Cut in half and serve immediately.

Makes 4 servings

SERVING SIZE 1 sandwich
PER SERVING Calories 320; Total Fat 16 g (Sat Fat 3.5 g, Mono Fat 8.7 g, Poly Fat 2.1 g); Protein 15 g; Carb 31 g; Fiber 9 g; Cholesterol 20 mg; Sodium 730 mg
EXCELLENT SOURCE OF Fiber, Folate, Manganese, Niacin, Phosphorus, Protein, Selenium, Thiamin, Vitamin A, Vitamin K
GOOD SOURCE OF Copper, Iron, Magnesium, Pantothenic Acid, Potassium, Riboflavin, Vitamin B6, Zinc

BEFORE	AFTER
460 cal. Sat. Fat 6g, Chol. 45mg Fiber 3g, Sodium 1390mg	Sat. Fat 3.5g, Chol. 20mg Fiber 9g, Sodium 730mg **320 cal.**

chapter four

MEAT MAIN DISHES

From down-home favorites like meatloaf and stew to more upscale delights like braised lamb shanks, these dishes give you that soul-warming, fall-off-the-bone tenderness that practically defines comfort.

BETTER BEEF LASAGNA

12 ounces whole-grain lasagna noodles (15 noodles)

8 ounces lean ground beef (90% lean or higher)

2 teaspoons olive oil

8 ounces portobello mushrooms, diced (about 3 large mushroom caps)

1 teaspoon salt

4 cups Quick Marinara Sauce (1½ recipes on page 63) or store-bought marinara

One 15-ounce container part-skim ricotta cheese

One 10-ounce package frozen chopped spinach, thawed and well drained

1 large egg, lightly beaten

½ teaspoon freshly ground black pepper

Pinch ground nutmeg

¼ cup freshly grated Parmesan cheese

3 ounces grated part-skim mozzarella cheese (about ⅔ cup)

This crowd-pleaser is beefed up with veggies in every layer, portobello mushrooms in the meat, spinach in the cheese, and of course tomato sauce in between. No will notice they're eating their vegetables, they'll be too busy devouring their cheesy beef lasagna.

Preheat the oven to 375°F.

Cook the noodles al dente according to the directions on the package. Drain well, then lay out on wax paper to prevent them from sticking to each other.

Heat a large nonstick skillet over medium-high heat. Add the beef and cook until no longer pink, breaking up the meat into small pieces with a wooden spoon, about 3 minutes. Transfer the meat to a plate, discarding any fat remaining in the skillet.

Heat the oil in the skillet over medium-high heat. Add the mushrooms and cook, stirring occasionally, until all the liquid is evaporated and they begin to brown, about 5 minutes. Return the meat to the pan. Season with ½ teaspoon salt, stir in 2 cups of the tomato sauce, and simmer for 2 minutes.

In a medium bowl, combine the ricotta cheese, spinach, egg, the remaining ½ teaspoon salt, the black pepper, and nutmeg.

continued on page 130

	BEFORE	AFTER	
800 cal.	Sat. Fat 23g, Chol. 200mg Fiber 3g, Sodium 1090mg	Sat. Fat 7g, Chol. 90mg Fiber 11g, Sodium 1000mg	**550 cal.**

continued from page 128

Spread 1 cup of the remaining tomato sauce on the bottom of a 9x13-inch baking dish. Place a layer of lasagna noodles over the sauce, touching but not overlapping. Spread half of the ricotta mixture on top of the noodles. Add another layer of noodles. Top with half the beef-mushroom mixture. Repeat with another layer of noodles, then the remaining cheese mixture, more noodles, the remaining beef mixture, and finally one more layer of noodles. Top the final layer of noodles with the remaining 1 cup tomato sauce, then sprinkle with the grated cheeses. Cover loosely with foil. Bake for 45 minutes, uncover, and bake 15 minutes more.

Makes 6 servings

SERVING SIZE 1 4x4-inch piece
PER SERVING Calories 550; Total Fat 18 g (Sat Fat 7 g, Mono Fat 5 g, Poly Fat 0.8 g); Protein 35 g; Carb 62 g; Fiber 11 g; Cholesterol 90 mg; Sodium 1000 mg
EXCELLENT SOURCE OF Calcium, Fiber, Iron, Niacin, Phosphorus, Potassium, Protein, Riboflavin, Selenium, Thiamin, Vitamin A, Vitamin B12, Vitamin C, Zinc
GOOD SOURCE OF Copper, Folate, Magnesium

SHEPHERD'S PIE

1 pound lean ground beef (90% lean or higher)

2 teaspoons olive oil

2 medium onions, chopped (about 3 cups)

3 medium carrots, diced (about 1½ cups)

½ pound white mushrooms, sliced

2 teaspoons chopped fresh thyme, or 1 teaspoon dried

2 tablespoons flour

1 cup low-sodium beef broth

1 teaspoon salt

Freshly ground black pepper

1 cup frozen peas

1½ pounds Yukon Gold potatoes

1 small head cauliflower, cut into florets (about 2 pounds)

⅔ cup low-fat (1%) milk

2 tablespoons unsalted butter

This rustic meal is double-decker meat-and-potatoes heaven—on the bottom, savory ground beef chock-full of vegetables, up top, a creamy mashed potato-and-cauliflower puree. It's a fresh take on old-world comfort.

In a large nonstick skillet, cook the beef over medium heat, stirring occasionally, until browned, about 5 minutes. Transfer the meat to a plate, discarding any fat remaining in the skillet.

Heat the oil in the skillet over medium heat. Add the onions and carrots, cover, and cook until the vegetables begin to soften, about 8 minutes. Increase the heat to medium high. Uncover and add the mushrooms and thyme and cook, uncovered, stirring occasionally, until the mushrooms are soft and their liquid is evaporated, about 8 minutes. Return the beef to the pan. Add the flour and cook, stirring, for 2 minutes. Stir in the broth, ½ teaspoon salt, and ⅛ teaspoon black pepper and bring to a simmer. Be sure to scrape up any brown bits from the bottom of the pan. Stir in the peas. Pour the mixture into a 12-cup shallow baking dish (about 9×13 inches).

Preheat the oven to 350°F. Scrub the potatoes and cut into 2-inch pieces. Arrange the potatoes in a steamer basket and steam for

continued on page 132

BEFORE		AFTER	
710 cal.	Sat. Fat 21g, Chol. 120mg Fiber 5g, Sodium 850mg	Sat. Fat 4.5g, Chol. 60mg Fiber 7g, Sodium 540mg	**340 cal.**

continued from page 131

10 minutes. Add the cauliflower to the basket and cook until the potatoes and cauliflower are tender when pierced with the tip of a knife, about 15 minutes longer. Transfer the potatoes and cauliflower to a bowl, then mash with a potato masher until smooth. Heat the milk, butter, the remaining ½ teaspoon salt, and a pinch of black pepper and stir into the potato mixture.

Spread the potato mixture on top of the meat. Bake until heated through, about 25 minutes.

Make 6 servings

SERVING SIZE 1¾ cups
PER SERVING Calories 340; Total Fat 10 g (Sat Fat 4.5 g, Mono Fat 3.5 g, Poly Fat 1 g); Protein 24 g; Carb 42 g; Fiber 7 g; Cholesterol 60 mg; Sodium 540 mg
EXCELLENT SOURCE OF Copper, Fiber, Folate, Iron, Manganese, Niacin, Potassium, Protein, Riboflavin, Vitamin A, Vitamin B6, Vitamin B12, Vitamin C, Vitamin K, Zinc
GOOD SOURCE OF Magnesium, Pantothenic Acid, Phosphorus, Thiamin

CRISPY BEEF AND BEAN TACOS

FOR THE CRISPY SHELLS:

Eight 6-inch corn tortillas

1 teaspoon olive oil

¼ teaspoon salt

FOR THE MEAT FILLING:

½ **pound lean ground beef (90% lean or higher)**

1 **cup canned black beans, preferably low-sodium, drained and rinsed**

2 cloves garlic, minced

2 teaspoons chili powder

½ teaspoon dried oregano

¼ teaspoon salt

⅛ teaspoon cayenne pepper, plus more to taste

¼ cup water

FOR THE TOPPINGS:

1 **medium tomato, seeded and diced**

¼ cup chopped red onion

½ **cup shredded cheddar cheese**

2 **cups shredded romaine lettuce**

¼ cup fresh cilantro leaves

It's no wonder taco night has become a beloved all-American tradition—it is such a fun, interactive, easy, and delicious meal. Just a few minor tweaks to the standard kit—using lean meat and beans in the filling and home-baked crispy corn shells—make it extra healthy too.

To make the taco shells, preheat the oven to 375°F.

Wrap the tortillas in damp paper towels and microwave on high until warm and softened, about 40 seconds. Brush the tortillas lightly on both sides with the oil, then sprinkle with the salt. Carefully drape each tortilla over two bars of the oven rack, so that the sides hang down and it forms into a flat-bottomed taco shape. (The sides will drape further as they cook.) Bake until crispy, about 7 minutes. Then, using tongs, transfer from the oven to a plate, or allow to cool completely, then wrap in foil for later use. Shells may be made up to 1 day ahead.

To make the meat, heat a large nonstick skillet over medium-high heat. Add the beef and cook until no longer pink, stirring occasionally and breaking up the meat into small pieces with a wooden spoon, about

continued on page 134

	BEFORE	AFTER	
470 cal.	Sat. Fat 13g, Chol. 90mg Fiber 2g, Sodium 660mg	Sat. Fat 6g, Chol. 50mg Fiber 8g, Sodium 460mg	**340 cal.**

continued from page 133

8 minutes. Add the beans and garlic and cook, stirring, for 2 minutes more. Add the chili powder, oregano, salt, cayenne pepper, and water and cook, stirring, until well combined and heated through, about 2 minutes more.

To assemble a taco, fill a shell with ¼ cup of the meat mixture, then top with tomato, onion, cheese, lettuce, and cilantro.

Makes 4 servings

SERVING SIZE 2 tacos
PER SERVING Calories 340; Total Fat 13 g (Sat Fat 6 g, Mono Fat 5 g, Poly Fat 1.3 g); Protein 22 g; Carb 35 g; Fiber 8 g; Cholesterol 50 mg; Sodium 460 mg
EXCELLENT SOURCE OF Fiber, Magnesium, Niacin, Phosphorus, Protein, Selenium, Vitamin A, Vitamin B6, Vitamin B12, Vitamin K, Zinc
GOOD SOURCE OF Calcium, Folate, Iron, Manganese, Potassium, Riboflavin, Thiamin, Vitamin C

HAMBURGER HEALTHIER

1 tablespoon olive oil

1 pound lean ground beef (90% lean or higher)

1 large onion, chopped

2 cloves garlic, minced

2 tablespoons chili powder

¾ teaspoon salt

½ teaspoon freshly ground black pepper

4 cups chopped cooked broccoli, thawed if frozen

One 14-ounce can no-salt-added diced tomatoes

One 8-ounce can no-salt-added tomato sauce

½ pound whole-wheat elbow macaroni

3 cups water

2 tablespoons chopped fresh parsley leaves

When I was a kid, a skillet dinner with hamburger, vegetables, and noodles was in regular rotation on my mom's menu. She always whipped hers up from scratch, but lots of families I knew used the boxed kit. This recipe has the same one-pan ease and family-friendly appeal, updated with lean meat, whole-grain pasta, fresh aromatics, and a generous helping of chopped broccoli.

Heat the oil in a large, deep skillet or pot (4 quarts) with a lid over medium-high heat. Add the beef and the onion and cook until no longer pink and the onion is softened, breaking up the meat with a wooden spoon, about 5 minutes. Add the garlic and cook for 1 minute more. Stir in the chili powder, salt, and black pepper until incorporated. Add the broccoli, tomatoes, tomato sauce, macaroni, and water, stir to combine well, and bring to a boil. Reduce the heat to medium low, cover, and cook until the pasta is tender, 10 to 12 minutes. Serve garnished with parsley.

Makes 4 servings

SERVING SIZE 2½ cups
PER SERVING Calories 520; Total Fat 17 g (Sat Fat 5 g, Mono Fat 7.7 g, Poly Fat 1.5 g); Protein 36 g; Carb 62 g; Fiber 11 g; Cholesterol 75 mg; Sodium 600 mg
EXCELLENT SOURCE OF Copper, Iron, Folate, Fiber, Magnesium, Manganese, Niacin, Phosphorus, Potassium, Protein, Riboflavin, Selenium, Thiamin, Vitamin A, Vitamin B6, Vitamin B12, Vitamin C, Vitamin K, Zinc
GOOD SOURCE OF Calcium, Pantothenic Acid

BEFORE		AFTER	
	Sat. Fat 14g, Chol. 150mg	Sat. Fat 5g, Chol. 75mg	
870 cal.	Fiber 2g, Sodium 1780mg	Fiber 11g, Sodium 600mg	**520 cal.**

HEARTY BEEF STEW

¼ cup all-purpose flour

¼ teaspoon salt

¼ teaspoon freshly ground black pepper

¼ teaspoon paprika

1 pound lean stew beef (round or chuck shoulder), cut into cubes

3 tablespoons olive oil

1 medium onion, chopped

1 small rutabaga or turnip, peeled and cubed (about 10 ounces)

1 large carrot, chopped

1 large russet potato, cubed (about 12 ounces)

2 tablespoons tomato paste

1 cup dry red wine

2 cups reduced-sodium beef broth

2 cups green peas (one 10-ounce box, frozen)

Something about having a big pot of stew on the stove, simmering away, fills me with contentment. It's one of life's simple pleasures—a wholesome, one-pot meal to satisfy the entire family or to have leftovers in the fridge for an even better next day's dinner. This one is especially homey with its familiar flavors: tender meat and hearty root vegetables simmered in beef gravy enriched with red wine and tomato.

Place the flour, salt, black pepper, and paprika in a large sealable plastic bag. Add the beef and shake to coat well. Heat 2 tablespoons of the oil in a large (at least 6-quart) saucepan or soup pot over medium-high heat. Add the beef and cook until browned on all sides, about 6 minutes total. Transfer the meat to a plate, leaving the juices in the saucepan.

Add the remaining 1 tablespoon oil to the pot. Add the onion and cook over medium heat, stirring occasionally, until the onion is golden but not browned, about 10 minutes. Add the rutabaga, carrot, and potato and cook until the vegetables soften slightly, about 10 minutes. Stir in the tomato paste and cook 1 minute more. Add the wine, bring

continued on page 138

	BEFORE	AFTER	
500 cal.	Sat. Fat 8g, Chol. 120mg Fiber 4g, Sodium 1200mg	Sat. Fat 3g, Chol. 50mg Fiber 8g, Sodium 340mg	**490 cal.**

continued from page 137

to a boil, and reduce for 3 minutes. Add the beef broth, return to a boil, then reduce the heat to medium low. Cover and simmer until the meat is tender, about 1 hour and 20 minutes. Add the peas and cook 5 minutes more. Remove from the heat and allow to rest for at least 15 minutes before serving.

Makes 4 servings

SERVING SIZE 2 cups
PER SERVING Calories 490; Total Fat 15 g (Sat Fat 3 g, Mono Fat 9.4 g, Poly Fat 1.6 g); Protein 36 g; Carb 42 g; Fiber 8 g; Cholesterol 50 mg; Sodium 340 mg
EXCELLENT SOURCE OF Fiber, Folate, Iron, Magnesium, Manganese, Niacin, Phosphorus, Potassium, Protein, Riboflavin, Selenium, Thiamin, Vitamin A, Vitamin B6, Vitamin B12, Vitamin C, Vitamin K, Zinc
GOOD SOURCE OF Copper, Pantothenic Acid

NEW CLASSIC MEATLOAF

1 tablespoon olive oil

1 small onion, diced (1 cup)

8 ounces white button mushrooms, finely diced

1 small carrot, finely grated

2 tablespoons tomato paste

½ teaspoon dried thyme

1 clove garlic, minced

1½ pounds extra-lean ground beef (90% lean or higher)

¾ cup quick-cooking oats

2 large eggs, beaten

2 teaspoons Worcestershire sauce

¾ teaspoon salt

½ teaspoon freshly ground black pepper

One 8-ounce can no-salt-added tomato sauce

1 tablespoon unsulfured molasses

1 tablespoon yellow mustard

Nothing says homey goodness like a classic, old-fashioned meatloaf. This one has all the familiar flavors you yearn for with a healthy update from meaty sautéed mushrooms that blend beautifully with lean ground beef and whole-grain oats instead of bread crumbs. For the full effect, serve with Smooth and Creamy Mashed Potatoes (page 233).

Preheat the oven to 350°F.

Heat the oil in a large skillet over medium-high heat. Add the onion and mushrooms and cook until the mushroom liquid is evaporated and they begin to brown, about 8 minutes. Add the carrot, tomato paste, thyme, and garlic and cook, stirring, for 2 minutes. Allow to cool completely.

In a large bowl, mix together the beef, oats, eggs, Worcestershire sauce, mushroom mixture, salt, and black pepper until well combined. Transfer the mixture to a 9×13-inch baking dish and shape into a loaf about 5 inches wide and 2 inches high.

continued on page 141

	BEFORE	AFTER	
340 cal.	Sat. Fat 9g, Chol. 110mg Fiber 1g, Sodium 370mg	Sat. Fat 4g, Chol. 110mg Fiber 2g, Sodium 370mg	250 cal.

continued from page 139

In a small bowl, whisk together the tomato sauce, molasses, and mustard and pour over the meatloaf.

Bake the meatloaf until a meat thermometer registers 160°F, 55 to 60 minutes. Remove from the oven and allow to rest 15 minutes before slicing.

Makes 8 servings

SERVING SIZE one 1-inch-thick slice
PER SERVING Calories 250; Total Fat 12 g (Sat Fat 4 g, Mono Fat 5.5 g, Poly Fat 1 g); Protein 21 g; Carb 14 g; Fiber 2 g; Cholesterol 110 mg; Sodium 370 mg
EXCELLENT SOURCE OF Niacin, Phosphorus, Protein, Selenium, Vitamin A, Vitamin B6, Vitamin B12, Zinc
GOOD SOURCE OF Copper, Iron, Pantothenic Acid, Potassium, Riboflavin, Vitamin C

COUNTRY FRIED STEAK WITH GRAVY

½ cup whole-wheat pastry flour

½ cup all-purpose flour

½ teaspoon smoked paprika

½ teaspoon salt

½ teaspoon freshly ground black pepper

1 large egg

1 large egg white

1 cup low-fat (1%) milk

¼ teaspoon hot pepper sauce, such as Tabasco

1 pound cube steak, cut into 4 equal pieces

3 tablespoons olive oil

½ cup low-sodium chicken broth

Like the best country meals, this one is both humble and downright satisfying. True to the standard recipe, this one calls for one of the leanest cuts of meat, the round, which is tenderized or "cubed" with a special machine and sold as cube steak. But here you get a crispy-fried coating without the grease, thanks to a nonstick pan and minimal oil, and you get a nice, thick country-style gravy made lighter with low-fat milk.

In a shallow bowl, combine the flours, paprika, ¼ teaspoon salt, and ¼ teaspoon black pepper. Remove 2 tablespoons of the flour mixture and set aside.

In a medium bowl, whisk together the egg, egg white, ¼ cup milk, and the hot pepper sauce. Dip each steak in the egg-milk mixture, then in the flour mixture, shaking off the excess. Dip each steak again in the liquid and flour, shaking off the excess.

Heat 1½ tablespoons of the oil in a large nonstick skillet over medium-high heat. Place 2 steaks in the pan and cook until golden brown, 2 to 3 minutes per side. Transfer to a plate. Repeat with the remaining oil and steaks. Transfer to the plate.

Add the chicken broth to the skillet, scraping up any browned bits from the bottom of the pan. In a small bowl, whisk together the

BEFORE	AFTER
510 cal. Sat. Fat 7g, Chol. 85mg Fiber 1g, Sodium 1000mg	Sat. Fat 4g, Chol. 120mg Fiber 2g, Sodium 430mg **400 cal.**

reserved 2 tablespoons seasoned flour into the remaining ¾ cup milk until the flour is dissolved. Slowly add the milk-flour mixture to the pan, whisking constantly, and bring to a simmer. Reduce the heat and cook, whisking, until the sauce thickens, an additional 1 to 2 minutes. Season with the remaining ¼ teaspoon salt and ¼ teaspoon black pepper. Serve the steak drizzled with gravy.

Makes 4 servings

SERVING SIZE 1 steak and ¼ cup gravy
PER SERVING Calories 400; Total Fat 18 g (Sat Fat 4 g, Mono Fat 10.2 g, Poly Fat 1.7 g) ; Protein 34 g; Carb 27 g; Fiber 2 g; Cholesterol 120 mg; Sodium 430 mg
EXCELLENT SOURCE OF Iron, Manganese, Niacin, Phosphorus, Protein, Riboflavin, Selenium, Thiamin, C Vitamin B6, Vitamin B12, Zinc
GOOD SOURCE OF Calcium, Copper, Folate, Iodine, Magnesium, Pantothenic Acid, Potassium, Vitamin K

BRAISED BRISKET WITH CAROLINA-STYLE BBQ SAUCE

FOR THE BARBECUE SAUCE:

½ cup yellow mustard

½ cup unsulfured molasses

¼ cup cider vinegar

2 teaspoons chili powder

½ teaspoon Worcestershire sauce

½ teaspoon hot pepper sauce, like Tabasco

¼ teaspoon freshly ground black pepper

FOR THE BRISKET:

2 tablespoons sugar

2 tablespoons chili powder

2 teaspoons smoked paprika

1½ teaspoons garlic powder

1½ teaspoons onion powder

1 teaspoon dry mustard

1 teaspoon ground cumin

1 teaspoon salt

1 teaspoon freshly ground black pepper

One 3-pound beef brisket, first-cut or flat-half, trimmed of all excess fat

2 tablespoons canola oil

½ cup water

If you crave low-and-slow barbecue but lack a backyard fire pit, this recipe lets you get that fabulous flavor at home. The brisket is rubbed generously with smoky spices, then simmered in the oven in a tangy-sweet, vinegar-based barbecue sauce until it is fork-tender. It's long-cooking but low maintenance, giving you plenty of time to kick back and relax before supper.

Preheat the oven to 300°F.

To make the sauce, in a medium bowl, whisk together the mustard, molasses, vinegar, chili powder, Worcestershire sauce, hot pepper sauce, and black pepper.

To make the brisket, in a small bowl, mix together the sugar, chili powder, paprika, garlic powder, onion powder, dry mustard, cumin, salt, and black pepper. Rub the mixture all over the brisket. Let the spices absorb into the meat for 1 hour and up to overnight.

Heat the oil in a large Dutch oven or heavy roasting pan over medium-high heat. Add the brisket and cook on one side until deep brown, about 8 minutes. Carefully flip the brisket so the browned side is now

continued on page 146

	BEFORE	AFTER	
590 cal.	Sat. Fat 13g, Chol. 110mg Fiber 1g, Sodium 1610mg	Sat. Fat 4g, Chol. 100mg Fiber 3g, Sodium 840mg	**470 cal.**

continued from page 145

on the top. Add the water and ½ cup of the barbecue sauce. Cover tightly, transfer to the oven, and cook until the meat is tender, 2½ to 3 hours.

Transfer the pan from the oven to the stovetop. Remove the meat and place on a cutting board. Add the remaining barbecue sauce to the liquid in the pan, and bring to a boil over medium-high heat. Reduce the heat to medium low and simmer until the sauce has reduced slightly, about 5 minutes. Slice the brisket into ¼-inch slices and serve with the sauce.

Makes 6 servings

SERVING SIZE 5 to 6 slices and ¼ cup sauce
PER SERVING Calories 470; Total Fat 16 g (Sat Fat 4 g, Mono Fat 7.6 g, Poly Fat 2.4 g); Protein 51 g; Carb 29 g; Fiber 3 g; Cholesterol 100 mg; Sodium 840 mg
EXCELLENT SOURCE OF Iron, Magnesium, Manganese, Niacin, Phosphorus, Potassium, Protein, Riboflavin, Selenium, Vitamin A, Vitamin B6, Vitamin B12, Zinc
GOOD SOURCE OF Calcium, Copper, Pantothenic Acid, Thiamin, Vitamin K

HORSERADISH, CHEDDAR, AND CARAMELIZED ONION–STUFFED BURGERS

2 teaspoons olive oil

1 medium onion, sliced into half-moons

1 pound lean ground beef (90% lean or higher)

4 teaspoons prepared white horseradish, drained of excess liquid

½ cup lightly packed shredded extra-sharp cheddar cheese (2 ounces)

¼ teaspoon salt

⅛ teaspoon freshly ground black pepper

Nonstick cooking spray

4 whole-wheat hamburger buns

4 medium leaves romaine lettuce, ribs removed

1 large tomato, sliced

Ketchup, optional

These burgers are big in every way—big in size, big in flavor, and big in wow! factor. It is incredible how small changes can add up to such a healthy difference while keeping all of the flavors you yearn for. By using a sensible amount of lean beef and stuffing it with a bit of aged cheese and lots of other high-impact flavors, you get the juicy, melted cheddar bun filler you crave without the downsides.

Heat the oil in a medium-size nonstick skillet over medium heat. Add the onion, reduce the heat to medium low and cook, stirring, until the onion is softened, about 5 minutes. Cover and cook, stirring occasionally, until the onion is a deep golden brown, about 20 minutes more.

In the meantime, shape the beef into 8 small patties, each about 4 inches in diameter.

To make a stuffed burger, spread 1 teaspoon horseradish on one of the patties. Top that with 2 tablespoons cheddar cheese and 1 tablespoon caramelized onions. Top with another meat patty and pinch around the edges of the patties to seal the burger closed. Repeat with

continued on page 148

BEFORE		AFTER	
810 cal.	Sat. Fat 26g, Chol. 150mg Fiber 2g, Sodium 1110mg	Sat. Fat 8g, Chol. 90mg Fiber 4g, Sodium 530mg	**410 cal.**

continued from page 147

the remaining patties. Season the stuffed burgers on both sides with salt and black pepper.

Spray a nonstick grill pan with cooking spray and heat over medium-high heat, or prepare a grill. Cook the burgers until the cheese is melted inside and the meat is at the desired doneness, about 4 minutes per side for medium doneness.

Serve on the buns with lettuce, tomato, and ketchup, if desired.

Makes 4 servings

SERVING SIZE 1 burger
PER SERVING Calories 410; Total Fat 21 g (Sat Fat 8 g, Mono Fat 8.5 g, Poly Fat 1.8 g); Protein 31g; Carb 27 g; Fiber 4 g; Cholesterol 90 mg; Sodium 530 mg
EXCELLENT SOURCE OF Iron, Protein, Manganese, Niacin, Phosphorus, Selenium, Vitamin A, Vitamin B6, Vitamin B12, Zinc
GOOD SOURCE OF Calcium, Copper, Fiber, Folate, Magnesium, Pantothenic Acid, Potassium, Riboflavin, Thiamin, Vitamin C, Vitamin K

STUFFED CABBAGE WITH SWEET-AND-SOUR TOMATO SAUCE

1 large head green cabbage (about 3 pounds)

1½ pounds lean ground beef (90% lean or higher)

2 medium carrots, finely grated (about ⅔ cup)

1 large onion, finely chopped

3 medium cloves garlic, minced

½ cup uncooked long-grain brown rice

1¼ teaspoons salt

1 teaspoon freshly ground black pepper

2 tablespoons olive oil

Two 15-ounce cans no-salt-added tomato sauce

½ cup cider vinegar

⅓ cup packed dark brown sugar

⅓ cup raisins

¼ cup water

When I eat this tender stuffed cabbage with its raisin-studded, sweet-tart tomato sauce I feel profoundly connected with the past. It is, after all, based on a dish my grandmother's grandmother used to make and it has nourished generations of my family. I admit I was a little intimidated making it the first time, but it is surprisingly easy, even fun, to do.

Fill a large soup pot about ⅔ full with water and bring to a boil. Using a small sharp knife, core the cabbage, then stick a long two-pronged carving fork into the core end to act as a handle. Submerge the cabbage in the boiling water until the outermost leaf separates easily from the cabbage head, about 15 seconds. Peel off the outmost leaf, then return the cabbage to the boiling water. Repeat until you have at least 12 large leaves for stuffing. Shred the remaining cabbage and place it at the bottom of a large, deep, ovenproof casserole dish (about 6 quarts).

Preheat the oven to 325°F. In a large bowl, combine the beef, carrots, half of the onion, half of the garlic, the rice, ¾ teaspoon salt, and ½ teaspoon pepper and mix to incorporate. Cut out and discard the thick part of the white central rib from each cabbage leaf. Place about ⅓ cup of the meat mixture onto a leaf in the area opposite the core end, then roll up burrito style: pull the bottom and top of the leaf over the

	BEFORE	AFTER	
700 cal.	Sat. Fat 12g, Chol. 190mg Fiber 8g, Sodium 1170mg	Sat. Fat 5g, Chol. 75mg Fiber 10g, Sodium 640mg	510 cal.

filling, fold over the side, then roll tightly. Place the stuffed cabbage, seam side down, into the casserole dish on top of the shredded cabbage. Repeat with the remaining cabbage leaves and meat mixture until you have used all the filling. Stack the rolls a bit, if needed, to get them all into the dish.

Heat the oil in a large skillet over medium heat. Add the remaining onion and cook, stirring, until softened and translucent, about 6 minutes. Add the remaining garlic and cook for 1 minute. Add the tomato sauce, vinegar, brown sugar, raisins, the water, the remaining ½ teaspoon salt, and the remaining ½ teaspoon black pepper and bring to a boil. Reduce the heat to medium low and simmer until the sauce thickens slightly, about 10 minutes. Pour the sauce over the stuffed cabbage, cover the casserole dish tightly, and place in the oven for 2 hours.

Makes 6 servings

SERVING SIZE 2 rolls and ¾ cup sauce
PER SERVING Calories 510; Total Fat 17 g (Sat Fat 5 g, Mono Fat 8.5 g, Poly Fat 1.2 g); Protein 30 g; Carb 61 g; Fiber 10 g; Cholesterol 75 mg; Sodium 640 mg
EXCELLENT SOURCE OF Copper, Folate, Fiber, Iron, Magnesium, Manganese, Niacin, Phosphorus, Potassium, Protein, Riboflavin, Selenium, Thiamin, Vitamin A, Vitamin B6, Vitamin B12, Vitamin C, Vitamin K, Zinc
GOOD SOURCE OF Calcium, Molybdenum, Pantothenic Acid

PORK AND TOMATILLO POSOLE

12 ounces fresh tomatillos, papery skins removed, rinsed well and dried

1 jalapeño pepper, halved and seeded

2 tablespoons olive oil

1 pound pork tenderloin, cut into ½-inch cubes

1 medium onion, halved and thinly sliced

3 cloves garlic, minced

1 teaspoon dried oregano

1 teaspoon ground cumin

½ teaspoon ground coriander

1 bay leaf

4 cups low-sodium chicken broth

Two 15-ounce cans white hominy, drained and rinsed

One 14.5-ounce can fire-roasted diced tomatoes, preferably no-salt-added

½ teaspoon salt, plus more to taste

¼ teaspoon freshly ground black pepper

4 radishes, diced

1 small ripe avocado, peeled, pitted, and cubed

¼ cup fresh cilantro leaves, chopped

Posole is a sumptuous Mexican stew, built on a foundation of large white corn kernels called hominy and typically made with pork and any number of flavor variations. I use lots of tomatillos in mine because I love their tangy flavor and fresh green color. The cilantro and avocado garnish give a cooling balance to the warm, full-flavored dish.

Preheat the broiler. Place the tomatillos and jalapeño on a baking sheet and broil, 5 to 6 inches from the flame, until the tomatillos collapse and the jalapeño is charred, about 10 minutes. Allow to cool slightly, then transfer to a blender or food processor and blend or process until smooth.

Heat 1 tablespoon of the oil in a soup pot over medium-high heat. Add the pork and cook until browned but still slightly pink in the center, about 5 minutes. Transfer the pork, with its juices, to a plate.

Heat the remaining 1 tablespoon oil over medium-high heat. Add the onion and cook, stirring, until softened, about 6 minutes. Add the garlic, oregano, cumin, coriander, and bay leaf and cook, stirring, until the spices become fragrant, about 1 minute. Return the pork with its juices to the pot and stir to combine. Add the pureed tomatillos, chicken broth, hominy, tomatoes, ½ teaspoon salt, and ¼ teaspoon black pepper and bring to a boil. Reduce the heat to medium low and simmer, skimming off any initial foam, for 15 minutes. Remove the bay leaf. Season with salt. Serve garnished with radishes, avocado, and cilantro.

Makes 4 servings

SERVING SIZE 2¼ cups
PER SERVING Calories 520; Total Fat 21 g (Sat Fat 3.5 g, Mono Fat 12 g, Poly Fat 3.5g); Protein 35 g; Carb 49 g; Fiber 12 g; Cholesterol 75 mg; Sodium 860 mg
EXCELLENT SOURCE OF Copper, Fiber, Iron, Magnesium, Manganese, Niacin, Pantothenic Acid, Phosphorus, Potassium, Protein, Riboflavin, Selenium, Thiamin, Vitamin B6, Vitamin C, Vitamin K, Zinc
GOOD SOURCE OF Folate, Vitamin A, Vitamin B12

BEFORE	AFTER
580 cal. Sat. Fat 7g, Chol. 70mg Fiber 12g, Sodium 1440mg	Sat. Fat 3.5g, Chol. 70mg Fiber 12g, Sodium 860mg **520 cal.**

GARLIC-ROSEMARY BRAISED LAMB SHANK WITH CREAMY POLENTA

FOR THE LAMB:

Two 1¼-pound lamb shanks, each cut across the bone into two 10-ounce pieces and trimmed of visible fat (ask your butcher to do this)

½ **teaspoon salt**

½ **teaspoon freshly ground black pepper**

1 **tablespoon olive oil**

1 **large onion, chopped**

6 **cloves garlic, minced**

2 **medium carrots, chopped**

2 **ribs celery, chopped**

1½ **cups dry red wine**

1½ **cups low-sodium beef broth**

One 14.5-ounce can no-salt-added diced tomatoes with their juices

One 8-ounce can no-salt-added tomato sauce

2 **tablespoons chopped fresh rosemary leaves**

FOR THE POLENTA:

3 **cups water or low-sodium chicken broth**

¼ **teaspoon salt**

¾ **cup polenta**

Here, succulent lamb is simmered with garlic, rosemary, wine, and tomatoes until the garlic softens, all the flavors meld completely into a rich, deeply flavorful sauce, and the meat falls off the bone with the slightest touch. It's all served atop creamy corn polenta making it a meal that is sure to warm you through and through.

Preheat the broiler. Season the lamb shanks with salt and black pepper. Place the lamb shanks on a broiling rack positioned about 6 inches from the flame, and broil until browned, 4 to 5 minutes per side.

Heat the oil in a large Dutch oven or pot over medium-high heat. Add the onion and cook, stirring, until softened, 5 minutes. Add the garlic and cook for 30 seconds. Add the carrots and celery and cook, stirring, until they begin to soften, about 4 minutes. Add the wine, broth, tomatoes, tomato sauce, and rosemary and bring to a boil. Reduce the heat to medium and boil until the liquid reduces by about ½ inch, about 5 minutes. Place the lamb shanks in the pot and press down so they are almost entirely covered in liquid. Reduce the heat to low, cover, and simmer until the lamb is fork-tender, about 2 hours.

continued on page 156

BEFORE	AFTER
560 cal. Sat. Fat 8g, Chol. 110mg Fiber 6g, Sodium 1760mg	Sat. Fat 1.5g, Chol. 95mg Fiber 6g, Sodium 920mg **460 cal.**

continued from page 155

Transfer the lamb shanks to a platter and tent with foil to keep warm. Increase the heat to medium and cook the liquid until it reduces and thickens slightly, about 10 minutes. Return the lamb to the pot and cover until ready to serve. The braised lamb may be made up to 2 days ahead and kept in the refrigerator.

Right before serving, make the polenta. Place the water and salt in a medium saucepan and bring to a boil. Whisking constantly, slowly add the polenta in an even stream. Continue to whisk until the mixture comes to a boil. Reduce the heat to medium low and cook, stirring constantly, until the polenta thickens and pulls away from the sides of the pan, 8 to 10 minutes.

Divide the polenta among four serving plates and top each with 1 piece of lamb shank and 1 cup of the braising liquid.

Makes 4 servings

SERVING SIZE ¾ cup polenta, 1 piece lamb shank, and 1 cup braising liquid/vegetables
PER SERVING Calories 460; Total Fat 7 g (Sat Fat 1.5 g, Mono Fat 5 g, Poly Fat 0.5 g); Protein 38 g; Carb 44 g; Fiber 6 g; Cholesterol 95 mg; Sodium 920 mg
EXCELLENT SOURCE OF Copper, Fiber, Iron, Manganese, Niacin, Phosphorus, Potassium, Protein, Riboflavin, Thiamin, Vitamin A, Vitamin B6, Vitamin B12, Vitamin C, Zinc
GOOD SOURCE OF Calcium, Magnesium, Selenium, Vitamin K

APPLE AND SPINACH–STUFFED PORK CHOPS WITH MUSTARD WINE SAUCE

2 tablespoons olive oil

1 small red onion, chopped

1 small red apple such as Rome or Empire, unpeeled, cored, and cut into ½-inch pieces

1 large clove garlic, minced

3 cups lightly packed fresh baby spinach leaves (about 3 ounces)

½ cup prepared sauerkraut, drained

Four ¾-inch-thick center-cut, bone-in pork loin chops (about 8 ounces each)

¼ teaspoon salt

½ teaspoon freshly ground black pepper

2 teaspoons all-purpose flour

1½ teaspoons ground turmeric

1 teaspoon caraway seeds

1 tablespoon Dijon mustard

½ cup fruity white wine, such as Riesling

1¼ cups low-sodium chicken broth

Pork and apple are a cozy duo elevated to fabulous by adding fresh spinach and zingy sauerkraut, stuffing it all into the chop, then serving drizzled with a simple yet luxurious pan sauce.

Heat 1 tablespoon of the oil in a large nonstick skillet over medium-high heat. Add the onion and cook, stirring occasionally, until softened, about 3 minutes. Add the apple and cook, stirring, until tender, about 4 minutes. Add the garlic and spinach and continue to cook until the spinach is just wilted, about 2 minutes. Stir in the sauerkraut until well combined. Transfer to a bowl and allow to cool, reserving the skillet.

Meanwhile, slice each pork chop horizontally to the bone, making a pocket for the stuffing. Stuff the spinach-apple mixture into the pockets, skewering to close with toothpicks, if necessary. Season the outside of the chops with salt and black pepper.

Heat the remaining 1 tablespoon oil in the reserved skillet over medium-high heat. Add the pork chops and cook until just cooked through, 3 to 4 minutes per side. Transfer to a plate and tent with foil to keep warm.

Add the flour to the skillet and cook, stirring constantly, until a shade darker, about 1 minute. Add the turmeric and caraway and cook, stirring, 1 minute more. Whisk in the mustard, wine, and broth and simmer, whisking occasionally, until reduced and thickened, about 5 minutes. Pour the mustard sauce over the pork and serve.

Makes 4 servings

SERVING SIZE 1 stuffed chop and ¼ cup sauce
PER SERVING Calories 430; Total Fat 16 g (Sat Fat 3.5 g, Mono Fat 8.3 g, Poly Fat 1.9g); Protein 53 g; Carb 13 g; Fiber 3 g; Cholesterol 155 mg; Sodium 530 mg
EXCELLENT SOURCE OF Magnesium, Niacin, Phosphorus, Potassium, Protein, Riboflavin, Selenium, Thiamin, Vitamin A, Vitamin B6, Vitamin B12, Vitamin C, Vitamin K, Zinc
GOOD SOURCE OF Copper, Fiber, Folate, Iron, Manganese, Molybdenum, Pantothenic Acid

	BEFORE	AFTER	
560 cal.	Sat. Fat 11g, Chol. 170mg Fiber 3g, Sodium 940mg	Sat. Fat 3.5g, Chol. 155mg Fiber 3g, Sodium 530mg	430 cal.

chapter five

POULTRY MAIN DISHES

Whether nestled in a potpie, crispy coated, à la Parmesan, or in a rich and hearty stew, humble chicken and turkey are transformed here into extraordinary, memory-making meals that are just the kind you come home for.

CHICKEN ALFREDO WITH ZUCCHINI RIBBONS

- 2 medium zucchini (about 8 ounces each)
- 3 tablespoons olive oil
- 2 garlic cloves, minced
- 4 pieces thinly sliced skinless boneless chicken breast cutlets (1 pound total)
- ¾ teaspoon salt
- ¼ teaspoon freshly ground black pepper
- 12 ounces fettuccine pasta, preferably whole wheat
- 1 tablespoon all-purpose flour
- 1 cup cold low-fat (1%) milk
- ½ cup evaporated skim milk (not condensed milk)
- ¾ cup freshly grated Parmesan cheese
- ¼ cup finely chopped fresh parsley leaves

Fettuccine Alfredo, with its ribbons of pasta coated in a luxurious cheese sauce, is the very definition of decadent comfort. This recipe is all that—redefined. Zucchini ribbons mingle harmoniously with the noodles, allowing a big serving, healthfully. The sauce is made creamy with thickened milk but kept full flavored with plenty of real, fresh grated cheese.

Slice the ends off the zucchini and discard. Using a mandoline or carefully with a sharp knife, slice the zucchini lengthwise into very thin slices. Stack the slices and cut lengthwise into ¼-inch-wide ribbons.

Heat 1 tablespoon of the oil in large nonstick skillet over medium heat. Add half the garlic and cook for 30 seconds. Add the zucchini ribbons, cover, stirring occasionally, and cook until the zucchini is just tender, about 3 minutes. Transfer to a bowl.

Heat 1 tablespoon of the oil in the skillet over medium-high heat. Season the chicken with ¼ teaspoon salt and the black pepper and cook until cooked through, 2 to 3 minutes per side. Transfer the chicken to a plate and tent with foil to keep warm.

continued on page 162

	BEFORE	AFTER	
1130 cal.	Sat. Fat 42g, Chol. 310mg Fiber 5g, Sodium 950mg	Sat. Fat 5g, Chol. 90mg Fiber 11g, Sodium 880mg	**660 cal.**

continued from page 161

Cook the pasta al dente according to the directions on the package. Reserve ½ cup of the pasta water. Drain the pasta and return it to the pasta pot.

Meanwhile, make the sauce. Combine the flour and low-fat milk, stirring until the flour is dissolved. Heat the remaining 1 tablespoon oil in the skillet over medium-high heat. Add the remaining garlic and cook for 30 seconds. Add the milk-flour mixture and cook, stirring constantly, until the mixture begins to boil. Reduce the heat to low and cook, stirring, for 2 minutes more. Add the evaporated skim milk, the remaining ½ teaspoon salt, and the cheese and cook, stirring, until the cheese is melted, about 1 minute.

Add 1 cup of the sauce, the zucchini, and 3 tablespoons of the parsley to the pasta in the pot and toss to combine. Add a little of the reserved pasta water as necessary to loosen the sauce.

To serve, place 2 cups of the pasta mixture on each plate. Top with a piece of chicken. Drizzle with the remaining sauce and garnish with the remaining parsley.

Makes 4 servings

SERVING SIZE 2 cups of pasta mixture and 1 piece of chicken breast
PER SERVING Calories 660; Total Fat 20 g (Sat Fat 5 g, Mono Fat 9.2 g, Poly Fat 1.7 g); Protein 49 g; Carb 79 g; Fiber 11 g; Cholesterol 90 mg; Sodium 880 mg
EXCELLENT SOURCE OF Calcium, Copper, Fiber, Folate, Iron, Magnesium, Manganese, Molybdenum, Niacin, Pantothenic Acid, Phosphorus, Potassium, Protein, Riboflavin, Selenium, Thiamin, Vitamin B6, Vitamin C, Vitamin K, Zinc
GOOD SOURCE OF Iodine, Vitamin A, Vitamin B12, Vitamin D

CHICKEN PARMESAN

1⅓ cups Light-and-Crisp Whole-Wheat Bread Crumbs (page 73)

1 teaspoon dried oregano

½ teaspoon garlic powder

½ teaspoon paprika

½ teaspoon salt

½ teaspoon freshly ground black pepper

2 large egg whites

½ cup nonfat milk

½ cup all-purpose flour

Four 5-ounce skinless boneless chicken breast halves, pounded to ½-inch thickness

Olive oil cooking spray

3 cups Quick Marinara Sauce (page 63) or store-bought marinara sauce

¾ cup shredded part-skim mozzarella cheese (3 ounces)

2 tablespoons freshly grated Parmesan cheese (½ ounce)

This dish comes out of the oven practically beckoning "you want me" with its bubbling, savory tomato sauce covered in melted mozzarella cheese, all atop a crisp breaded chicken cutlet. Because the chicken is baked, not fried, and the amount of cheese is just right, it's a want you absolutely can have.

Preheat the oven to 400°F.

In a shallow bowl or pie plate, toss the bread crumbs with the oregano, garlic powder, paprika, ¼ teaspoon salt, and ¼ teaspoon black pepper. In another bowl, whisk together the egg whites and milk. In another shallow bowl, stir together the flour and the remaining ¼ teaspoon salt and ¼ teaspoon black pepper. One at a time, dip each chicken breast half in the flour, shaking off the excess, then dip into the egg mixture, then the bread crumbs.

Place the breaded chicken in a 9x13-inch baking dish and spray each side for 5 seconds with cooking spray. Bake until the chicken is cooked through and the coating is crisped and browned, about 15 minutes. Top with the marinara sauce and the cheeses and continue to bake until the cheeses are melted and bubbling, about 10 minutes more.

Makes 4 servings

SERVING SIZE 1 piece of chicken with sauce and cheese
PER SERVING Calories 390; Total Fat 12 g (Sat Fat 4 g, Mono Fat 4.3 g, Poly Fat 1.1 g); Protein 43 g; Carb 25 g; Fiber 3 g; Cholesterol 105 mg; Sodium 940 mg
EXCELLENT SOURCE OF Calcium, Pantothenic Acid, Phosphorus, Potassium, Protein, Niacin, Riboflavin, Selenium, Vitamin A, Vitamin B6, Vitamin C
GOOD SOURCE OF Fiber, Iodine, Iron, Magnesium, Manganese, Thiamin, Vitamin B12, Vitamin K, Zinc

BEFORE		AFTER	
630 cal.	Sat. Fat 13g, Chol. 320mg Fiber 2g, Sodium 1480mg	Sat. Fat 4g, Chol. 105mg Fiber 3g, Sodium 940mg	390 cal.

CHICKEN AND BISCUIT POTPIE

Any dish with the word "pie" in it immediately qualifies as comfort food to me. Pie, of course, means there's a crust—here, a golden-brown, tender drop-biscuit topping—and it means there's a warm filling—in this case an herb-scented cream sauce carrying hearty chunks of chicken and vegetables. Mostly, though, pie means the loving care that goes into making it.

FOR THE FILLING:

Nonstick cooking spray

1½ pounds skinless boneless chicken breasts, cut into ½-inch chunks

¾ teaspoon salt

½ teaspoon freshly ground black pepper

4 teaspoons olive oil

1 medium onion, chopped

2 medium carrots, chopped

2 ribs celery, chopped

½ pound green beans, trimmed and chopped into ½-inch pieces

2 cloves garlic, minced

1½ cups low-fat (1%) milk

¼ cup all-purpose flour

1 cup low-sodium chicken broth

1 cup fresh or frozen (thawed) peas

1½ tablespoons chopped fresh thyme

FOR THE BISCUIT CRUST:

½ cup whole-wheat pastry flour or whole-wheat flour

¼ cup all-purpose flour

¾ teaspoon baking powder

¼ teaspoon baking soda

¼ teaspoon salt

3 tablespoons cold unsalted butter, cut into small pieces

½ cup low-fat buttermilk

2 tablespoons canola oil

Preheat the oven to 375°F. Spray a large shallow casserole dish or six individual casserole dishes with cooking spray.

Season the chicken with ¼ teaspoon salt and ¼ teaspoon black pepper. In a large nonstick skillet, heat 2 teaspoons oil over medium-high heat. Add the chicken and cook, stirring occasionally, for 5 minutes. Transfer the chicken with its juices to a bowl.

Heat the remaining 2 teaspoons oil in the skillet over medium-high heat. Add the onion, carrots, and celery and cook, stirring, until the vegetables begin to soften, about 3 minutes. Add the green beans, garlic, and the remaining ½ teaspoon salt and ¼ teaspoon pepper and cook, stirring, for 2 minutes more. Add the milk. Combine the flour and broth and stir until the flour is dissolved. Add the broth-flour mixture to the

continued on page 166

	BEFORE	AFTER	
640 cal.	Sat. Fat 19g, Chol. 110mg Fiber 4g, Sodium 800mg	Sat. Fat 6g, Chol. 80mg Fiber 5g, Sodium 600mg	**400 cal.**

continued from page 164

skillet and cook, stirring, until the mixture begins to boil. Reduce the heat to medium low and cook for 2 minutes more. Return the chicken with its juices back to the pan. Add the peas and thyme and stir to combine. Spoon the mixture into the baking dish or individual dishes.

To make the crust, place the flours, baking powder, baking soda, and salt into a food processor and pulse a few times to combine. Add the butter and pulse about 12 times, or until pebble-size pieces form.

In a small bowl or pitcher, whisk together the buttermilk and oil. Add the buttermilk-oil mixture to the food processor and pulse until just moistened. Do not overmix. Drop the batter in 6 mounds on top of the chicken mixture (one mound on each individual dish, if using), spreading the batter out slightly. Bake until the filling is bubbling and the biscuit topping is golden brown, about 20 minutes.

Makes 6 servings

SERVING SIZE 1¾ cups or 1 individual potpie
PER SERVING Calories 400; Total Fat 18 g (Sat Fat 6 g, Mono Fat 8 g, Poly Fat 2.7 g); Protein 31 g; Carb 30 g; Fiber 5 g; Cholesterol 80 mg; Sodium 600 mg
EXCELLENT SOURCE OF Fiber, Manganese, Niacin, Phosphorus, Potassium, Protein, Riboflavin, Selenium, Vitamin A, Vitamin B6, Vitamin K
GOOD SOURCE OF Calcium, Folate, Iodine, Iron, Magnesium, Pantothenic Acid, Thiamin, Vitamin B12, Vitamin C, Zinc

CHICKEN MARSALA

¼ cup all-purpose flour

¼ teaspoon paprika

½ teaspoon salt

½ teaspoon freshly ground black pepper

Four 5-ounce skinless boneless chicken breast halves, pounded to ½-inch thickness

2 tablespoons olive oil

1 large shallot, finely minced (about ¼ cup)

1½ pounds white button mushrooms, thinly sliced

½ cup Marsala wine

1 cup low-sodium chicken broth

1 tablespoon unsalted butter, optional

4 teaspoons finely chopped fresh parsley leaves

Since childhood I have celebrated many happy occasions at small family-owned Italian restaurants in Queens, where I grew up. This recipe is inspired by one of my regular orders. It is probably not a coincidence that it's also one of the first dishes I learned to cook when I began living on my own at college. It's a simple but luxurious meal of tender sautéed chicken in a full-bodied mushroom-wine sauce. Typically made with loads of butter, just a dab at the finish does the trick just fine. It is both a comfort and a celebration—all made in one pan.

Combine the flour, paprika, ¼ teaspoon salt, and ¼ teaspoon black pepper in a large sealable plastic bag. Add 2 pieces of chicken and toss in the flour mixture until well coated. Remove the chicken from the bag, shaking off any excess, and repeat with the remaining 2 chicken pieces. Reserve 1 tablespoon of the remaining flour mixture.

Heat 1 tablespoon of oil in a very large nonstick skillet over medium-high heat. Add the chicken and cook until browned, about 2 minutes per side. Transfer the chicken to a plate.

Add the remaining 1 tablespoon oil to the pan and heat over medium-high heat. Add the shallot and cook until softened but not browned,

continued on page 168

	BEFORE	AFTER	
510 cal.	Sat. Fat 12g, Chol. 130mg Fiber 1g, Sodium 1030mg	Sat. Fat 4g, Chol. 100mg Fiber 2g, Sodium 490mg	**380 cal.**

continued from page 167

about 2 minutes. Add half the mushrooms and cook until they begin to soften, about 2 minutes. Then add the remaining mushrooms and cook until they release their water, about 5 minutes. Add the reserved 1 tablespoon dredging flour and stir until the flour is dissolved into the mushroom-shallot mixture, about 1 minute.

Add the Marsala wine to the pan and bring to a boil. Cook until about half the wine is evaporated, about 30 seconds. Add the chicken broth and the remaining ¼ teaspoon salt and ¼ teaspoon pepper and bring to a boil. Continue cooking until the sauce is reduced slightly, about 2 minutes. Add the chicken, spooning the sauce over to cover, and cook until the mixture thickens slightly, about 10 minutes. Transfer the chicken to a serving plate. Cook the sauce to the desired thickness, 2 to 3 minutes more. Add the butter, if using, and stir until melted. Drizzle the sauce over the chicken and garnish with the parsley.

Makes 4 servings

SERVING SIZE 1 piece of chicken and ¼ cup sauce
PER SERVING Calories 380; Total Fat 14 g (Sat Fat 4 g, Mono Fat 7 g, Poly Fat 1.8 g); Protein 38 g; Carb 18 g; Fiber 2 g; Cholesterol 100 mg; Sodium 490 mg
EXCELLENT SOURCE OF Copper, Pantothenic Acid, Phosphorus, Potassium, Protein, Selenium, Thiamin, Riboflavin, Niacin, Vitamin B6, Vitamin K
GOOD SOURCE OF Folate, Iron, Magnesium, Manganese, Molybdenum, Vitamin C, Zinc

HERBED CHICKEN SALAD

1 lemon, halved

1 pound skinless boneless chicken breast, pounded to ½-inch thickness

2 sprigs fresh tarragon, plus 2 tablespoons chopped

3 tablespoons plain Greek-style nonfat yogurt

3 tablespoons mayonnaise

¼ teaspoon salt, plus more to taste

¼ teaspoon freshly ground black pepper

2 ribs celery, chopped

3 tablespoons chopped fresh chives

Whether it's for a summer picnic, a home-packed sandwich, or a ladies' lunch, there is something so basic and feel-good about chicken salad. This one takes it to another level with the easy addition of fresh tarragon and chives.

Juice half the lemon (about 1½ tablespoons) and reserve; thinly slice the other half. Place the chicken, lemon slices, and tarragon sprigs in a saucepan, cover with water by 2 inches, and bring to a boil over medium heat. Reduce the heat to low, cover, and cook until the chicken is cooked through, about 15 minutes. Transfer the chicken to a plate and place in the refrigerator to cool. Cut the chicken into small cubes.

In a large bowl, combine the lemon juice, yogurt, mayonnaise, ¼ teaspoon salt, and the black pepper. Add the chicken cubes, celery, chopped tarragon, and chives and toss to combine. Place in the refrigerator and chill for 1 hour to allow the flavors to meld. Season with salt and serve.

Makes 4 servings

SERVING SIZE ½ cup
PER SERVING Calories 190; Total Fat 7 g (Sat Fat 1 g, Mono Fat 1.9 g, Poly Fat 2.3 g); Protein 26 g; Carb 5 g; Fiber 1 g; Cholesterol 75 mg; Sodium 380 mg
EXCELLENT SOURCE OF Niacin, Phosphorus, Protein, Selenium, Vitamin B6
GOOD SOURCE OF Pantothenic Acid, Vitamin C, Vitamin K

	BEFORE	AFTER	
220 cal.	Sat. Fat 1.5g, Chol. 80mg Fiber 1g, Sodium 600mg	Sat. Fat 1g, Chol. 75mg Fiber 1g, Sodium 380mg	**190 cal.**

HONEY-CRISP OVEN-FRIED CHICKEN

4 skinless bone-in chicken thighs (about 1½ pounds)

⅔ cup low-fat buttermilk

4 cups cornflakes cereal

½ teaspoon paprika

½ teaspoon garlic powder

½ teaspoon salt

¼ teaspoon freshly ground black pepper

¼ teaspoon cayenne pepper

Olive oil cooking spray

2 tablespoons honey

Glazed with honey, coated in crushed cornflakes, then baked to crisp golden perfection—this is your fried chicken craving satisfied.

Place the chicken in a bowl with the buttermilk and toss to coat. Marinate in the refrigerator for at least 1 hour and up to 4 hours.

Place the cornflakes in a food processor and process until crumbs form (you should have about 1 cup of crumbs). Transfer to a shallow dish and mix in the paprika, garlic powder, salt, black pepper, and cayenne pepper.

Preheat the oven to 350°F. Spray a baking sheet with cooking spray.

Remove the chicken from the buttermilk, shaking off excess buttermilk from the chicken. Discard the remaining buttermilk. Brush each piece of chicken with honey, then dip in the cornflake crumbs, pressing hard so the crumbs adhere to the chicken. Place the coated chicken on the prepared baking sheet. Lightly spray the top of each chicken thigh with cooking spray. Bake until the chicken is crisped and cooked through, 45 to 50 minutes.

Makes 4 servings

SERVING SIZE 1 piece
PER SERVING Calories 330; Total Fat 10 g (Sat Fat 3 g, Mono Fat 3.7 g, Poly Fat 2.3 g); Protein 27 g; Carb 35 g; Fiber 1 g; Cholesterol 85 mg; Sodium 600 mg
EXCELLENT SOURCE OF Folate, Iron, Niacin, Protein, Riboflavin, Selenium, Thiamin, Vitamin B6, Vitamin B12
GOOD SOURCE OF Phosphorus, Vitamin A, Vitamin C, Vitamin D, Zinc

BEFORE	AFTER
560 cal. Sat. Fat 8g, Chol. 130mg Fiber 1g, Sodium 730mg	Sat. Fat 3g, Chol. 85mg Fiber 1g, Sodium 600mg 330 cal.

SESAME CHICKEN WITH **BROCCOLI**

5 tablespoons reduced-
  sodium soy sauce

4 teaspoons toasted sesame
  oil

5 teaspoons honey

1¼ pounds skinless boneless
  chicken breast, cut into
  1-inch chunks

2 tablespoons canola oil

2 scallions, thinly sliced,
  2 tablespoons greens
  reserved

1 tablespoon grated fresh
  ginger

3 cloves garlic, minced

1½ cups low-sodium chicken
  broth

4 teaspoons cornstarch

1 tablespoon rice vinegar

1 teaspoon chili paste

1 small head broccoli, cut into
  florets, steamed until crisp-
  tender, 4 to 5 minutes

3 tablespoons toasted
  sesame seeds

  Cooked brown rice, for
  serving, optional

There is mouthwatering magic in the sweet-tart, spicy-salty balance of Chinese sauces like this one. Here it is poured over tender marinated chicken, sprinkled with a generous helping of toasted sesame seeds and served with the crisp clean contrast of steamed broccoli. It's just like the dish you get from the local takeout, only so much more delicious—and better for you.

In a medium bowl, whisk together 3 tablespoons soy sauce, 2 teaspoons sesame oil, and 2 teaspoons honey. Add the chicken, toss to coat, and marinate for 20 minutes. Remove the chicken from the marinade with a slotted spoon and discard the marinade.

    Heat 2 teaspoons canola oil in a large nonstick skillet or wok over medium-high heat. Add half of the chicken pieces to the pan and cook until browned and cooked through, turning once or twice, about 6 minutes. Transfer the cooked chicken to a large serving plate. Repeat with 2 more teaspoons of canola oil and the remaining chicken. Transfer to the serving plate.

    Heat the remaining 2 teaspoons canola oil in the skillet over medium-high heat. Add the scallions, ginger, and garlic and cook, stirring, until

	BEFORE	AFTER	
610 cal.	Sat. Fat 4g, Chol. 105mg Fiber 1g, Sodium 1850mg	Sat. Fat 2.5g, Chol. 90mg Fiber 4g, Sodium 730mg	**410 cal.**

fragrant, 1 to 2 minutes. In a small bowl, whisk together the broth, the remaining 2 tablespoons soy sauce, the remaining 3 teaspoons honey, the cornstarch, vinegar, and chili paste until the cornstarch and honey are dissolved. Add the mixture to the pan and cook, stirring, until the mixture is thickened and darkened in color, 2 to 3 minutes. Stir in the remaining 2 teaspoons sesame oil.

Pour the sauce over the chicken. Surround the chicken with the steamed broccoli. Sprinkle the chicken with the sesame seeds and 2 tablespoons scallion greens. Serve with brown rice, if desired.

Makes 4 servings

SERVING SIZE 1 cup chicken and sauce, and 1 cup broccoli
PER SERVING Calories 410; Total Fat 18 g (Sat Fat 2.5 g, Mono Fat 8.2 g, Poly Fat 5.3 g); Protein 36 g; Carb 29 g; Fiber 4 g; Cholesterol 90 mg; Sodium 730 mg
EXCELLENT SOURCE OF Magnesium, Manganese, Niacin, Pantothenic Acid, Potassium, Phosphorus, Protein, Selenium, Vitamin B6, Vitamin C, Vitamin K
GOOD SOURCE OF Copper, Folate, Fiber, Iron, Riboflavin, Thiamin, Vitamin A, Zinc

SPICY CHICKEN FRIED RICE WITH PEANUTS

3 tablespoons low-sodium soy sauce

1 tablespoon dark brown sugar

2 teaspoons toasted sesame oil

¾ teaspoon red chili flakes

2 tablespoons canola oil

1 small onion, diced

3 scallions, finely sliced

2 medium red bell peppers, diced

3 cloves garlic, minced

1 tablespoon finely grated fresh ginger

One 5-ounce can water chestnuts, diced

2 cups diced cooked chicken

4 cups very cold cooked brown rice

⅓ cup coarsely chopped unsalted peanuts

This aromatic rice dish is a meal-in-a-bowl you can really cozy up with. It is chock-full of tasty treasures—sweet bell peppers, crunchy water chestnuts, peanuts, and chunks of chicken, all stir-fried with just the right spicy kick. Made with a fraction of the oil typically used, you certainly won't miss the grease—or the extra calories.

In a small bowl, whisk together the soy sauce, brown sugar, sesame oil, and chili flakes until the sugar is dissolved.

Heat the canola oil in a very large skillet or wok over high heat. Add the onion, scallions, and bell peppers and cook until they begin to soften, about 2 minutes. Add the garlic and ginger and cook for 1 minute. Add the water chestnuts, chicken, and rice and cook until heated through, about 5 minutes. Stir in the soy sauce mixture and toss to coat evenly. Garnish with the peanuts and serve.

Makes 4 servings

SERVING SIZE 2 cups
PER SERVING Calories 580; Total Fat 20 g (Sat Fat 3 g, Mono Fat 9.81 g, Poly Fat 6.04 g); Protein 32 g; Carb 68 g; Fiber 9 g; Cholesterol 60 mg; Sodium 360 mg
EXCELLENT SOURCE OF Fiber, Magnesium, Manganese, Niacin, Phosphorus, Potassium, Protein, Selenium, Thiamin, Vitamin A, Vitamin B6, Vitamin C, Vitamin K
GOOD SOURCE OF Copper, Folate, Iron, Pantothenic Acid, Riboflavin, Zinc

	BEFORE	AFTER	
820 cal.	Sat. Fat 7g, Chol. 290mg Fiber 3g, Sodium 840mg	Sat. Fat 3g, Chol. 60mg Fiber 9g, Sodium 360mg	580 cal.

CINCINNATI TURKEY CHILI

In Cincinnati they heat things up with heaping bowls of chili cooked until practically melted, with additions such as warm spices like cinnamon, cocoa powder, allspice, and cloves, and a touch of sweet molasses. Served over spaghetti and topped with hearty beans, cheese, and onion, it's like no chili you have had before, but definitely one you'll make over and over again.

1 tablespoon olive oil
1 large onion, chopped
3 cloves garlic, minced
1 pound lean ground turkey
2 green bell peppers, diced
2 tablespoons chili powder
1 tablespoon unsweetened natural cocoa
2 teaspoons paprika
1 teaspoon ground cumin
1 teaspoon dried oregano
1 teaspoon ground cinnamon
½ teaspoon ground allspice
½ teaspoon cayenne pepper
½ teaspoon salt
¼ teaspoon freshly ground black pepper
¼ teaspoon ground cloves
One 15-ounce can no-salt-added tomato sauce
One 14.5-ounce can no-salt-added diced tomatoes with their juices
½ cup water
1 tablespoon unsulfured molasses

1 bay leaf
8 ounces whole-grain spaghetti, cooked according to package directions
1 cup canned kidney beans, preferably low-sodium, drained and rinsed
¼ cup grated, lightly packed extra-sharp cheddar cheese
4 teaspoons finely diced red onion

Heat the oil in a large Dutch oven or soup pot over medium-high heat. Add the chopped onion and cook, stirring, until softened, about 5 minutes. Add the garlic and cook for 30 seconds. Add the turkey and cook, breaking it up with a wooden spoon into small pieces, until just cooked through and no longer pink, about 5 minutes. Add the bell peppers and cook until they begin to soften, about 2 minutes. Add the chili powder, cocoa, paprika, cumin, oregano, cinnamon, allspice, cayenne pepper, salt, black pepper, and cloves and cook, stirring, until fragrant, about 1 minute. Add the tomato sauce, tomatoes with their juice, water, molasses, and bay leaf and bring to a boil. Reduce the heat

continued on page 178

	BEFORE	AFTER	
970 cal.	Sat. Fat 26g, Chol. 190mg Fiber 13g, Sodium 2190mg	Sat. Fat 2.5g, Chol. 50mg Fiber 19g, Sodium 480mg	**570 cal.**

continued from page 177

to low and simmer until the mixture has thickened considerably but is still soupy, about 2 hours. Remove the bay leaf. Serve over the spaghetti, topped with the kidney beans, cheese, and diced red onion.

Makes 4 servings

SERVING SIZE 1 cup spaghetti, 1½ cups chili, ¼ cup kidney beans, 1 tablespoon grated cheddar cheese, and 1 teaspoon diced red onion

PER SERVING Calories 570; Total Fat 10 g (Sat Fat 2.5 g, Mono Fat 3.5 g, Poly Fat 1.3 g); Protein 47 g; Carb 83 g; Fiber 19 g; Cholesterol 50 mg; Sodium 480 mg

EXCELLENT SOURCE OF Copper, Fiber, Iron, Magnesium, Manganese, Niacin, Phosphorus, Potassium, Protein, Selenium, Thiamin, Vitamin A, Vitamin B6, Vitamin C, Vitamin K

GOOD SOURCE OF Calcium, Folate, Riboflavin, Zinc

EASY CASSOULET

This savory herbed bean casserole, baked with rustic pieces of sausage and poultry, and topped with garlicky bread crumbs, is comfort French-country-style. Classically a complicated, long cooking dish made with duck, I have imported it here, keeping its deep flavor and homey spirit but making it simple and healthy enough for the everyday American table.

¾ cup Light-and-Crisp Whole-Wheat Bread Crumbs (page 73)

3 cloves garlic, minced

1 tablespoon plus 1 teaspoon olive oil

6 skinless bone-in chicken thighs (about 1¾ pounds)

½ teaspoon salt, plus more to taste

¼ teaspoon freshly ground black pepper

4 ounces low-fat or turkey kielbasa, sliced into ¼-inch-thick rounds

2 ribs celery, chopped

1 large onion, chopped

3 medium parsnips, peeled and chopped

1 tablespoon finely chopped fresh rosemary

1 tablespoon chopped fresh thyme

1 bay leaf

½ teaspoon ground allspice

1 tablespoon all-purpose flour

1 cup dry white wine

One 14.5-ounce can no-salt-added diced tomatoes, drained

2 cups low-sodium chicken broth

Three 15-ounce cans cannellini beans, preferably low-sodium, drained and rinsed

Preheat the oven to 375°F.

In a small bowl, toss the bread crumbs with the garlic and 1 teaspoon olive oil.

Heat the oil in a large Dutch oven or ovenproof pot over medium-high heat. Season the chicken with ¼ teaspoon salt and ⅛ teaspoon black pepper. Brown the chicken on both sides until golden brown, about 3 minutes per side. Transfer to a plate. Add the sausage and cook, stirring occasionally, until browned, about 3 minutes. Transfer to the plate with the chicken.

Reduce the heat to medium, add the celery, onion, parsnips, rosemary, thyme, bay leaf, and the remaining ¼ teaspoon salt and ⅛ teaspoon pepper, and cook, stirring, until the vegetables are softened, about 3 minutes. Stir in the allspice, then sprinkle with the flour and stir until

continued on page 180

	BEFORE	AFTER	
860 cal.	Sat. Fat 15 g, Chol. 195 mg Fiber 13 g, Sodium 1290 mg	Sat. Fat 2g, Chol. 75 mg Fiber 13 g, Sodium 610 mg	**540 cal.**

continued from page 179

well incorporated, about 1 minute. Add the wine and simmer until the liquid is thickened and reduced by half, about 5 minutes. Stir in the tomatoes, broth, and beans and return the chicken and sausage to the pot, tucking them into the bean mixture. Sprinkle the top with the garlic bread crumbs and bake in the middle of the oven until the chicken is cooked through, about 40 minutes. Allow to stand 10 minutes before serving.

Makes 6 servings

SERVING SIZE 2 cups
PER SERVING Calories 540; Total Fat 11 g (Sat Fat 2 g, Mono Fat 4.1g, Poly Fat 1.9 g); Protein 36 g; Carb 70 g; Fiber 13 g; Cholesterol 75 mg; Sodium 610 mg
EXCELLENT SOURCE OF Calcium, Copper, Fiber, Iron, Magnesium, Manganese, Niacin, Phosphorus, Potassium, Protein, Riboflavin, Selenium, Thiamin, Vitamin B6, Vitamin C, Vitamin K, Zinc
GOOD SOURCE OF Pantothenic Acid, Vitamin A

chapter six

SEAFOOD MAIN DISHES

Inspired by classic seaside favorites like rich gumbo, crispy crab cakes, succulent shrimp and grits, and satisfying fisherman's stew, the dishes here make the most of the water's bounty and bring to mind relaxed days of sun-soaked sand and briny breezes.

OVEN-FRIED SHRIMP

Olive oil cooking spray

¼ cup whole-wheat pastry flour or all-purpose flour

2 large egg whites

1⅓ cup Light-and-Crisp Whole-Wheat Bread Crumbs (page 73)

1 tablespoon chopped fresh thyme

2 teaspoons finely grated lemon zest

¼ teaspoon salt

Pinch cayenne pepper

1 pound large shrimp (20-25 per pound) peeled and deveined, tails on

Lemon wedges, for serving

Every bite of this dish is pure enjoyment, from the initial herb-and-lemon–laced crunch to the succulent shrimp center. Whether served simply with citrus or dunked in decadent Avocado Green Goddess Dipping Sauce (recipe follows), it hits that fried shrimp craving square on the head.

Preheat the oven to 425°F. Spray a baking sheet with cooking spray.

Place the flour on a plate. Beat the egg whites in a shallow bowl.

On another plate, combine the bread crumbs, thyme, lemon zest, salt, and cayenne.

Rinse the shrimp and pat dry with paper towels. A few pieces at a time, dip the shrimp into the flour, dusting off the excess. Then dip the shrimp into the egg whites, and coat with the bread crumbs. Set the breaded shrimp onto a large plate.

When all the shrimp are breaded, place the prepared baking tray into the oven to preheat for 3 minutes. Remove the tray from the oven and place the breaded shrimp on it. Spray the tops of the shrimp with cooking spray. Bake until crispy outside and cooked through, 12 to 15 minutes. Serve with Avocado Green Goddess Dipping Sauce (recipe follows) or lemon wedges.

Makes 4 servings

SERVING SIZE 5 to 6 shrimp
PER SERVING Calories 220; Total Fat 3 g (Sat Fat 0.5 g, Mono Fat 0.8 g, Poly Fat 1 g); Protein 30 g; Carb 18 g; Fiber 3 g; Cholesterol 170 mg; Sodium 470 mg
EXCELLENT SOURCE OF Copper, Iron, Protein, Manganese, Niacin, Phosphorus, Selenium, Vitamin B12
GOOD SOURCE OF Fiber, Magnesium, Vitamin B6, Zinc

	BEFORE	AFTER	
410 cal.	Sat. Fat 5g, Chol. 180mg Fiber 1g, Sodium 1170mg	Sat. Fat 0.5g, Chol. 170mg Fiber 3g, Sodium 470mg	220 cal.

AVOCADO GREEN GODDESS DIPPING SAUCE

½ ripe medium avocado
1 scallion, coarsely chopped
1 tablespoon fresh lemon juice
⅓ cup low-fat buttermilk
¼ cup fresh parsley leaves
1 teaspoon anchovy paste

Avocado makes a decadent, creamy, nutrient-rich base for fresh herbs and citrus in this stunning dip. The touch of anchovy paste ties it tastily to seafood dishes like the Oven-Fried Shrimp (page 185). It also pairs perfectly with the Herbed Salmon Croquettes (page 193), and it is an outstanding substitute for mayo in a tuna sandwich.

Place all the ingredients in the small bowl of a food processor and process until smooth.

Makes 4 servings

SERVING SIZE 2 tablespoons
PER SERVING Calories 50; Total Fat 4 g (Sat Fat 0.5 g, Mono Fat 2.5 g, Poly Fat 0.5 g); Protein 2 g; Carb 4 g; Fiber 2 g; Cholesterol 0 mg; Sodium 25 mg
EXCELLENT SOURCE OF Vitamin K
GOOD SOURCE OF Vitamin C

BEFORE*	AFTER
90 cal. Sat. Fat 1g, Chol. 5mg Fiber 1g, Sodium 240mg	Sat. Fat 0.5g, Chol. 0mg Fiber 2g, Sodium 25mg **50 cal.**

* compared to tartar sauce

CREAMY SHRIMP AND GRITS

FOR THE GRITS:

2 cups water

1 cup grits (not quick-cooking)

3 cups low-fat (1%) milk

1 tablespoon unsalted butter

¼ teaspoon salt

FOR THE SHRIMP:

2 tablespoons olive oil

6 slices Canadian bacon, sliced into 1½-inch strips (3 ounces)

1 pound large shrimp, peeled and deveined

1 medium onion, diced

1 red bell pepper, diced

1 clove garlic, minced

1½ teaspoons chopped fresh thyme or ¼ teaspoon dried

¾ teaspoon paprika

¼ teaspoon salt, plus more to taste

2 teaspoons all-purpose flour

1 cup low-sodium chicken broth

½ cup low-fat (1%) milk

Freshly ground black pepper to taste

When I was researching traditional shrimp and grits recipes I learned that the only ingredients they all have in common are shrimp and grits. After that, the variations are endless. All the better to make my own shrimp and grits dreams come true, and they certainly do here, with smoky bacon-laced shrimp in a fragrant herb and paprika–infused sauce poured over slow-cooked, ultra creamy grits. I hate to play favorites with my recipes but this one is so outstanding I have to make an exception.

To make the grits, bring the water to a boil in a medium saucepan. Gradually add the grits, whisking constantly. Add the milk, butter, and salt and simmer, whisking constantly. Reduce the heat to low, cover, and simmer, stirring occasionally, until smooth and creamy, about 40 minutes.

To make the shrimp and sauce, heat 1 tablespoon oil in a large nonstick skillet over medium-high heat. Add the Canadian bacon and cook until the bacon is browned and crisped, about 4 minutes. Add the shrimp and cook until pink on the outside but not quite cooked through, about 3 minutes. Transfer the shrimp and bacon to a plate.

continued on page 188

	BEFORE	AFTER	
660 cal.	Sat. Fat 21g, Chol. 275mg Fiber 2g, Sodium 1260mg	Sat. Fat 5g, Chol. 200mg Fiber 3g, Sodium 880mg	**510 cal.**

continued from page 187

Heat the remaining 1 tablespoon oil in the same pan over medium heat. Add the onion and bell pepper and cook, stirring, until the vegetables soften, about 6 minutes. Add the garlic, thyme, paprika, and ¼ teaspoon salt and cook for 1 minute. Sprinkle the flour over the vegetable mixture and stir until incorporated, about 1 minute. Add the chicken broth and milk and bring to a boil, stirring constantly. Cook over medium-high heat, stirring occasionally, until the sauce thickens, about 3 minutes. Return the shrimp and Canadian bacon to the pan and simmer until the shrimp is cooked through, about 1 minute. Season with salt and black pepper.

Spoon the grits onto plates and serve topped with the shrimp mixture.

Makes 4 servings

SERVING SIZE 1 cup grits and 1 cup shrimp mixture
PER SERVING Calories 510; Total Fat 16 g (Sat Fat 5 g, Mono Fat 7.5 g, Poly Fat 2.3 g); Protein 40 g; Carb 50 g; Fiber 3 g; Cholesterol 200 mg; Sodium 880 mg
EXCELLENT SOURCE OF Calcium, Copper, Folate, Iodine, Iron, Magnesium, Niacin, Phosphorus, Potassium, Protein, Riboflavin, Selenium, Thiamin, Vitamin A, Vitamin B6, Vitamin B12, Vitamin C, Vitamin D
GOOD SOURCE OF Manganese, Molybdenum, Pantothenic Acid, Zinc

SHELLFISH AND OKRA GUMBO

3 tablespoons olive oil

1 link (4 ounces) andouille sausage, finely diced (about 1 cup)

⅓ cup all-purpose flour

2 ribs celery, diced

1 medium green bell pepper, diced

1 medium onion, diced

4 cloves garlic, minced

1 bay leaf

2 large sprigs fresh thyme

½ teaspoon cayenne pepper

One 8-ounce bottle clam juice

6 cups water

½ pound fresh okra, sliced (about 1½ cups)

1½ pounds large shrimp (20 to 25 per pound), peeled and deveined

8 ounces lump crabmeat, drained and picked over for cartilage

½ cup chopped fresh parsley leaves

½ cup chopped scallion greens

1 teaspoon salt

8 cups cooked long-grain white rice

Hot pepper sauce, such as Tabasco, for serving

This is comfort Louisiana style—an okra-thickened stew loaded with crabmeat and shrimp, accented with spicy sausage and fresh herbs. It's one case where I veer from my usual whole grain and serve it with long-grain white rice in keeping with the traditional taste.

Heat the oil in a large nonstick skillet over medium-high heat. Add the sausage and cook, stirring, until browned, about 3 minutes. Transfer to a bowl with a slotted spoon. Remove the skillet from the heat and allow the remaining oil to cool slightly, about 5 minutes. Sprinkle the flour over the oil and stir. Cook over medium-low heat, stirring constantly, until the mixture (now a roux) is deep brown (a shade darker than peanut butter), about 20 minutes. If the mixture begins to stick while cooking, lower the heat.

Add the celery, bell pepper, and onion, and cook over medium heat, stirring occasionally, until the vegetables are tender, about 7 minutes. Add the garlic, bay leaf, thyme, and cayenne pepper and cook 1 minute more. Transfer the mixture to a large 6-quart pot. Slowly add the clam juice, then the water in a stream, whisking well to combine, and bring

	BEFORE	AFTER	
640 cal.	Sat. Fat 4.5g, Chol. 195mg Fiber 3g, Sodium 2140mg	Sat. Fat 2.5g, Chol. 165mg Fiber 3g, Sodium 780mg	450 cal.

the mixture to a boil. Add the okra and simmer over medium-low heat until the okra is just tender, about 20 minutes. Add the shrimp and cook, stirring occasionally, for 1 minute. Stir in the crabmeat, parsley, scallion greens, and andouille and simmer until the shrimp are just cooked through, about 2 minutes more. Remove the thyme sprigs and bay leaf, and season with the salt. Serve over the rice with the hot sauce as an accompaniment.

Makes 8 servings

SERVING SIZE 1½ cups gumbo and 1 cup rice
PER SERVING Calories 450; Total Fat 10 g (Sat Fat 2.5 g, Mono Fat 4.1 g, Poly Fat 1.4 g); Protein 32 g; Carb 57 g; Fiber 3 g; Cholesterol 165 mg; Sodium 780 mg
EXCELLENT SOURCE OF Copper, Folate, Iron, Magnesium, Manganese, Niacin, Phosphorus, Protein, Selenium, Thiamin, Vitamin B6, Vitamin B12, Vitamin C, Vitamin K, Zinc
GOOD SOURCE OF Calcium, Fiber, Pantothenic Acid, Potassium, Vitamin A

HERBED SALMON CROQUETTES

2 slices whole-wheat bread

2 tablespoons olive oil

1 small onion, minced

2 cloves garlic, minced

　Two 5-ounce pouches skinless, boneless salmon, drained of any excess water

1 tablespoon Dijon mustard

1 rib celery, very finely diced

2 large egg whites

3 tablespoons chopped fresh parsley leaves

2 tablespoons chopped fresh dill

⅛ teaspoon salt

¼ teaspoon freshly ground black pepper

　Olive oil cooking spray

1 recipe Creamy Mustard Dip with Chives (page 197) or Avocado Green Goddess Dipping Sauce (page 186), optional

It's no surprise that the salmon patty has been a constant at the family table for generations. It's a simple and affordable crowd-pleaser made with healthful canned salmon, enhanced with accessible seasonings like garlic and onion, and cooked up tender inside and crisp outside. Here, the addition of aromatic herbs is like hitting the refresh button on Grandma's recipe.

Place the bread in a food processor and process until fine crumbs are formed. You should wind up with about 1¾ cups of crumbs.

Heat 2 teaspoons oil in a small nonstick skillet over medium heat. Add the onion and cook, stirring, until softened and translucent, about 5 minutes. Add the garlic and cook for 30 seconds. Remove from the heat and allow to cool slightly, about 5 minutes.

In a large bowl, combine 1 cup of the bread crumbs, the onion mixture, the salmon, mustard, celery, egg whites, parsley, dill, salt, and black pepper, mixing well to combine. Form into eight 2½-inch patties and gently press each patty in the remaining ¾ cup bread crumbs. Heat the remaining 4 teaspoons oil in a large nonstick skillet over medium heat. Cook the croquettes until browned on one side, about 3 minutes. Spray the tops with oil spray, flip, and cook 3 minutes more, until browned and warmed through. Serve with Creamy Mustard Dip with Chives or Avocado Green Goddess Dipping Sauce, if desired.

Makes 4 servings

SERVING SIZE 2 croquettes
PER SERVING Calories 230; Total Fat 10 g (Sat Fat 1.5 g, Mono Fat 5.9 g, Poly Fat 1.9 g); Protein 20 g; Carb 13 g; Fiber 2 g; Cholesterol 40 mg; Sodium 320 mg
EXCELLENT SOURCE OF Manganese, Niacin, Phosphorus, Protein, Selenium, Vitamin B12, Vitamin K
GOOD SOURCE OF Magnesium, Potassium, Riboflavin, Thiamin, Vitamin B6, Vitamin C

	BEFORE	AFTER	
370 cal.	Sat. Fat 4g, Chol. 145mg Fiber 2g, Sodium 700mg	Sat. Fat 1.5g, Chol. 40mg Fiber 2g, Sodium 320mg	**230 cal.**

CRISPY CRAB CAKES

1 tablespoon plus 2 teaspoons olive oil

2 scallions, thinly sliced

1 medium green bell pepper, finely diced

1 jalapeño pepper, finely diced

1 tablespoon finely grated fresh ginger

2 cloves garlic

1 cup panko (Japanese bread crumbs)

1 large egg, beaten

2 tablespoons nonfat milk

1 pound lump crab or crab claw meat, drained and picked over for cartilage

1 teaspoon finely grated lime zest

2 tablespoons fresh lime juice

¼ cup finely chopped fresh cilantro leaves

½ teaspoon salt

Olive oil cooking spray

1 recipe Creamy Chili-Garlic Dipping Sauce (recipe follows), optional

The secret to getting these crab cakes super-crisp without the grease is a good nonstick skillet and panko, Japanese bread crumbs, which you can now find in most supermarkets. Running with the Asian theme, I seasoned these with aromatic ginger, garlic, lime, and cilantro. They all come together—so the cakes are moist and tender on the inside without a drop of mayo—to enhance the real star: the sweet, succulent crab.

Heat 2 teaspoons oil in a large nonstick skillet over medium-high heat. Add the scallions and pepper and cook, stirring, until the pepper softens slightly, about 3 minutes. Add the ginger and garlic and cook for 30 seconds. Set aside to cool slightly.

In a large bowl, stir together ½ cup panko, the egg, and milk until well combined. Fold in the pepper-scallion mixture, crab, lime zest, lime juice, cilantro, and salt. Shape into 8 patties and refrigerate for 30 minutes.

Place the remaining ½ cup panko on a plate. Dredge the crab cakes in the panko to coat. Heat the remaining 1 tablespoon oil in the skillet over medium-high heat. Cook the crab cakes until golden brown on the bottom, 3 to 4 minutes. Spray the tops with cooking spray to coat, then flip and cook 3 to 4 minutes more. Serve with Creamy Chili-Garlic Dipping Sauce, if desired.

Makes 4 servings

SERVING SIZE 2 crab cakes
PER SERVING Calories 270; Total Fat 9 g (Sat Fat 1.5 g, Mono Fat 5.6 g, Poly Fat 2.9 g); Protein 27 g; Carb 19 g; Fiber 1 g; Cholesterol 165 mg; Sodium 690 mg
EXCELLENT SOURCE OF Copper, Phosphorus, Protein, Selenium, Vitamin B12, Vitamin C, Vitamin K, Zinc
GOOD SOURCE OF Calcium, Folate, Iron, Magnesium, Manganese, Niacin, Potassium, Thiamin, Vitamin B6

	BEFORE	AFTER	
430 cal.	Sat. Fat 10g, Chol. 175mg Fiber 2g, Sodium 810mg	Sat. Fat 1.5g, Chol. 165mg Fiber 1g, Sodium 690mg	270 cal.

CREAMY CHILI-GARLIC DIPPING SAUCE

2 tablespoons mayonnaise

⅓ cup plain Greek-style nonfat yogurt

1 teaspoon chili-garlic sauce, such as Sriracha, plus more to taste

I use Sriracha chili-garlic sauce to add zing to everything from eggs to roast chicken. Here it turns a yogurt and mayo base into a deliciously spicy dipping sauce that's not only excellent with the Crispy Crab Cakes, it also adds excitement to simply grilled fish.

In a small bowl, stir together the mayonnaise, yogurt, and chili-garlic sauce until well combined.

Makes 4 servings

SERVING SIZE 2 tablespoons
PER SERVING Calories 40; Total Fat 2.5 g (Sat Fat 0 g, Mono Fat 0.7 g, Poly Fat 1.3 g); Protein 2 g; Carb 3 g; Fiber 0 g; Cholesterol 0 mg; Sodium 60 mg
EXCELLENT SOURCE OF N/A
GOOD SOURCE OF N/A

	BEFORE*	AFTER	
90 cal.	Sat. Fat 1g, Chol. 5mg Fiber 1g, Sodium 240mg	Sat. Fat 0g, Chol. 0mg Fiber 0g, Sodium 60mg	**40 cal.**

* compared to tartar sauce

FAVORITE FISH FINGERS

Olive oil cooking spray

1¼ cup Light-and-Crisp Whole-Wheat Bread Crumbs (page 73)

½ teaspoon salt

⅛ teaspoon freshly ground black pepper

½ cup whole-wheat pastry flour or all-purpose flour

1 large egg

1 large egg white

1 pound tilapia fillets or other white fish fillets (such as flounder)

1 recipe Creamy Mustard Dip with Chives (recipe follows), optional

This is what those frozen fish sticks you had as a kid, and perhaps serve your own kids, aspire to be—crunchy outside, with a whole chunk of tender, mild fish fillet inside. It's fun finger food you can feel good about. Feel free to dip in ketchup for old time's sake or upgrade to the Creamy Mustard Dip with Chives.

Preheat the oven to 400°F. Spray a baking sheet with cooking spray.

On a plate, combine the bread crumbs, salt, and pepper. Place the flour on another plate. In a small bowl, beat together the egg and egg white to combine.

Pat the fish dry, then cut it into 4×1-inch strips. A couple of pieces at a time, dip the fish into the flour mixture, dusting off the excess. Dip the fish in the egg and then coat in the bread crumbs. Arrange on the prepared baking sheet. Repeat with the remaining fish strips. Spray the coated fish strips with cooking spray to coat. Bake until golden brown and cooked through,12 to 15 minutes. Serve with Creamy Mustard Dip with Chives, if desired.

Makes 4 servings

SERVING SIZE 5 to 6 pieces
PER SERVING Calories 210; Total Fat 4 g (Sat Fat 1.5 g, Mono Fat 1.5 g, Poly Fat 0.8 g); Protein 29 g; Carb 14 g; Fiber 2 g; Cholesterol 110 mg; Sodium 420 mg
EXCELLENT SOURCE OF Manganese, Niacin, Phosphorus, Protein, Selenium, Vitamin B12, Vitamin D
GOOD SOURCE OF Copper, Folate, Magnesium, Potassium, Riboflavin, Thiamin, Vitamin B6, Vitamin K

BEFORE		AFTER	
390 cal.	Sat. Fat 2.5g, Chol. 195mg Fiber 1g, Sodium 930mg	Sat. Fat 1.5g, Chol. 110mg Fiber 2g, Sodium 420mg	210 cal.

CREAMY MUSTARD DIP WITH CHIVES

⅓ cup plain Greek-style
   nonfat yogurt

2 tablespoons mayonnaise

1 tablespoon Dijon mustard

½ teaspoon Worcestershire
   sauce

1 tablespoon snipped fresh
   chives

   Pinch cayenne pepper,
   optional

Use this tangy, chive-flecked dip anywhere you might use tartar sauce—on fish cakes or croquettes, on a grilled fish-fillet sandwich, or as a shrimp cocktail dip.

In a small bowl, stir together the yogurt, mayonnaise, mustard, Worcestershire sauce, chives, and cayenne pepper, if using.

Makes 4 servings

SERVING SIZE 2 tablespoons
PER SERVING Calories 45; Total Fat 2.5 g (Sat Fat 0 g, Mono Fat 0.7 g, Poly Fat 1.3 g); Protein 2 g; Carb 3 g; Fiber 0 g; Cholesterol 0 mg; Sodium 160 mg
EXCELLENT SOURCE OF N/A
GOOD SOURCE OF N/A

	BEFORE*	AFTER	
90 cal.	Sat. Fat 1g, Chol. 5mg Fiber 1g, Sodium 240mg	Sat. Fat 0g, Chol. 0mg Fiber 0g, Sodium 160mg	45 cal.

* compared to tartar sauce

CODFISH STEW WITH FENNEL AND ORANGE ESSENCE

1 tablespoon olive oil

1 large onion, chopped

3 cloves garlic, minced

2 ribs celery, diced

1 large green bell pepper, chopped

1 fennel bulb, trimmed and chopped, fronds reserved and chopped for garnish

One 28-ounce can no-salt-added diced tomatoes with their juices

3½ cups water or fish stock

1 bay leaf

1 whole dried red chile

Two 1-inch-wide strips orange zest

½ teaspoon salt

¼ teaspoon freshly ground black pepper

1½ pounds skinless cod fillet, cut into 1-inch chunks

1 tablespoon fresh lemon juice

A bowl of this hearty fisherman's stew is perfect for an evening at the shore (or when you want to be transported there) when, even if the day has been warm, the cool breeze after sunset makes you want to cozy up in your hooded sweatshirt. Although the stew is delightfully rustic, its hint of anise from the fennel and the gentle touch of citrus make it special enough for company.

Heat the oil in a large Dutch oven or soup pot over medium-high heat. Add the onion and cook until softened, about 5 minutes. Add the garlic and cook for 30 seconds. Add the celery and cook until tender-firm, about 3 minutes. Add the bell pepper and fennel and cook for 1 minute. Add the tomatoes and their juices, water, bay leaf, chile, orange zest, salt, and black pepper and bring to a boil. Reduce the heat to

BEFORE	AFTER
420 cal. Sat. Fat 2.5g, Chol. 100mg Fiber 5g, Sodium 590mg	Sat. Fat 0.5g, Chol. 75mg Fiber 5g, Sodium 470mg **270 cal.**

medium low and cook until the broth thickens a little and the fennel is tender, 15 to 20 minutes. Add the fish and cook until just done, about 5 minutes. Remove the bay leaf, chile, and orange zest. Stir in the lemon juice. Serve garnished with the chopped fennel fronds.

Makes 4 servings

SERVING SIZE 2½ cups
PER SERVING Calories 270; Total Fat 5 g (Sat Fat 0.5 g, Mono Fat 2.7 g, Poly Fat 0.8 g); Protein 34 g; Carb 22 g; Fiber 5 g; Cholesterol 75 mg; Sodium 470 mg
EXCELLENT SOURCE OF Fiber, Magnesium, Niacin, Phosphorus, Potassium, Protein, Selenium, Vitamin A, Vitamin B6, Vitamin B12, Vitamin C, Vitamin K
GOOD SOURCE OF Folate, Iron, Manganese, Molybdenum, Thiamin, Riboflavin, Vitamin D

SOLE ALMONDINE

½ cup sliced almonds

⅓ cup all-purpose flour

½ teaspoon paprika

¼ teaspoon salt

¼ teaspoon freshly ground black pepper

Four 6-ounce sole or flounder fillets

3 tablespoons plus 1 teaspoon olive oil

2 medium shallots, finely chopped

¾ cup dry white wine

¼ cup fresh lemon juice

1 tablespoon unsalted butter

2 tablespoons chopped fresh parsley leaves

This luxurious dish is the kind of old-world, fancy restaurant entrée you would have had as you gazed over candlelight into the eyes of your adoring date. No wonder it reminds me of being in love. Just a touch of butter, instead of the typical pool of it, enriches the sauce and highlights the buttery crunch of the toasted almonds.

Toast the almonds in a dry skillet over medium-high heat, stirring frequently, until fragrant and golden brown, 2 to 3 minutes.

In a large shallow dish, combine the flour, paprika, salt, and black pepper. Dredge the fish in the flour to coat lightly.

Heat 2 teaspoons oil in a large nonstick skillet over medium-high heat. Add 2 fish fillets and cook until browned, about 2 minutes. Gently flip, add 2 teaspoons oil to the pan, and cook until browned and the fish flakes easily with a fork. Transfer the fish to a plate and tent with foil to keep warm. Repeat with the remaining 2 fish fillets.

Heat the remaining 2 teaspoons oil in the skillet over medium-high heat. Add the shallots and cook until translucent, about 2 minutes. Add

BEFORE	AFTER
980 cal. Sat. Fat 13g, Chol. 315mg Fiber 7g, Sodium 590mg	Sat. Fat 4.5g, Chol. 90mg Fiber 2g, Sodium 290mg **450 cal.**

the wine and lemon juice and bring to a boil. Reduce the heat to medium low and simmer until the sauce thickens slightly, about 3 minutes. Whisk in the butter until melted, then stir in the parsley. To serve, pour the sauce over the fish and sprinkle with the toasted almonds.

Makes 4 servings

SERVING SIZE 1 fillet, 3 tablespoons sauce, and 2 tablespoons almonds
PER SERVING Calories 450; Total Fat 22 g (Sat Fat 4.5 g, Mono Fat 13g, Poly Fat 3.3 g); Protein 37 g; Carb 18 g; Fiber 2 g; Cholesterol 90 mg; Sodium 290 mg
EXCELLENT SOURCE OF Magnesium, Manganese, Niacin, Phosphorus, Potassium, Protein, Selenium, Vitamin B6, Vitamin B12, Vitamin C, Vitamin D, Vitamin K
GOOD SOURCE OF Folate, Iron, Pantothenic Acid, Riboflavin, Thiamin, Vitamin A

chapter seven

VEGETARIAN MAIN DISHES

Here decadent pastas, creamy risotto, deeply flavorful and filling vegetable
stews, and hearty bean chili dishes prove you don't need meat to have a
seriously satisfying comfort food experience.

SMOKY BLACK BEAN CHILI

1 tablespoon olive oil

1 medium onion, diced

2 cloves garlic, minced

Two 15-ounce cans black beans, preferably low-sodium, drained and rinsed

Two 14.5-ounce cans crushed fire-roasted tomatoes with their juices

3 large roasted red peppers, drained and rinsed, if jarred, and chopped

1½ teaspoons ground cumin

1 teaspoon ancho chili powder

½ teaspoon salt

½ teaspoon hot pepper sauce, such as Tabasco

¼ cup reduced-fat sour cream or plain Greek-style nonfat yogurt

2 tablespoons chopped fresh cilantro leaves

4 lime wedges

The trio of fire-roasted tomatoes, roasted red peppers, and ancho pepper gives this satisfying chili an alluring smoky aroma and multilayered taste. It's edible proof that you don't have to lean on lots of salt for fantastic flavor.

Heat the oil in a large saucepan over medium-high heat. Add the onion and cook, stirring occasionally, until softened and translucent, about 3 minutes. Add the garlic and cook for 30 seconds. Add the beans, tomatoes, red peppers, cumin, chili powder, salt, and hot sauce and stir to combine. Increase the heat and bring to a boil. Reduce the heat, cover, and simmer for 15 minutes. Ladle into individual bowls and garnish each with a dollop of sour cream, some cilantro, and 1 lime wedge.

Makes 4 servings

SERVING SIZE 1¼ cups
PER SERVING Calories 320; Total Fat 6 g (Sat Fat 2 g, Mono Fat 3.1 g, Poly Fat 0.6 g); Protein 17 g; Carb 54 g; Fiber 15 g; Cholesterol 5 mg; Sodium 980 mg
EXCELLENT SOURCE OF Fiber, Iron, Magnesium, Phosphorus, Protein, Vitamin A, Vitamin C
GOOD SOURCE OF Calcium, Iodine, Potassium, Riboflavin, Thiamin, Vitamin B6, Zinc

BEFORE	AFTER
370 cal. Sat. Fat 2.5g, Chol. 10mg Fiber 16g, Sodium 1600mg	Sat. Fat 2g, Chol. 5mg Fiber 15g, Sodium 980mg **320 cal.**

CHILI BEAN AND CORN BREAD PIE

Chili and corn bread go so well together, why not combine them into one wonderful pie? The hearty bean-and-tomato filling is mildly spiced with green chiles and aromatic Southwestern spices. The topping is a moist buttermilk corn bread that bakes up beautifully to golden brown. Together they bring out the absolute best in each other.

FOR THE FILLING:

- 1 tablespoon olive oil
- 1 large onion, chopped
- 3 cloves garlic, minced
- 2 tablespoons tomato paste
- 1 teaspoon ground cumin
- 1 teaspoon dried oregano
- 1 teaspoon ancho chili powder
- ½ teaspoon dried coriander
- One 15-ounce can low-sodium kidney beans, drained and rinsed
- One 15-ounce can low-sodium pink or red beans, drained and rinsed
- One 14.5-ounce can no-salt-added diced tomatoes with their juices
- Two 4-ounce cans diced green chiles, drained
- ½ teaspoon salt
- ¼ teaspoon freshly ground black pepper
- 2 tablespoons chopped fresh cilantro leaves

FOR THE TOPPING:

- 1¼ cups yellow cornmeal
- 1 cup whole-wheat pastry flour or whole-wheat flour
- 1 teaspoon baking powder
- ¾ teaspoon baking soda
- ½ teaspoon salt
- 1⅓ cups low-fat buttermilk
- 1 large egg
- 2 tablespoons honey
- 1 tablespoon canola oil

Preheat the oven to 350°F.

To make the filling, heat the oil in a large pot over medium-high heat. Add the onion and cook, stirring, until softened and lightly browned, about 8 minutes. Add the garlic and cook for 30 seconds. Add the tomato paste, cumin, oregano, chili powder, and coriander and cook, stirring, about 1 minute. Add the beans, tomatoes with their liquid, green chiles, salt, and black pepper and bring to a boil. Reduce the heat to medium and simmer until the liquid is reduced by about half, about 10 minutes. Stir in the cilantro, then transfer the filling to an 8-inch square baking dish.

	BEFORE	AFTER	
430 cal.	Sat. Fat 7g, Chol. 50mg Fiber 7g, Sodium 1450mg	Sat. Fat 1.5g, Chol. 35mg Fiber 15g, Sodium 790mg	**410 cal.**

To make the topping, in a medium bowl, whisk together the cornmeal, flour, baking powder, baking soda, and salt. In another medium bowl, whisk together the buttermilk, egg, honey, and oil. Add the wet ingredients to the dry and stir to combine. Pour the cornmeal batter over the bean mixture, then smooth the surface with a spatula. Bake until the top is browned around the edges and a toothpick inserted into the corn bread layer comes out clean, about 30 minutes.

Makes 6 servings

SERVING SIZE about 2 cups
PER SERVING Calories 410; Total Fat 8 g (Sat Fat 1.5 g, Mono Fat 3.9 g, Poly Fat 1.2 g); Protein 17 g; Carb 71 g; Fiber 15 g; Cholesterol 35 mg; Sodium 790 mg
EXCELLENT SOURCE OF Fiber, Iodine, Iron, Magnesium, Manganese, Molybdenum, Phosphorus, Potassium, Protein, Selenium, Thiamin, Vitamin C, Zinc
GOOD SOURCE OF Calcium, Folate, Niacin, Riboflavin, Vitamin A

AUTUMN VEGETABLE CURRY

This golden stew is a vegetable treasure, brimming with carrots, sweet potatoes, cauliflower, tomatoes, spinach, and chickpeas, all simmered with intoxicatingly fragrant curry spices in a coconut milk–enriched broth. Pureeing the onion, garlic, and spices relieves you of a lot of chopping, so you can get right to the heady aroma of them cooking in the pot. It's kept optimally healthy by using light coconut milk and skipping the heavy clarified butter found in many curries.

1 large onion, coarsely chopped

4 cloves garlic, peeled

1 1½-inch length fresh ginger, peeled and cut into chunks

1½ tablespoons yellow curry powder

¼ teaspoon cayenne pepper, plus more to taste

2 tablespoons canola oil

2 tablespoons tomato paste

2 cups low-sodium vegetable broth

1 cup light coconut milk

1 cinnamon stick

¾ teaspoon salt, plus more to taste

¼ teaspoon freshly ground black pepper, plus more to taste

½ head cauliflower, broken into 1½-inch-wide florets (about 3 cups)

1 pound sweet potatoes (garnet yams), peeled and cut into 1-inch cubes

2 large carrots, peeled and cut into 1-inch rounds

2 tomatoes, cored and chopped

Grated zest of 1 lime

2 tablespoons fresh lime juice

One 15-ounce can chickpeas, preferably low-sodium, drained and rinsed

5 cups fresh baby spinach leaves (5 ounces)

¼ cup chopped fresh cilantro leaves

Cooked rice, for serving, optional

Place the onion, garlic, ginger, curry powder, and cayenne pepper in a food processor and process to combine. Add the oil and process until a smooth puree is formed. Transfer the curry puree to a large pot and cook over medium heat, stirring frequently, about 5 minutes. Add the tomato paste and cook, stirring frequently, until the mixture begins to darken, about 5 minutes more.

continued on page 210

BEFORE		AFTER	
750 cal.	Sat. Fat 25g, Chol. 10mg Fiber 13g, Sodium 1060mg	Sat. Fat 3.5g, Chol. 0mg Fiber 16g, Sodium 780mg	**420 cal.**

continued from page 208

Add the vegetable broth, coconut milk, cinnamon stick, ¾ teaspoon salt, and ¼ teaspoon black pepper and bring to a boil. Reduce the heat and simmer for 10 minutes. Add the cauliflower, sweet potatoes, carrots, and tomatoes, season with salt and pepper, and return to a boil. Reduce the heat to medium low, cover, and simmer until the vegetables are tender, about 25 minutes. Remove the cinnamon stick. Stir in the lime zest and juice, chickpeas, and spinach and cook until the spinach is wilted, about 5 minutes. Season with more salt to taste.

Serve garnished with cilantro and over rice, if desired.

Makes 4 servings

SERVING SIZE about 2½ cups curry
PER SERVING Calories 420; Total Fat 12 g (Sat Fat 3.5 g, Mono Fat 4.6 g, Poly Fat 2.3 g); Protein 13 g; Carb 70 g; Fiber 16 g; Cholesterol 0 mg; Sodium 780 mg
EXCELLENT SOURCE OF Copper, Fiber, Folate, Iron, Magnesium, Molybdenum, Manganese, Phosphorus, Potassium, Protein, Vitamin A, Vitamin B6, Vitamin C, Vitamin K
GOOD SOURCE OF Calcium, Niacin, Riboflavin, Pantothenic Acid, Thiamin, Zinc

BROCCOLI AND CHEESE CALZONES

- 2 cups chopped cooked broccoli, thawed if from frozen
- 8 sun-dried tomatoes, thinly sliced (about ½ cup), reconstituted in hot water if very dry
- 1 cup part-skim ricotta cheese
- ½ teaspoon crushed red pepper flakes
- ¼ teaspoon salt
- ¼ teaspoon freshly ground black pepper
- 1 pound store-bought whole-wheat pizza dough, thawed if frozen
- 1 cup shredded part-skim mozzarella cheese
- 1⅓ cups Quick Marinara Sauce (page 63) or good-quality store-bought marinara
- 2 tablespoons chopped fresh basil leaves

These crusty golden pockets stuffed with creamy ricotta, melted mozzarella, and a tasty broccoli and sun-dried tomato mix is contentment you can hold in your hand. The basil-laced marinara sauce for dipping or spooning adds even more enjoyment. Using a satisfying but not heavy amount of cheese means you'll feel good after eating it too.

Preheat the oven to 425°F.

In a medium bowl, combine the broccoli, sun-dried tomatoes, ¼ cup ricotta cheese, the crushed red pepper, salt, and black pepper.

Divide the dough into 4 balls. On a lightly floured surface, roll out one dough ball into an 8-inch round. Sprinkle ¼ cup of the mozzarella cheese onto half of the round, leaving a 1½-inch border at the edge of the dough. Dollop 3 tablespoons of the remaining ricotta cheese on top of the mozzarella. Top with about ¾ cup of the broccoli mixture. Moisten the edges of the dough with water, then fold the unfilled dough over the filling to form a half-moon. Fold the edge of the dough and crimp to seal the calzone. Repeat with the remaining 3 dough balls, cheeses, and broccoli mixture.

Bake on a baking sheet or pizza stone until golden brown and puffed, 20 to 25 minutes.

Meanwhile, heat the marinara sauce in a small saucepan. Stir in the basil and remove from the heat. Serve the calzone with the tomato sauce alongside.

Makes 4 servings

SERVING SIZE 1 calzone and ⅓ cup sauce
PER SERVING Calories 510; Total Fat 17 g (Sat Fat 7 g, Mono Fat 6.6 g, Poly Fat 0.7 g); Protein 27 g; Carb 66 g; Fiber 10 g; Cholesterol 35 mg; Sodium 1250 mg
EXCELLENT SOURCE OF Calcium, Fiber. Folate, Phosphorus, Protein, Selenium, Vitamin A, Vitamin C
GOOD SOURCE OF Iron, Magnesium, Manganese, Potassium, Riboflavin, Vitamin B6, Vitamin B12, Zinc

	BEFORE	AFTER	
770 cal.	Sat. Fat 17g, Chol. 140mg Fiber 8g, Sodium 1950mg	Sat. Fat 7g, Chol. 35mg Fiber 10g, Sodium 1250mg	**510 cal.**

SKILLET MAC AND CHEESE

2 cups 1-inch-wide cauliflower florets

1¼ cups Light-and-Crisp Whole-Wheat Bread Crumbs (page 73)

3 tablespoons freshly grated Parmesan cheese

2 teaspoons olive oil

3 cups cold low-fat (1%) milk

3 tablespoons all-purpose flour

1¼ cups shredded extra-sharp cheddar cheese (5 ounces)

¼ cup shredded Gruyère cheese (1 ounce)

2 teaspoons mustard powder

¾ teaspoon paprika

½ teaspoon salt

½ teaspoon freshly ground black pepper

¼ teaspoon cayenne pepper

6 ounces (1½ cups) whole-grain elbow macaroni, cooked for 3 minutes less than the package directions (about 3 cups cooked)

Nonstick cooking spray

Serving mac and cheese in the skillet it's baked in amps up the homey comfort factor. The secret ingredient in this bread crumb–topped beauty is the finely chopped cauliflower that blends in subtly with the pasta. Using three different cheeses guarantees maximum flavor and meltability.

Preheat the oven to 375°F.

Place the cauliflower into a steamer basket fitted over the pot, cover, and steam until just tender, about 5 minutes. Finely chop the steamed cauliflower.

In a small bowl, combine the bread crumbs, Parmesan, and oil.

In a large saucepan, whisk together the milk and flour until the flour is dissolved. Whisking constantly, bring the mixture to a gentle boil over medium heat. Reduce the heat to medium low and simmer until the mixture thickens slightly, 2 to 3 minutes. Stir in the cheddar, Gruyère, mustard powder, paprika, salt, black pepper, and cayenne pepper. Whisk until the cheeses are melted and the mixture is smooth, 1 to 2 minutes. Add the chopped cauliflower and macaroni and stir until well coated.

Spray an ovenproof 10-inch high-sided skillet with cooking spray. Pour the mixture into the prepared skillet. Sprinkle with the bread crumb mixture, place on a baking sheet, and bake until the top is browned and the cheese is bubbly, 35 to 40 minutes.

Makes 6 servings

SERVING SIZE 1¼ cups
PER SERVING Calories 360; Total Fat 14 g (Sat Fat 8 g, Mono Fat 4.7 g, Poly Fat 0.8 g); Protein 20 g; Carb 40g; Fiber 5 g; Cholesterol 40 mg; Sodium 540 mg
EXCELLENT SOURCE OF Calcium, Iodine, Magnesium, Manganese, Phosphorus, Protein, Riboflavin, Selenium, Vitamin C
GOOD SOURCE OF Copper, Fiber, Folate, Iron, Niacin, Pantothenic Acid, Potassium, Thiamin, Vitamin A, Vitamin B6, Vitamin B12, Vitamin D, Vitamin K, Zinc

	BEFORE	AFTER	
540 cal.	Sat. Fat 20g, Chol. 195mg Fiber 1g, Sodium 940mg	Sat. Fat 8g, Chol. 40mg Fiber 5g, Sodium 540mg	**360 cal.**

EGGPLANT ROLLATINI

Olive oil cooking spray

1½ pounds eggplant, trimmed and cut lengthwise into twelve ¼-inch-thick slices

½ teaspoon salt

½ teaspoon freshly ground black pepper

2 cups Quick Marinara Sauce (page 63) or good-quality store-bought marinara sauce

1 cup part-skim ricotta cheese

1 large egg, lightly beaten

½ cup lightly packed chopped fresh arugula

1 teaspoon freshly grated lemon zest

1 clove garlic, minced

12 large basil leaves

2 tablespoons finely grated Parmesan cheese

I know Nonna would approve of this luscious version of her homey favorite. The eggplant is baked, rather than breaded and fried, until soft and tender, so it's not only better for you, its easier and less messy to make. It's then rolled with smooth ricotta, fresh arugula, and basil leaves before baking—just like Nonna would do it—nestled in a bed of tomato sauce and sprinkled with Parmesan.

Preheat the oven to 375°F.

Line two baking sheets with foil and coat with cooking spray. Arrange the eggplant in one layer and spray with oil. Season with ¼ teaspoon salt and ¼ teaspoon black pepper. Broil one tray at a time on high, about 5 inches from the flame, until golden brown on both sides and tender, about 3 minutes per side. Allow the eggplant to cool.

Spoon 1 cup marinara sauce into the bottom of a 9-inch square glass baking dish.

Whisk together the ricotta, egg, arugula, lemon zest, garlic, and the remaining ¼ teaspoon salt and ¼ teaspoon black pepper. Arrange the

BEFORE	AFTER
340 cal. Sat. Fat 11g, Chol. 145mg Fiber 6g, Sodium 970mg	Sat. Fat 4.5g, Chol. 75mg Fiber 7g, Sodium 630mg 240 cal.

basil leaves on each slice of eggplant and top with about 2 tablespoons ricotta filling, spreading it evenly. Starting at one short end, roll up the eggplant and arrange, seam side down, in the prepared baking dish. Spoon the remaining 1 cup marinara sauce over the eggplant rolls and sprinkle with the Parmesan.

Bake, uncovered, in the middle of the oven, until the sauce is bubbling and heated through, 25 to 30 minutes.

Makes 4 servings

SERVING SIZE 3 eggplant rollatini and ½ cup sauce
PER SERVING Calories 240; Total Fat 12 g (Sat Fat 4.5 g, Mono Fat 5.4 g, Poly Fat 1 g); Protein 13 g; Carb 22 g; Fiber 7 g; Cholesterol 75 mg; Sodium 630 mg
EXCELLENT SOURCE OF Calcium, Fiber, Manganese, Phosphorus, Protein, Selenium, Vitamin A, Vitamin C, Vitamin K
GOOD SOURCE OF Copper, Folate, Iodine, Magnesium, Molybdenum, Potassium, Riboflavin

BUTTERNUT SQUASH **RISOTTO**

- 5 cups low-sodium vegetable or chicken broth
- 1 tablespoon olive oil
- 1 medium onion, finely diced
- 1½ cups Arborio rice
- ½ cup dry white wine
- 1 cup pureed butternut squash (one 10-ounce package frozen butternut squash puree, thawed)
- 2 tablespoons chopped fresh sage
- ½ cup freshly grated Parmesan cheese (1½ ounces)
- ½ teaspoon salt, plus more to taste
- Freshly ground black pepper to taste

This dish is pure luxury made with the simplest ingredients. Its decadent creaminess comes from the natural starch of the Arborio rice and the butternut squash puree. A generous sprinkle of Parmesan and a hint of fresh sage make it unforgettably delicious.

Heat the broth in a pan on the stove until it is hot but not boiling. Reduce the heat to low and cover to keep warm.

Heat the oil in a large saucepan over medium heat. Add the onion and cook, stirring, until softened but not browned, 6 to 8 minutes. Add the rice and cook, stirring, for 1 minute. Add the wine and simmer until it is absorbed, stirring constantly, about 2 minutes.

Add ½ cup of the hot broth and simmer over medium heat, stirring frequently, until it is absorbed. Repeat with the remaining broth, ½ cup at a time, allowing each addition to be absorbed before adding more, about 30 minutes total. When all the broth is incorporated and the rice is tender and creamy, add the squash, sage, all but 2 tablespoons of the cheese, the salt, and pepper. Season with additional salt to taste. Serve immediately, garnished with the reserved cheese.

Makes 4 servings

SERVING SIZE 1½ cups
PER SERVING Calories 440; Total Fat 9 g (Sat Fat 3 g, Mono Fat 4.2 g, Poly Fat 0.9 g); Protein 17 g; Carb 70 g; Fiber 5 g; Cholesterol 10 mg; Sodium 550 mg
EXCELLENT SOURCE OF Fiber, Niacin, Protein, Vitamin A
GOOD SOURCE OF Calcium, Copper, Manganese, Phosphorus, Potassium, Riboflavin

BEFORE	AFTER
480 cal. Sat. Fat 8g, Chol. 35mg Fiber 2g, Sodium 1500mg	Sat. Fat 3g, Chol. 10mg Fiber 5g, Sodium 550mg **440 cal.**

chapter eight

SIDES AND SALADS

From classic slaws and casseroles to creamy mashed potatoes and sweet-savory baked beans, these sides don't just stand on the sidelines—they are stars in their own right, destined to become signature dishes and part of your family tradition.

SCALLOPED POTATOES AU GRATIN

Nonstick cooking spray

3 **pounds yellow potatoes, like Yukon Gold, unpeeled, sliced into ⅛-inch slices**

3 **cups cold low-fat (1%) milk**

¼ **cup all-purpose flour**

2 **cloves garlic, minced**

1 **large or 2 small sprigs thyme**

1¾ **cups grated Gruyère cheese (6 ounces)**

1½ **teaspoons salt**

Nothing says comfort like a bubbling casserole of cheesy potatoes. These will make you swoon with their garlic-and-thyme–scented sauce layered with nutty Swiss Gruyère cheese.

Preheat the oven to 350°F. Spray a 2-quart shallow baking dish with cooking spray.

Place the potatoes in a large pot and cover with water. Bring to a boil, then reduce the heat and simmer until the potatoes are just tender, about 8 minutes. Drain, set aside, and allow to cool slightly.

Place the milk and flour into a large saucepan and whisk until the flour is dissolved. Add the garlic and thyme and heat over medium-high heat, stirring constantly, until the mixture comes to a boil and is thickened, about 8 minutes. Remove from the heat and discard the thyme sprig. Add the salt and 1 cup cheese, stirring until the cheese is melted.

continued on page 222

	BEFORE	AFTER	
380 cal.	Sat. Fat 14g, Chol. 65mg Fiber 2g, Sodium 630mg	Sat. Fat 5g, Chol. 30mg Fiber 4g, Sodium 570mg	**280 cal.**

continued from page 221

Arrange half of the potatoes in the baking dish. Pour over half of the cheese sauce. Add the remaining potatoes and top with the remaining sauce. Sprinkle with the remaining ¾ cup cheese and bake until bubbling, about 25 minutes. Set under the broiler and broil on high until the top is browned, about 2 minutes.

Makes 8 servings

SERVING SIZE about 1 cup
PER SERVING Calories 280; Total Fat 9 g (Sat Fat 5 g, Mono Fat 2.6 g, Poly Fat 0.5 g); Protein 14 g; Carb 38 g; Fiber 4 g; Cholesterol 30 mg; Sodium 570 mg
EXCELLENT SOURCE OF Calcium, Phosphorus, Potassium, Protein, Vitamin B6, Vitamin C
GOOD SOURCE OF Copper, Fiber, Folate, Iodine, Magnesium, Manganese, Niacin, Riboflavin, Selenium, Thiamin, Vitamin B12, Vitamin D, Zinc

CREAMED CORN

1 cup cold low-fat (1%) milk
1 tablespoon cornstarch
2 cups corn kernels (from about 3 fresh cobs or one 10-ounce box frozen)
½ teaspoon salt
¼ teaspoon freshly ground black pepper

A quick whir of corn and milk in the blender creates a luxuriously creamy puree—creamlessly. Sunny yellow and studded with whole sweet corn, it's the ultimate feel-good food.

In a medium saucepan, whisk together the milk and cornstarch until the cornstarch is dissolved. Bring to a simmer over medium-high heat, stirring constantly. Add the corn and return to a simmer. Reduce the heat to medium low and cook, stirring occasionally, for 5 minutes.

Transfer ½ cup of the corn to another medium saucepan. Working in 2 batches and using a blender, puree the remaining liquid and corn until smooth. Add the corn puree to the kernels in the saucepan, stir to combine, and warm through over medium-high heat. Season with the salt and black pepper.

Makes 4 servings

SERVING SIZE ½ cup
PER SERVING Calories 100; Total Fat 1 g (Sat Fat 0 g, Mono Fat 0.3 g, Poly Fat 0.3 g); Protein 4 g; Carb 20 g; Fiber 2 g; Cholesterol 5 mg; Sodium 330 mg
EXCELLENT SOURCE OF N/A
GOOD SOURCE OF N/A

220 cal.

BEFORE
Sat. Fat 11g, Chol. 55mg
Fiber 2g, Sodium 350mg

AFTER
Sat. Fat 0g, Chol. 5mg
Fiber 2g, Sodium 330mg

100 cal.

HERBED SQUASH CASSEROLE

Nonstick cooking spray

2 tablespoons olive oil

2 medium onions, chopped

1 tablespoon minced garlic

5 medium yellow squash, cut into ⅛-inch-thick rounds (2¼ pounds)

1 large zucchini, cut into ⅛-inch-thick rounds (1 pound)

½ teaspoon salt

¼ teaspoon freshly ground black pepper

1½ cups cold low-fat (1%) milk

2 tablespoons all-purpose flour

¾ cup grated extra-sharp cheddar cheese (3 ounces)

½ cup finely grated Parmesan cheese (1½ ounces)

¼ cup plus 1 tablespoon chopped fresh basil

¼ cup plus 1 tablespoon chopped fresh chives

2 cups Light-and-Crisp Whole-Wheat Bread Crumbs (page 73)

Here tender summer squash and golden onions are tossed with toasted bread crumbs, fresh herbs, cheddar, and Parmesan, then baked until melded together into a rich cheesy casserole.

Preheat the oven to 350°F. Spray a 9×13-inch baking dish with cooking spray.

Heat the oil in a large, deep, nonstick skillet over medium heat. Add the onions and cook, stirring, until golden, about 5 minutes. Add the garlic, yellow squash, zucchini, salt, and black pepper and stir. Reduce the heat to medium low, cover, and cook, stirring occasionally, until just tender, about 8 minutes.

With a slotted spoon, transfer the vegetables to a large bowl, leaving any accumulated liquid in the skillet. Whisk together the milk and flour until the flour is dissolved. Slowly add the milk-flour mixture to the skillet. Whisking constantly, bring the mixture to a simmer. Reduce heat to medium-low and continue to cook, whisking occasionally, until thickened, about 8 minutes. Remove the skillet from the heat and stir in ½ cup cheddar and ¼ cup Parmesan. Transfer the cheese mixture to the

	BEFORE	AFTER	
450 cal.	Sat. Fat 17g, Chol. 70mg Fiber 3g, Sodium 790mg	Sat. Fat 4g, Chol. 20mg Fiber 4g, Sodium 420mg	**220 cal.**

bowl with the vegetables. Gently stir in the ¼ cup basil, the ¼ cup chives, and 1 cup bread crumbs until well combined.

Spoon the squash mixture evenly into the prepared baking dish. In a small bowl, stir together the remaining ¼ cup cheddar and Parmesan cheeses, the remaining 1 cup bread crumbs, the remaining 1 tablespoon basil, and the remaining 1 tablespoon chives and sprinkle the mixture evenly over the squash mixture. Bake until bubbling and golden brown on top, about 30 minutes.

Makes 8 servings

SERVING SIZE 1 cup
PER SERVING Calories 220; Total Fat 10 g (Sat Fat 4 g, Mono Fat 4.4 g, Poly Fat 0.9 g); Protein 12 g; Carb 22 g; Fiber 4 g; Cholesterol 20 mg; Sodium 420 mg
EXCELLENT SOURCE OF Calcium, Manganese, Molybdenum, Phosphorus, Protein, Riboflavin, Vitamin B6, Vitamin C, Vitamin K
GOOD SOURCE OF Copper, Fiber, Folate, Iodine, Magnesium, Niacin, Potassium, Selenium, Thiamin, Vitamin A, Zinc

GREEN BEAN CASSEROLE WITH CRISPY SHALLOTS

¼ cup olive oil

6 medium shallots, sliced into rings (about 1 cup)

1½ pounds thin fresh string beans or haricots verts, trimmed

1 pound button mushrooms, sliced

6 large cloves garlic, minced

1 tablespoon chopped fresh thyme

3 cups cold low-fat (1%) milk

3 tablespoons all-purpose flour

⅓ cup plus 2 tablespoons freshly grated Parmesan cheese

½ cup finely chopped fresh parsley leaves

¼ teaspoon ground nutmeg

¾ teaspoon salt

½ teaspoon freshly ground black pepper

Nonstick cooking spray

This dish is the fresh-from-scratch version of the holiday classic that requires lots of can opening but not much actual cooking. This one is not hard to make and the taste payoff is big—the snap of fresh beans, lots of meaty mushrooms, fresh garlic and herbs, and real Parmesan—all topped with crispy shallot rings. Once you try it you'll never go back.

Preheat the oven to 375°F. Heat the oil in a small skillet over medium-high heat until very hot but not smoking. Add ¼ cup shallots and cook, stirring, until golden brown and crisp, about 2 minutes. Transfer with a slotted spoon to paper towels to drain. Repeat with the remaining shallots, cooking ¼ cup at a time. Reserve the oil in the skillet.

Place the green beans in a steamer basket fitted over a pot of boiling water. Cover and steam until bright green and still crisp, about 3 minutes.

Heat 1 tablespoon of the reserved shallot oil in a large, deep nonstick skillet over medium-high heat. Add the mushrooms and cook,

continued on page 228

	BEFORE	AFTER	
290 cal.	Sat. Fat 10g, Chol. 35mg Fiber 2g, Sodium 890mg	Sat. Fat 2g, Chol. 10mg Fiber 3g, Sodium 330mg	**150 cal.**

continued from page 226

stirring occasionally, until the mushroom liquid is evaporated and they begin to brown, about 12 minutes. Add the garlic and thyme and cook, stirring, for 1 minute. Transfer the mushroom mixture to a bowl.

Whisk together the milk and flour until the flour is dissolved. Add the mixture to the skillet and, whisking constantly, bring to a simmer. Reduce the heat to medium low, whisking occasionally, until thickened, about 10 minutes. Remove the pan from the heat and stir in the green beans, mushroom mixture, the ⅓ cup cheese, the parsley, nutmeg, salt, and black pepper.

Coat a 2-quart baking dish with cooking spray. Spoon the green bean mixture into the prepared dish and sprinkle the top with the crispy shallots and remaining 2 tablespoons cheese. Bake until golden on top and bubbling, about 20 minutes.

Makes 8 servings

SERVING SIZE 1 cup
PER SERVING Calories 150; Total Fat 6 g (Sat Fat 2 g, Mono Fat 3.1 g, Poly Fat 0.7 g); Protein 9 g; Carb 18 g; Fiber 3 g; Cholesterol 18 mg; Sodium 330 mg
EXCELLENT SOURCE OF Calcium, Phosphorus, Riboflavin, Vitamin A, Vitamin C, Vitamin K
GOOD SOURCE OF Copper, Folate, Fiber, Iodine, Iron, Magnesium, Manganese, Molybdenum, Niacin, Pantothenic Acid, Potassium, Protein, Selenium, Thiamin, Vitamin B6, Vitamin D

BUCKWHEAT AND BOW TIES (KASHA VARNISHKAS)

1 tablespoon olive oil

1 large onion, diced

1 large egg

¾ cup kasha

2 cups low-sodium chicken broth or water

1 cup whole-grain bow tie pasta, cooked according to package directions and drained

½ teaspoon salt

¼ teaspoon freshly ground black pepper, plus more to taste

Buckwheat, also called kasha, is a hearty whole grain with a nutty taste and aroma that, along with tender pasta and browned onions, make up this satisfying side dish. My Russian great-grandmother often made it with chicken fat and regular noodles. I have brought it to the New World with healthier olive oil and whole-grain pasta.

Heat the oil in a medium saucepan over medium heat. Add the onion and cook until softened and the edges are slightly charred, 10 to 12 minutes. Transfer to a plate and set the pan aside.

In a medium bowl, beat the egg. Add the kasha and stir until the kasha is well coated. Place the kasha mixture in the pan and cook over medium heat, stirring constantly, until the egg is absorbed and the kasha separates into individual grains, 3 to 4 minutes.

Add the chicken broth and bring to a boil. Reduce the heat to low, cover, and cook until all the liquid is absorbed, about 10 minutes. Remove from the heat. Stir in the onion, pasta, salt, and black pepper and allow to sit, covered, for 5 minutes before serving.

Makes 4 servings

SERVING SIZE 1¼ cups
PER SERVING Calories 280; Total Fat 7 g (Sat Fat 1.5 g, Mono Fat 3.6 g, Poly Fat 1.1 g); Protein 12 g; Carb 48 g; Fiber 6 g; Cholesterol 55 mg; Sodium 350 mg
EXCELLENT SOURCE OF Copper, Fiber, Magnesium, Manganese, Niacin, Phosphorus, Protein
GOOD SOURCE OF Folate, Iron, Riboflavin, Thiamin, Vitamin B6, Zinc

BEFORE
420 cal.
Sat. Fat 2.5g, Chol. 80mg
Fiber 8g, Sodium 710mg

AFTER
Sat. Fat 1.5g, Chol. 55mg
Fiber 6g, Sodium 350mg
280 cal.

SWEET POTATO CASSEROLE WITH MERINGUE TOPPING

Nonstick cooking spray

3½ pounds sweet potatoes (5 medium), peeled and cut into 1-inch chunks

⅓ cup honey

1 large egg

½ teaspoon ground cinnamon

¼ teaspoon ground nutmeg

½ teaspoon salt

1 large egg white

¼ teaspoon cream of tartar

¼ cup superfine sugar

This sweet potato bake is creamy and light without a drop of butter because it is whipped up with an egg and just enough honey to bring out the tuber's natural sweetness. Dollops of meringue make a stunning alternative to the typical marshmallow topper. If you don't want to make the meringue, this is also wonderful simply sprinkled with chopped pecans mixed with a touch of brown sugar.

Preheat the oven to 350°F. Spray an 8 x 8-inch casserole dish with cooking spray.

Place the sweet potatoes in a large steamer basket fitted over a pot of boiling water. Cover and steam until tender, 20 to 25 minutes. Transfer the sweet potatoes to a large bowl and allow to cool slightly. Add the honey, egg, cinnamon, nutmeg, and salt and whip using an electric mixer. Spread the sweet potato mixture into the prepared dish.

In a small bowl, using the electric mixer, beat together the egg white and cream of tartar until foamy. Add the sugar, 1 tablespoon at a time,

continued on page 232

BEFORE		AFTER	
420 cal.	Sat. Fat 9g, Chol. 80mg Fiber 2g, Sodium 190mg	Sat. Fat 0g, Chol. 25mg Fiber 3g, Sodium 190mg	**150 cal.**

continued from page 230

beating for about 10 seconds between each addition. Then continue to whip until stiff peaks are formed and the mixture is glossy and smooth, 4 to 5 minutes. Using a pastry bag or a plastic bag with the corner snipped off, pipe 1-inch dollops on top of the casserole. Bake until the meringue is browned on top and the casserole is warmed through, 40 to 45 minutes.

Makes 8 servings

SERVING SIZE ¾ cup
PER SERVING Calories 150; Total Fat 1 g (Sat Fat 0 g, Mono Fat 0.2 g, Poly Fat 0.1 g); Protein 3 g; Carb 36 g; Fiber 3 g; Cholesterol 25 mg; Sodium 190 mg
EXCELLENT SOURCE OF Vitamin A, Vitamin C
GOOD SOURCE OF Fiber, Manganese

SMOOTH AND CREAMY MASHED POTATOES

1½ **pounds russet potatoes (3 medium), peeled and cut into 1-inch pieces**

⅔ **cup low-fat (1%) milk**

1 **tablespoon unsalted butter**

¼ **cup reduced-fat sour cream**

¼ **teaspoon salt, plus more to taste**

These are the classic fluffy, smooth mashed potatoes you dream of, only better because they're so much better for you. Just a touch of butter and a dollop of reduced-fat sour cream is all it takes to make them taste luxuriously creamy.

Place the potatoes in a steamer basket fitted over a large pot of boiling water. Cover and steam until the potatoes are knife-tender, 12 to 15 minutes. Meanwhile, heat the milk and butter in a saucepan over low heat until hot and the butter is melted.

Drain the potato steaming water from the pot. Working in batches, press the potatoes through a food mill or ricer into the still warm pot. Add the milk-butter mixture and stir until well combined. Gently stir in the sour cream and salt. Serve immediately.

Makes 4 servings

SERVING SIZE ¾ cup
PER SERVING Calories 210; Total Fat 6 g (Sat Fat 3.5 g, Mono Fat 1.5 g, Poly Fat 0.3 g); Protein 5 g; Carb 35 g; Fiber 3 g; Cholesterol 15 mg; Sodium 180 mg
EXCELLENT SOURCE OF Vitamin B6
GOOD SOURCE OF Copper, Fiber, Manganese, Niacin, Phosphorus, Potassium, Protein, Thiamin, Vitamin C

BEFORE	AFTER
330 cal. Sat. Fat 13g, Chol. 60mg / Fiber 3g, Sodium 630mg	Sat. Fat 3.5g, Chol. 15mg / Fiber 3g, Sodium 180mg **210 cal.**

GARLIC BREADSTICKS

2 tablespoons olive oil
1 tablespoon unsalted butter
3 cloves garlic, minced
½ teaspoon salt
1 loaf whole-grain Italian bread or baguette (about 12 ounces)
¼ cup finely chopped fresh parsley leaves

One of my first jobs helping Mom in the kitchen was to slather the Italian bread with butter and sprinkle it with garlic powder for the toasted bread with dinner. As a grown-up, I discovered you could make it even better by mixing a touch of butter with olive oil and infusing it all with chopped fresh garlic. Cut into "breadsticks," baked until the aroma calls you and the bread is golden brown, it is one of the simple pleasures that make life so delicious.

Preheat the oven to 350°F. In a small saucepan, combine the oil, butter, garlic, and salt and heat over medium-low heat until the butter is melted. Remove from the heat.

Cut the bread in half lengthwise, then cut each half crosswise into 3 pieces. Then cut each piece into four ½-inch-thick sticks. Brush the breadsticks with the garlic-infused mixture, sprinkle with the parsley, and place on a baking sheet. Bake until the edges are golden brown, about 20 minutes.

Makes 6 servings

SERVING SIZE 3 breadsticks
PER SERVING Calories 170; Total Fat 9 g (Sat Fat 2 g, Mono Fat 4 g, Poly Fat 0.8 g); Protein 9 g; Carb 22 g; Fiber 4 g; Cholesterol 5 mg; Sodium 450 mg
EXCELLENT SOURCE OF Niacin, Vitamin K
GOOD SOURCE OF Protein, Fiber, Thiamin, Riboflavin

BEFORE		AFTER	
240 cal.	Sat. Fat 6g, Chol. 25mg Fiber 2g, Sodium 500mg	Sat. Fat 2g, Chol. 5mg Fiber 4g, Sodium 450mg	**170 cal.**

CRISPY BAKED ZUCCHINI-POTATO PANCAKES

Olive oil cooking spray
2 teaspoons olive oil
1 small onion, thinly sliced
1 medium russet potato (about 8 ounces), unpeeled
1 medium zucchini (about 8 ounces), unpeeled, ends removed
2 large eggs
2 large egg whites
1 teaspoon fresh lemon juice
¼ cup all-purpose flour
½ teaspoon salt
¼ teaspoon freshly ground black pepper

Making fried potato pancakes is practically a competitive sport in my family, with my dad and his brother constantly sparring for the championship. I am more than happy to judge their challenge once or twice a year, but I take comfort knowing I can enjoy my greaseless version anytime the craving hits. Making these two bites–size allows them to crisp beautifully on the baking tray while the zucchini lightens them and adds lovely flavor and color. They are perfect as a side with roasted meat but you can also serve them as an upscale appetizer with a dollop of crème fraîche and some caviar.

Preheat the oven to 400°F. Coat a baking sheet with cooking spray.

Heat the oil in a large skillet over medium heat. Add the onion and cook, stirring, until softened and golden, about 5 minutes. Remove from the heat and allow to cool completely.

Grate the potato and zucchini on the large holes of a box grater. Place the grated potato and zucchini in a kitchen towel or cheesecloth, and twist over the sink to squeeze out as much liquid as possible. Transfer the zucchini and potato to a bowl. In a small bowl, beat together the eggs and egg whites to combine. Add the eggs, lemon juice, flour, salt,

BEFORE		AFTER
260 cal.	Sat. Fat 2.5g, Chol. 105mg Fiber 3g, Sodium 920mg	Sat. Fat 1g, Chol. 105mg Fiber 3g, Sodium 360mg **160 cal.**

and black pepper to the zucchini-potato mixture and stir until well combined.

Heat the prepared baking sheet in the oven for 3 to 5 minutes, until hot but before the oil begins to smoke. Remove the baking sheet from the oven and immediately begin to make the pancakes and place them on the tray. Use about 2 tablespoons of batter for each, forming it into a flat, 2-inch pancake. You should wind up with 16 pancakes.

Bake until the edges begin to crisp, 7 to 8 minutes. Remove from the oven, spray the tops of the pancakes with cooking spray, and flip the pancakes. Bake until browned and crisp, about 5 minutes more.

Makes 4 servings

SERVING SIZE 4 pancakes
PER SERVING Calories 160; Total Fat 5 g (Sat Fat 1 g, Mono Fat 2.6 g, Poly Fat 0.7 g); Protein 8 g; Carb 22 g; Fiber 3 g; Cholesterol 105 mg; Sodium 360 mg
EXCELLENT SOURCE OF Vitamin C
GOOD SOURCE OF Fiber, Folate, Iodine, Manganese, Molybdenum, Phosphorus, Potassium, Protein, Riboflavin, Selenium, Thiamin, Vitamin B6

RUSTIC MASHED POTATOES WITH BLUE CHEESE

1½ pounds Yukon Gold potatoes (4 medium), unpeeled and cut into 1-inch pieces

⅔ cup low-fat (1%) milk

1 tablespoon unsalted butter

1½ ounces blue cheese (3 tablespoons)

⅛ teaspoon salt

Freshly ground black pepper to taste

Yukon Gold potatoes have a natural creaminess and thin skin, making them perfect for this rustic mash. A little real blue cheese goes a long way to make it all the more decadent.

Place the potatoes in a steamer basket fitted over a large pot of boiling water. Cover and steam until the potatoes are knife-tender, 12 to 15 minutes. Meanwhile, heat the milk and butter in a saucepan over low heat until hot and the butter is melted.

Drain the potato steaming water from the still hot pot and transfer the steamed potatoes into the pot. Add the milk-butter mixture and mash with a masher to the desired consistency. Stir in the blue cheese and season with salt and black pepper. Serve immediately.

Makes 4 servings

SERVING SIZE ¾ cup
PER SERVING Calories 210; Total Fat 6 g (Sat Fat 4 g, Mono Fat 1.7 g, Poly Fat 0.3 g); Protein 7 g; Carb 32 g; Fiber 4 g; Cholesterol 20 mg; Sodium 250 mg
EXCELLENT SOURCE OF Potassium, Vitamin B6, Vitamin C
GOOD SOURCE OF Calcium, Fiber, Magnesium, Manganese, Phosphorus, Protein, Riboflavin

BEFORE	AFTER
330 cal. Sat. Fat 13g, Chol. 60mg Fiber 3g, Sodium 630mg	Sat. Fat 4g, Chol. 20mg Fiber 4g, Sodium 250mg **210 cal.**

CORN AND CHEDDAR SPOON BREAD

Nonstick cooking spray

2 cups low-fat (1%) milk

1½ cups fresh or frozen thawed corn kernels

⅔ cup yellow cornmeal

½ teaspoon salt

½ cup grated extra-sharp cheddar cheese (2 ounces)

2 large eggs, yolks and whites separated

¼ teaspoon cream of tartar

This homey dish, spiked with fresh corn and extra-sharp cheddar cooks up soft and golden with the satisfaction of corn bread and the lightness of a soufflé.

Preheat the oven to 375°F. Spray a 2-quart baking dish with cooking spray.

In a medium saucepan, combine the milk, corn, cornmeal, and salt over medium-high heat and, stirring constantly, bring to a gentle boil. Reduce the heat to medium and simmer until the mixture thickens, 3 to 4 minutes. Remove from the heat and stir in the cheese. Allow to cool for 10 minutes. Add the egg yolks to the cornmeal mixture and stir until well combined.

BEFORE		AFTER
270 cal.	Sat. Fat 10g, Chol. 135mg Fiber 2g, Sodium 430mg	Sat. Fat 3g, Chol. 85mg Fiber 2g, Sodium 320mg	**180 cal.**

In a stand mixer or using a handheld electric mixer, beat the egg whites and cream of tartar until soft peaks are formed, 1 to 2 minutes. Fold the egg whites into the corn mixture until just incorporated and pour into the prepared dish. Bake until browned on top and set but still slightly loose in the center, 40 to 45 minutes.

Makes 6 servings

SERVING SIZE ¾ cup
PER SERVING Calories 180; Total Fat 7 g (Sat Fat 3 g, Mono Fat 2 g, Poly Fat 0.8 g); Protein 10 g; Carb 22 g; Fiber 2 g; Cholesterol 85 mg; Sodium 320 mg
EXCELLENT SOURCE OF Iodine
GOOD SOURCE OF Calcium, Magnesium, Molybdenum, Phosphorus, Protein, Riboflavin, Selenium, Thiamin, Vitamin B12, Vitamin D

STOVE-TOP BAKED BEANS

2 teaspoons olive oil
1 small onion, finely chopped
1 clove garlic, minced
One 8-ounce can no-salt-added tomato sauce
¼ cup dark brown sugar
1 tablespoon tomato paste
1 tablespoon white vinegar
1 teaspoon prepared yellow mustard
½ teaspoon garlic powder
½ teaspoon onion powder
½ teaspoon paprika
½ teaspoon salt
¼ teaspoon freshly ground black pepper
One 15-ounce can navy beans, preferably low-sodium, drained and rinsed
1 cup water

These beans have that slow-baked taste, but since they're cooked on the stove they are perfect for a summer supper when the grill is going outside and you don't want to heat up the house.

Heat the oil in a large saucepan over medium-high heat. Add the onion and cook, stirring, until translucent, 3 minutes. Add the garlic and cook for 30 seconds. Add the tomato sauce, brown sugar, tomato paste, vinegar, mustard, garlic powder, onion powder, paprika, salt, and black pepper and whisk to combine. Add the beans and water and bring to a boil. Reduce the heat to medium low and simmer until the liquid has thickened slightly, about 30 minutes.

Makes 4 servings

SERVING SIZE ⅔ cup
PER SERVING Calories 200; Total Fat 3 g (Sat Fat 0 g, Mono Fat 1.7 g, Poly Fat 0.3 g); Protein 7 g; Carb 38 g; Fiber 7 g; Cholesterol 0 mg; Sodium 360 mg
EXCELLENT SOURCE OF Fiber, Folate, Manganese, Potassium, Protein, Thiamin
GOOD SOURCE OF Calcium, Copper, Iron, Magnesium, Phosphorus, Vitamin A, Vitamin B6, Vitamin C

BEFORE	AFTER
290 cal. Sat. Fat 3g, Chol. 15mg Fiber 7g, Sodium 740mg	Sat. Fat 0g, Chol. 0mg Fiber 7g, Sodium 360mg **200 cal.**

COLORFUL COLESLAW

3 tablespoons grainy mustard

2 tablespoons honey

2 tablespoons fresh lime juice, plus more to taste

2 tablespoons cider vinegar

2 tablespoons extra-virgin olive oil

½ teaspoon salt, plus more to taste

¼ teaspoon freshly ground black pepper, plus more to taste

¼ large head red cabbage, cored and thinly sliced (about 4 cups)

2 large carrots, shredded

1 medium fennel bulb, halved, cored, and thinly sliced (1½ cups)

1 small red onion, thinly sliced

½ cup chopped fresh cilantro leaves

1 tablespoon poppy seeds

This dish is like putting your regular "white" coleslaw through a prism and having a rainbow of exciting color and flavor emerge on the other side. The sweet-tart honey mustard dressing, fresh cilantro, and peppy poppy seeds make it all the more extraordinary.

In a large serving bowl, whisk together the mustard, honey, 2 tablespoons lime juice, cider vinegar, oil, ½ teaspoon salt, and ¼ teaspoon black pepper. Add the cabbage, carrots, fennel, onion, cilantro, and poppy seeds and toss well to combine. Season with more lime juice, salt, and black pepper.

Makes 6 servings

SERVING SIZE 1 cup
PER SERVING Calories 120; Total Fat 5 g (Sat Fat 0.5g, Mono Fat 3.4 g, Poly Fat 1 g); Protein 2 g; Carb 19 g; Fiber 4 g; Cholesterol 0 mg; Sodium 350 mg
EXCELLENT SOURCE OF Vitamin A, Vitamin B6, Vitamin C, Vitamin K
GOOD SOURCE OF Fiber, Manganese, Potassium

	BEFORE	AFTER	
375 cal.	Sat. Fat 6g, Chol. 30mg Fiber 3g, Sodium 930mg	Sat. Fat 0.5g, Chol. 0mg Fiber 4g, Sodium 350mg	120 cal.

CARROT-RAISIN SALAD WITH PINEAPPLE

- ⅓ cup plain Greek-style nonfat yogurt
- 2 tablespoons mayonnaise
- 2 tablespoons fresh lemon juice
- 1 tablespoon honey
- ¼ teaspoon salt, plus more to taste
- ¼ teaspoon freshly ground black pepper
- 1 pound carrots (3 medium), peeled and shredded (about 4 cups)
- ¼ cup canned crushed pineapple, drained
- ¼ cup golden raisins

This salad has all the familiar creamy-crunchy sweetness you expect in a much healthier way, thanks to the yogurt-based dressing. The pineapple adds a juicy colorful twist. Just make sure you use canned because the active enzymes in fresh pineapple will react with the protein in the yogurt.

In a large bowl, whisk together the yogurt, mayonnaise, lemon juice, honey, ¼ teaspoon salt, and black pepper. Add the carrots, pineapple, and raisins and toss to coat. Season with additional salt if desired.

Makes 4 servings

SERVING SIZE ¾ cup
PER SERVING Calories 140; Total Fat 3 g (Sat Fat 0 g, Mono Fat 0.7 g, Poly Fat 1.5 g); Protein 3 g; Carb 27 g; Fiber 4 g; Cholesterol 0 mg; Sodium 280 mg
EXCELLENT SOURCE OF Vitamin A, Vitamin K
GOOD SOURCE OF Fiber, Manganese, Potassium, Vitamin C

BEFORE	AFTER
200 cal. Sat. Fat 2g, Chol. 10mg Fiber 4g, Sodium 440mg	Sat. Fat 0g, Chol. 0mg Fiber 4g, Sodium 280mg **140 cal.**

SOUTHERN-STYLE GREENS

- 1 tablespoon olive oil
- 1 large onion, chopped
- 2 cloves garlic, minced
- 1 pound collard greens, trimmed and thinly shredded
- 1 pound kale, trimmed and thinly shredded
- 1½ cups water
- 3 tablespoons white vinegar
- 2 tablespoons pure maple syrup
- ½ teaspoon salt
- ½ teaspoon smoked paprika
- ¼ teaspoon freshly ground black pepper
- Dash cayenne pepper

Long-cooked greens like collards and kale bring up the healthy end of Southern soul food, but even they can be loaded with pork fat, salt, and sugar. These mouthwatering greens, spiked with smoked paprika, cayenne, and a dash of maple syrup, prove you can have that down-home flavor without the downsides. Make sure you serve them with the liquid or "pot liquor" in the pan. After the low-and-slow cooking, that's where the big flavor and nutrients are.

Heat the oil in a large (at least 6-quart) pot over medium-high heat. Add the onion and cook, stirring, until translucent, about 5 minutes. Add the garlic and cook for 30 seconds. Add the collards, kale, and water and cook, stirring occasionally, until the greens begin to wilt and reduce in

	BEFORE	AFTER	
390 cal.	Sat. Fat 9g, Chol. 40mg Fiber 7g, Sodium 1280mg	Sat. Fat 0.5g, Chol. 0mg Fiber 7g, Sodium 370mg	**170 cal.**

volume, about 5 minutes. Add the vinegar, maple syrup, salt, paprika, black pepper, and cayenne pepper and stir to combine. Reduce the heat to low, cover, and cook until the greens are softened and the liquid in the pot has turned dark green, about 2 hours. Serve the greens with the "pot liquor."

Makes 4 servings

SERVING SIZE ¾ cup
PER SERVING Calories 170; Total Fat 5 g (Sat Fat 0.5 g, Mono Fat 2.6 g, Poly Fat 1 g); Protein 7 g; Carb 29 g; Fiber 7 g; Cholesterol 0 mg; Sodium 370 mg
EXCELLENT SOURCE OF Calcium, Copper, Fiber, Folate, Manganese, Potassium, Vitamin A, Vitamin B6, Vitamin C, Vitamin K
GOOD SOURCE OF Iron, Magnesium, Molybdenum, Niacin, Protein, Riboflavin, Thiamin

CREAMY POTATO SALAD
WITH EGGS, PEAS, AND CHIVES

1½ **pounds Yukon Gold potatoes, unpeeled (about 4 medium)**

4 **large eggs**

⅓ **cup plain Greek-style nonfat yogurt**

2 **tablespoons mayonnaise**

1 **tablespoon Dijon mustard**

1 **tablespoon white wine vinegar**

½ **teaspoon salt**

¼ **teaspoon freshly ground black pepper**

1 **cup green peas, steamed until tender (2 to 5 minutes) if fresh or thawed if frozen**

3 **tablespoons chopped fresh chives**

Come summertime, the beautiful farm-fresh ingredients inevitably lead me to this sumptuous potato salad, which is perfect for a picnic or a barbecue.

Place the potatoes in a steamer basket fitted over a large pot of boiling water. Cover and steam until the potatoes are knife-tender, 25 to 30 minutes. Remove from the steamer and allow to cool completely. Cut the potatoes into ½-inch cubes.

Place the eggs in a medium pot, cover with water, and bring to a boil. Reduce the heat to medium low and simmer for 9 minutes. Drain and rinse the eggs under cold water, or refrigerate until cool enough to handle, and peel them. Discard 2 yolks and then coarsely chop the remaining eggs.

In a large bowl, whisk together the yogurt, mayonnaise, mustard, vinegar, salt, and black pepper. Add the eggs, potatoes, peas, and chives and gently fold until combined. Cover and refrigerate to allow the flavors to meld for at least 1 hour and up to overnight.

Makes 6 servings

SERVING SIZE ¾ cup
PER SERVING Calories 160; Total Fat 3.5 g (Sat Fat 1 g, Mono Fat 1.1 g, Poly Fat 1.2 g); Protein 8 g; Carb 26 g; Fiber 4 g; Cholesterol 70 mg; Sodium 370 mg
EXCELLENT SOURCE OF Vitamin C, Vitamin K
GOOD SOURCE OF Fiber, Folate, Manganese, Phosphorus, Potassium, Protein, Riboflavin, Selenium, Thiamin, Vitamin A, Vitamin B6

	BEFORE	AFTER	
220 cal.	Sat. Fat 1.5g, Chol. 85mg Fiber 2g, Sodium 650mg	Sat. Fat 1g, Chol. 70mg Fiber 4g, Sodium 370mg	**160 cal.**

PASTA SALAD WITH GARDEN VEGETABLES

½ pound whole-grain rotini or other corkscrew-shaped pasta

⅓ cup plain Greek-style nonfat yogurt

3 tablespoons mayonnaise

¼ cup cider vinegar

4 medium carrots, shredded

1½ cups finely shredded purple cabbage

1½ cups cherry or grape tomatoes, halved (8 ounces)

2 ribs celery, chopped

½ cup chopped red onion

¼ cup chopped fresh cilantro leaves

½ teaspoon salt

¼ teaspoon freshly ground black pepper

This salad's creamy dressing is a nod to the deli-style standard so many of us are used to, but its bounty of colorful garden vegetables gives it a fresh appeal that puts it in another league altogether.

Cook the pasta al dente according to package directions. Drain and refrigerate to allow to cool.

In a large serving bowl, whisk together the yogurt, mayonnaise, and vinegar.

Add the cooled pasta, carrots, cabbage, tomatoes, celery, onion, cilantro, salt, and black pepper and toss well to combine.

Makes 6 servings

SERVING SIZE 1⅓ cups
PER SERVING Calories 210; Total Fat 3.5 g (Sat Fat 0.5 g, Mono Fat 0.8 g, Poly Fat 1.7 g); Protein 8 g; Carb 40 g; Fiber 6 g; Cholesterol 0 mg; Sodium 310 mg
EXCELLENT SOURCE OF Fiber, Manganese, Vitamin A, Vitamin C, Vitamin K
GOOD SOURCE OF Copper, Folate, Iron, Magnesium, Phosphorus, Potassium, Protein, Thiamin, Niacin, Vitamin B6

BEFORE		AFTER	
390 cal.	Sat. Fat 3.5g, Chol. 160mg Fiber 2g, Sodium 760mg	Sat. Fat 0.5g, Chol. 0mg Fiber 6g, Sodium 310mg	210 cal.

WALDORF SALAD

¼ cup walnut pieces

¾ cup plain Greek-style nonfat yogurt

2 tablespoons mayonnaise

1 tablespoon fresh lemon juice

2 teaspoons Dijon mustard

¼ teaspoon salt

¼ teaspoon freshly ground black pepper

1 large red apple, cored and diced (about 2 cups)

3 ribs celery, diced (1 cup)

½ cup halved seedless grapes

Crunchy walnuts and apples, juicy sweet grapes, and crisp celery folded together in a thick creamy dressing: this recipe has all the taste and texture that made this dish a classic, only it's much better for you.

Toast the walnuts in a dry skillet over medium-high heat, stirring, until fragrant and golden. Set aside and allow to cool, then chop coarsely.

In a medium bowl, stir together the yogurt, mayonnaise, lemon juice, mustard, salt, and black pepper. Fold in the walnuts, apple, celery, and grapes.

Makes 4 servings

SERVING SIZE 1 cup
PER SERVING Calories 150; Total Fat 8 g (Sat Fat 1 g, Mono Fat 1.4 g, Poly Fat 4.9 g); Protein 5 g; Carb 18 g; Fiber 3 g; Cholesterol 0 mg; Sodium 290 mg
EXCELLENT SOURCE OF N/A
GOOD SOURCE OF Fiber, Manganese, Protein, Vitamin C, Vitamin K

BEFORE	AFTER
430 cal. Sat. Fat 4.5g, Chol. 15mg, Fiber 3g, Sodium 510mg	Sat. Fat 1g, Chol. 0mg, Fiber 3g, Sodium 290mg **150 cal.**

SWEET-AND-TANGY THREE-BEAN SALAD

½ small red onion, thinly sliced into half-moons

¾ pound green beans, trimmed

¾ pound wax beans, trimmed

¼ cup honey

½ cup cider vinegar

3 tablespoons extra-virgin olive oil

½ teaspoon salt

¼ teaspoon freshly ground black pepper

One 15-ounce can kidney beans, preferably low-sodium, drained and rinsed

1 medium red bell pepper, trimmed and sliced into matchsticks

If you are usually a fan of three-bean salad, be prepared to be wowed. This dish, with its fresh green and wax beans, bright red bell peppers, and perfectly sweet-tart dressing, is what the jarred stuff always aspired to be.

To mellow the bite of the onion, place it in a bowl of ice water and allow it to soak for 30 minutes. Drain.

Place the green and wax beans in a steamer basket fitted over a pot of boiling water. Cover and steam until crisp-tender, about 4 minutes. Remove from the heat and allow to cool. Cut into 2-inch lengths.

In a large bowl, whisk together the honey, vinegar, oil, salt, and black pepper. Add the onion, green and wax beans, kidney beans, and bell pepper and toss to combine. Cover and refrigerate for at least 1 hour before serving.

Makes 8 servings

SERVING SIZE 1 cup
PER SERVING Calories 150; Total Fat 5 g (Sat Fat 0.5 g, Mono Fat 3.7 g, Poly Fat .06 g); Protein 5 g; Carb 23 g; Fiber 7 g; Cholesterol 0 mg; Sodium 160 mg
EXCELLENT SOURCE OF Fiber, Vitamin C
GOOD SOURCE OF Magnesium, Manganese, Potassium, Protein, Thiamin, Vitamin A, Vitamin K

BEFORE		AFTER	
200 cal.	Sat. Fat 2g, Chol. 0mg Fiber 4g, Sodium 860mg	Sat. Fat 0.5g, Chol. 0mg Fiber 7g, Sodium 160mg	**150 cal.**

CHOPPED FIXINS SALAD

2 cups chopped green leaf lettuce

2 cups chopped seeded tomato (about 2 medium)

½ cup chopped half-sour or full-sour dill pickle

½ cup chopped red onion

1 tablespoon extra-virgin olive oil

2 teaspoons red wine vinegar

½ teaspoon yellow mustard

⅛ teaspoon freshly ground black pepper

Sandwich fixins are familiar comfort food sides that don't often get the spotlight. I thought it would be fun to combine them all into one easy salad that makes them really shine. Try it as an unexpected alternative to coleslaw.

In a medium bowl, combine the lettuce, tomato, pickle, and onion. In a small bowl, whisk together the oil, vinegar, mustard, and black pepper. Right before serving, pour the dressing over the salad and toss to coat.

Makes 4 servings

SERVING SIZE 1 cup
PER SERVING Calories 50; Total Fat 3.5 g (Sat Fat 0.5 g, Mono Fat 2.5 g, Poly Fat .04 g); Protein 1 g; Carb 5 g; Fiber 2 g; Cholesterol 0 mg; Sodium 170 mg
EXCELLENT SOURCE OF Vitamin A, Vitamin C, Vitamin K
GOOD SOURCE OF N/A

BEFORE*	AFTER
375 cal. Sat. Fat 6g, Chol. 30mg / Fiber 3g, Sodium 930mg	Sat. Fat 0.5g, Chol. 0mg / Fiber 2g, Sodium 170mg **50 cal.**

* compared to coleslaw

chapter nine

DESSERTS

With scrumptious pies galore, creamy puddings, decadent cakes, and irresistible cookies, these homey desserts truly hit the sweet spot. They will make you feel like a kid again, nose pressed against the bakery glass or in your grandma's kitchen, carefree and delighted by life's delicious possibilities.

CHOCOLATE CHUNK COOKIES

3 tablespoons unsalted butter, softened

½ cup packed light brown sugar

¼ cup granulated sugar

2 tablespoons canola oil

1 large egg, lightly beaten

1 teaspoon vanilla extract

½ cup all-purpose flour

½ cup whole-wheat pastry flour or whole-wheat flour

½ teaspoon baking soda

¼ teaspoon salt

3 ounces dark chocolate (60% to 70% cocoa solids), chopped into chunks

These treats are dunkable happiness you can hold in your hand. They have the perfect tender-crunchy texture of a classic chocolate chip cookie, only these are studded with big chunks of top-quality chocolate. Eat them while they are still warm for their full gooey, melted impact.

Preheat the oven to 350°F. Line two baking sheets with parchment paper.

In a large bowl, mash together the butter and sugars with a fork until well combined. Add the oil and egg and beat until creamy. Stir in the vanilla.

In a medium bowl, whisk together the flours, baking soda, and salt. Add the flour mixture to the butter mixture and mix well. Gently fold in the chocolate.

Scoop rounded tablespoons of the dough onto the prepared cookie sheets, leaving at least 1½ inches between cookies to allow for spreading. Bake until the cookies are just set, about 12 minutes. Transfer the cookies on parchment to a rack and allow to cool. The cookies will crisp as they cool. Store at room temperature in an airtight container, where they will keep for up to 4 days.

Makes about 20 cookies

SERVING SIZE 1 cookie
PER SERVING Calories 110; Total Fat 5 g (Sat Fat 2.5 g, Mono Fat 2 g, Poly Fat 0.6 g); Protein 1 g; Carb 14 g; Fiber 1 g; Cholesterol 15 mg; Sodium 65 mg
EXCELLENT SOURCE OF N/A
GOOD SOURCE OF Manganese

BEFORE		AFTER	
120 cal.	Sat. Fat 4g, Chol. 20mg Fiber 0.5g, Sodium 85mg	Sat. Fat 2.5g, Chol. 15mg Fiber 1g, Sodium 65mg	**110 cal.**

KITCHEN SINK COOKIES

¼ cup natural almonds

2 tablespoons unsalted butter, softened

2 tablespoons canola oil

⅓ cup firmly packed light brown sugar

¼ cup natural unsweetened applesauce

1 large egg white

1 teaspoon vanilla extract

⅔ cup whole-wheat pastry flour or whole-wheat flour

½ cup old-fashioned rolled oats

¼ teaspoon salt

¼ teaspoon ground cinnamon

¼ cup chopped dried tart cherries

¼ cup chopped dried apricots

2 ounces dark chocolate (60% to 70% cocoa solids), chopped into chunks

Nonstick cooking spray

These toothsome cookies are loaded with goodies: two kinds of dried fruits, chocolate chunks, and almonds. With oatmeal and applesauce as well, they have nearly everything but the kitchen sink and boy, are they delicious!

Preheat the oven to 375°F.

Toast the almonds in a dry skillet over medium-high heat, stirring frequently, until fragrant, 3 to 5 minutes. Allow to cool, then coarsely chop.

In a large bowl, beat together the butter, oil, and brown sugar until well combined. Add the applesauce, egg white, and vanilla and stir to combine. In a medium bowl, whisk together the flour, oats, salt, and cinnamon. Add the dry ingredients to the wet ingredients and mix just enough to combine them. Stir in the almonds, cherries, apricots, and chocolate.

BEFORE	AFTER
150 cal. Sat. Fat 2.5g, Chol. 15mg Fiber 1g, Sodium 55mg	Sat. Fat 2g, Chol. 5mg Fiber 2.5g, Sodium 40mg **120 cal.**

Coat a baking sheet with cooking spray. Using 1 tablespoon of dough at a time, roll into balls and place 2 inches apart on the baking sheet. Press the cookies down with the palm of your hand to flatten slightly, which will help to keep them from spreading too much. Bake until lightly browned but still soft, 12 to 14 minutes. Transfer the cookies to a wire rack and allow to cool.

Makes about 18 cookies

SERVING SIZE 1 cookie
PER SERVING Calories 120; Total Fat 5.5 g (Sat Fat 2 g, Mono Fat 2.5 g, Poly Fat 0.9 g); Protein 2 g; Carb 15 g; Fiber 2.5 g; Cholesterol 5 mg; Sodium 40 mg
EXCELLENT SOURCE OF Manganese
GOOD SOURCE OF Copper, Fiber, Iron, Magnesium, Molybdenum, Phosphorus, Selenium

PEANUT BUTTER COOKIES

Nonstick cooking spray
¾ cup all-purpose flour
½ cup whole-wheat pastry flour or whole-wheat flour
1 teaspoon baking soda
¼ cup unsalted butter, softened
¾ cup smooth natural peanut butter
⅓ cup packed light brown sugar
⅓ cup granulated sugar
½ teaspoon vanilla extract
1 large egg

It's like magic the way a few simple ingredients can turn a basic pantry staple—creamy peanut butter—into this fabulous, melt-in-your-mouth, sweet-salty cookie.

Preheat the oven to 375°F. Spray two baking sheets with cooking spray.

In a large bowl, whisk together the flours and baking soda. In another large bowl, beat together the butter, peanut butter, and sugars until fluffy. Add the vanilla and egg and beat until well combined. Gradually stir in the flour mixture, blending well.

Shape the dough into ¾-inch balls, and place on the baking sheets. Use the tines of a fork to lightly flatten each ball, making a crisscross pattern. Bake until lightly browned, 10 to 12 minutes. Allow to cool on a wire rack.

Makes 42 cookies

SERVING SIZE 2 cookies
PER SERVING Calories 130; Total Fat 7g (Sat Fat 2 g, Mono Fat 0.8 g, Poly Fat 1 g); Protein 3 g; Carb 14 g; Fiber 1 g; Cholesterol 14 mg; Sodium 100 mg

BEFORE			AFTER	
170 cal.	Sat. Fat 4g, Chol. 20mg Fiber 1g, Sodium 100mg		Sat. Fat 2g, Chol. 14mg Fiber 1g, Sodium 100mg	130 cal.

DARK CHOCOLATE BROWNIES

Nonstick cooking spray

8 ounces bittersweet chocolate, coarsely chopped

2 tablespoons unsalted butter

1 cup whole-grain pastry flour or whole-wheat flour

¼ cup unsweetened natural cocoa powder

¼ teaspoon salt

¼ teaspoon baking soda

4 large eggs

1 cup packed light brown sugar

½ cup plain low-fat yogurt

¼ cup canola oil

2 teaspoons vanilla extract

¾ cup chopped walnuts, optional

With their intense chocolate punch, these super-moist, cakey brownies are meant for serious chocolate lovers only. All others need not apply.

Preheat the oven to 350°F. Coat a 9×13-inch baking pan with cooking spray.

Melt the chocolate and butter in a double boiler or heatproof bowl set over a pot of barely simmering water, stirring occasionally.

In a medium bowl, whisk together the flour, cocoa, salt, and baking soda.

In a large bowl, whisk together the eggs and sugar until smooth. Add the yogurt, oil, and vanilla and whisk to combine. Add the chocolate-butter mixture and whisk until blended. Add the dry ingredients to the wet ingredients, mixing just enough to moisten.

Transfer the mixture to the prepared pan and sprinkle with nuts, if desired. Bake until a wooden toothpick inserted into the center comes out with a few moist crumbs, 20 to 25 minutes. Allow to cool completely in the pan on a wire rack before cutting into 24 pieces.

Makes 24 servings

SERVING SIZE 1 piece
PER SERVING Calories 150; Total Fat 8 g (Sat Fat 3 g, Mono Fat 2 g, Poly Fat 0.8 g); Protein 3 g; Carb 18 g; Fiber 1.5 g; Cholesterol 40 mg; Sodium 55 mg

	BEFORE	AFTER	
190 cal.	Sat. Fat 7g, Chol. 55mg Fiber 1g, Sodium 35mg	Sat. Fat 3g, Chol. 40mg Fiber 1.5g, Sodium 55mg	150 cal.

LITTLE DEVIL'S FOOD CUPCAKES

FOR THE CUPCAKES:

24 mini paper cupcake liners
(1¼ inches in diameter)

½ cup whole-wheat pastry
flour

½ cup cake flour

½ cup unsweetened natural
cocoa powder

¾ teaspoon baking soda

¼ teaspoon salt

½ cup reduced-fat sour cream

⅓ cup low-fat buttermilk

½ cup canola oil

⅔ cup dark brown sugar

1 large egg

1 large egg white

FOR THE ICING:

¾ cup confectioners' sugar

4 teaspoons low-fat (1%)
milk, plus more if needed

2 ounces dark chocolate
(60% to 70% cocoa solids),
finely chopped

FOR SQUIGGLE DECORATION:

3 tablespoons whipped
cream cheese

¼ cup confectioners' sugar

Each of these adorably decorated cupcakes is the perfect portion of dense, moist chocolate cake topped with a dark chocolate frosting. A natural with a glass of cold milk, it makes you feel like a kid again.

Move the oven rack to the center of the oven and preheat to 350°F.

To make the cupcakes, put a cupcake liner into each section of 2 mini-muffin tins.

In a medium bowl, whisk together the flours, cocoa powder, baking soda, and salt. In a small bowl, stir together the sour cream and buttermilk well to combine. In a large bowl, beat together the oil, brown sugar, egg, and egg white until smooth and the color begins to lighten. Add one-third of the flour-cocoa mixture to the oil-sugar mixture and stir to combine. Add half of the sour cream–buttermilk mixture and stir until well combined. Repeat with half of the remaining flour mixture, the remaining sour cream–buttermilk mixture, and finally the remaining flour mixture, mixing well after each addition.

Distribute the batter evenly among the cupcake liners. Bake until a toothpick inserted into one of the cupcakes comes out clean, 13 to 14 minutes. Allow to cool slightly in the pan, then transfer to wire racks to cool completely, 10 to 15 minutes.

	BEFORE	AFTER	
200 cal.	Sat. Fat 6g, Chol. 55mg Fiber 0.5g, Sodium 50mg	Sat. Fat 2g, Chol. 10mg Fiber 1g, Sodium 85mg	**140 cal.**

Meanwhile, make the icing. In a small saucepan, combine the confectioners' sugar and milk and heat over low heat until the sugar is dissolved. Add the chocolate and stir until melted and the icing is the consistency of thick pancake batter; add more milk, if necessary. While the icing is still warm, spread about 1 teaspoon of icing on top of each cupcake. Let the icing harden completely, about 10 minutes.

For the squiggle decoration, put the cream cheese in a small microwave-safe bowl and microwave on high for approximately 10 to 15 seconds, until the cream cheese is melted but before it begins to bubble. Add the confectioners' sugar and stir until the sugar is dissolved. Allow the mixture to cool slightly and transfer to a small plastic bag. Snip just the very bottom corner of the bag, then force the icing to the bottom of the bag. Pipe a squiggle of icing down the center of each cupcake.

Makes 24 cupcakes

SERVING SIZE 1 cupcake
PER SERVING Calories 140; Total Fat 7 g (Sat Fat 2 g, Mono Fat 3.7 g, Poly Fat 1.5 g); Protein 2 g; Carb 18 g; Fiber 1 g; Cholesterol 10 mg; Sodium 85 mg
GOOD SOURCE OF Manganese

MINI CHEESECAKES WITH STRAWBERRIES

12 graham crackers (3 full sheets/45g)

1 tablespoon unsalted butter, melted

1 tablespoon water

2 tablespoons packed brown sugar

⅛ teaspoon salt

¾ cup part-skim ricotta cheese

6 ounces Neufchâtel cheese (reduced-fat cream cheese; ¾ bar)

⅓ cup sugar

¼ cup reduced-fat sour cream

Grated zest of 1 lemon

1 teaspoon vanilla extract

1 teaspoon gelatin powder

Nonstick cooking spray

6 small strawberries, thinly sliced

How nice to be able to indulge in an entire cheesecake and feel good about it after. These creamy little cakes with their crumbly graham cracker crust and crown of fresh berries are sized just right for one.

Move the oven rack to the center of the oven and preheat to 300°F. Place 6 cupcake liners in a 6-cup cupcake tin.

Place the graham crackers in a food processor and process until fine crumbs are formed. You will wind up with about ¾ cup of crumbs. Add the butter, water, brown sugar, and salt and pulse to combine. Distribute the crumbs evenly among the cupcake holders, pressing down to pack in firmly. Bake until just set, about 8 minutes. Allow to cool completely.

In a stand mixer or with a hand mixer on medium-high, beat together the ricotta cheese, cream cheese, sugar, sour cream, lemon zest, and vanilla until light and fluffy, about 1 minute. Place the gelatin in a small bowl and dissolve completely in 1 tablespoon boiling water. Spray the cupcake holders containing the baked crusts lightly with cooking spray. Spoon about ⅓ cup of the batter into each prepared cupcake holder on top of the crust. Place in the refrigerator and allow to cool completely, at least 4 hours. Garnish with fresh strawberry slices.

Makes 6 servings

SERVING SIZE 1 cheesecake
PER SERVING Calories 250; Total Fat 13 g (Sat Fat 7 g, Mono Fat 3.6 g, Poly Fat 0.8 g); Protein 8 g; Carb 26 g; Fiber 0 g; Cholesterol 40 mg; Sodium 240 mg
GOOD SOURCE OF Calcium, Phosphorus, Protein, Selenium

BEFORE		AFTER	
390 cal.	Sat. Fat 14g, Chol. 140mg Fiber 0g, Sodium 240mg	Sat. Fat 7g, Chol. 40mg Fiber 0g, Sodium 240mg	**250 cal.**

BANANA PUDDING WITH VANILLA WAFERS

2 cups cold low-fat (1%) milk

2 large eggs

⅓ cup plus 1 teaspoon granulated sugar

3 tablespoons cornstarch

2 teaspoons vanilla extract

24 vanilla wafer cookies

3 large ripe bananas, sliced

⅓ cup heavy cream

This classic Southern comfort is a parfait of custard-like vanilla pudding layered with slices of banana and vanilla wafer cookies. As the pudding sets, the wafers soften around the edges but their centers maintain a lovely crunch. I have lightened it here with low-fat milk, but have not eased up one bit on the sweet creamy indulgence of it.

In a medium bowl, whisk together the milk and eggs. In a medium saucepan, whisk together ⅓ cup sugar and the cornstarch until well combined. Gradually add the milk-egg mixture, whisking until smooth. Turn the heat to medium and cook, whisking constantly, until the mixture thickens and comes to a boil, about 6 minutes. Boil for 1 minute. Stir in the vanilla and remove from the heat. Chill in the refrigerator for 30 minutes.

Place 6 vanilla wafers in a layer on the bottom of a 1½-quart bowl or casserole dish. Layer with one-third of the banana slices. Top the bananas with one-third of the pudding. Repeat with two more layers

continued on page 270

	BEFORE	AFTER	
400 cal.	Sat. Fat 9g, Chol. 135mg Fiber 2g, Sodium 160mg	Sat. Fat 4.5g, Chol. 95mg Fiber 2g, Sodium 110mg	**300 cal.**

continued from page 269

of wafers, then bananas, then pudding. Cover tightly with plastic wrap and refrigerate until ready to serve, at least 3 hours.

Whip the cream with an electric beater until it begins to thicken. Add the remaining 1 teaspoon sugar and continue to beat until soft peaks are formed. Right before serving top the pudding with the whipped cream and crumble the remaining 6 vanilla wafers for garnish.

Makes 6 servings

SERVING SIZE 1 cup
PER SERVING Calories 300; Total Fat 10 g (Sat Fat 4.5 g, Mono Fat 3 g, Poly Fat 0.5 g); Protein 6 g; Carb 47 g; Fiber 2 g; Cholesterol 95 mg; Sodium 110 mg
EXCELLENT SOURCE OF Iodine
GOOD SOURCE OF Calcium, Potassium, Phosphorus, Protein, Riboflavin, Selenium, Vitamin B6, Vitamin B12, Vitamin D

SOFT AND CHEWY OATMEAL-RAISIN COOKIES

Nonstick cooking spray

2 tablespoons unsalted butter, melted

¼ cup canola oil

½ cup honey

¼ cup packed light brown sugar

1 large egg

¼ cup smooth unsalted almond butter

¾ teaspoon vanilla extract

1 cup whole-wheat pastry flour or whole-wheat flour

½ teaspoon baking soda

¾ teaspoon ground cinnamon

¼ teaspoon salt

2 cups old-fashioned rolled oats

⅔ cup raisins

These chewy, honey-sweetened cookies are my absolute favorite way to eat oatmeal! They taste incredibly decadent but they are 100-percent whole grain and have nutrient-rich almond butter instead of much of the usual butter.

Preheat the oven to 350°F. Spray two cookie sheets with cooking spray.

In a large bowl, beat together the butter, oil, honey, brown sugar, egg, almond butter, and vanilla until well combined.

In another bowl, whisk together the flour, baking soda, cinnamon, and salt. Stir the dry ingredients into the wet ingredients and mix to combine. Stir in the oats and raisins.

Scoop rounded tablespoons of the dough onto the prepared baking sheets. Bake for 6 minutes, placing one tray on the top shelf and the second on the bottom, then switch the trays and bake, until the cookies are golden brown around the edges but are still quite soft, 6 to 7 minutes more. Allow to cool on the tray for 2 minutes, then transfer the cookies to a wire rack to cool completely. The cookies will firm up as they cool. Store flat in a loosely covered container for up to 3 days.

Makes about 30 cookies

SERVING SIZE 1 cookie
PER SERVING Calories 110; Total Fat 4.5 g (Sat Fat 1 g, Mono Fat 2.3 g, Poly Fat 0.9g); Protein 2 g; Carb 16 g; Fiber 1 g; Cholesterol 10 mg; Sodium 55 mg
GOOD SOURCE OF Manganese

	BEFORE	AFTER	
120 cal.	Sat. Fat 2.5g, Chol. 20mg Fiber 1g, Sodium 55mg	Sat. Fat 1g, Chol. 10mg Fiber 1g, Sodium 55mg	110 cal.

DOUBLE CHOCOLATE BREAD PUDDING

Nonstick cooking spray
3½ cups low-fat (1%) milk
2 large eggs
2 large egg whites
2 teaspoons vanilla extract
2 tablespoons unsweetened natural cocoa powder
1 teaspoon instant espresso powder
2 tablespoons hot water
⅓ cup sugar
3 ounces dark chocolate (60% to 70% percent cocoa solids), coarsely chopped
½ loaf whole-grain Italian or French bread (8 ounces), preferably day-old, cut into 1-inch cubes

There is no better way to use leftover bread than to transform it into this sweet, custardy cocoa-infused pudding that's soft inside, crusty on top, and loaded with melted dark chocolate.

Preheat the oven to 325°F. Spray an 8-inch square baking dish with cooking spray.

In a large bowl, whisk together the milk, eggs, egg whites, and vanilla. Place the cocoa powder and espresso into a small bowl, add the hot water, and stir to dissolve, then add to the egg-milk mixture. Add the sugar and whisk well until dissolved. Stir in the chocolate.

Place the prepared baking dish on a rimmed baking sheet and arrange the bread cubes evenly in the dish. Pour the egg-chocolate mixture evenly over the top, tilting the dish to make sure the liquid is distributed evenly among the bread cubes and there are no dry spots. Allow to sit for 20 minutes for the bread to absorb some of the liquid. Bake until the top is browned and the inside is warmed through but is still moist, about 45 minutes.

Makes 8 servings

SERVING SIZE ⅔ cup
PER SERVING Calories 240; Total Fat 8 g (Sat Fat 4 g, Mono Fat 2.4g, Poly Fat 0.9 g); Protein 11 g; Carb 32 g; Fiber 4 g; Cholesterol 60 mg; Sodium 200 mg
EXCELLENT SOURCE OF Iodine, Manganese, Riboflavin, Selenium, Phosphorus, Protein
GOOD SOURCE OF Calcium, Copper, Fiber, Folate, Magnesium, Potassium, Iron, Vitamin B12, Vitamin D, Zinc

BEFORE		AFTER	
470 cal.	Sat. Fat 7g, Chol. 120mg Fiber 3g, Sodium 290mg	Sat. Fat 4g, Chol. 60mg Fiber 4g, Sodium 200mg	**240 cal.**

RUM-RAISIN RICE PUDDING

½ cup raisins

¼ cup dark rum

1 cup long-grain white rice

2 cups water

3½ cups low-fat (1%) milk

One 12-ounce can low-fat evaporated milk

⅓ cup honey

2 teaspoons vanilla extract

Rice pudding is one of my husband's most craved desserts and a good dark rum is one of his favorite drinks, so I put them together to really get on his good side. This vanilla-scented pudding is spiked with sweet plump raisins and just enough liquor to give it a deep flavor and tingly warmth.

In a small bowl, toss together the raisins and rum. Let the raisins soak in the rum as the pudding cooks.

In a large saucepan, combine the rice and water and bring to a boil. Reduce the heat to low and simmer, uncovered, until most of the water is absorbed but the rice is still a little wet, about 10 minutes.

Add 3 cups low-fat milk, the evaporated milk, and honey and bring to a simmer. Reduce the heat to low and cook, uncovered, stirring occasionally, until the rice is very soft and most of the liquid is absorbed but the mixture is still quite wet, 20 to 25 minutes. Stir in the vanilla, the raisins and rum, and the remaining ½ cup low-fat milk. Transfer to a container and chill completely. The pudding will thicken as it cools. Stir well before serving.

Makes 8 servings

SERVING SIZE ¾ cup
PER SERVING Calories 240; Total Fat 1.5 g (Sat Fat 1.4 g, Mono Fat 0.3 g, Poly Fat 0 g); Protein 8 g; Carb 46 g; Fiber 0.5 g; Cholesterol 10 mg; Sodium 95 mg
EXCELLENT SOURCE OF Calcium, Phosphorus, Riboflavin, Vitamin D
GOOD SOURCE OF Potassium, Protein

BEFORE		AFTER	
330 cal.	Sat. Fat 7g, Chol. 35mg Fiber 0.5g, Sodium 140mg	Sat. Fat 1.4g, Chol. 10mg Fiber 0.5g, Sodium 95mg	**240 cal.**

GRANDMA'S CHOCOLATE PUDDING

⅓ cup sugar

2 tablespoons unsweetened cocoa powder

3 tablespoons cornstarch

2 cups cold low-fat (1%) milk

1 ounce dark chocolate (60% to 70% cocoa solids), finely chopped

Some of my fondest food memories are of making pudding with my grandma—standing next to her on my step stool, stirring patiently and watching as the mixture warmed and thickened. The sweet aroma and anticipation was a pleasure in itself. To this day, I reserve the right to lick the spoon. This very chocolaty, velvety pudding is dedicated to her.

In a medium saucepan, whisk together the sugar, cocoa, and cornstarch. Gradually add the milk, whisking until smooth. Turn the heat to medium and cook, whisking constantly, until the mixture thickens and comes to a boil, about 6 minutes. Boil for 1 minute.

Place the chopped chocolate into a medium bowl. Pour the pudding over the chocolate and allow to sit for 2 minutes. Stir until the chocolate is melted and smooth. Transfer the mixture to a serving bowl, cover, and refrigerate until set, at least 3 hours.

Makes 4 servings

SERVING SIZE ¾ cup
PER SERVING Calories 180; Total Fat 4.5 g (Sat Fat 2.5 g, Mono Fat 1.4 g, Poly Fat 0.1 g); Protein 5 g; Carb 31 g; Fiber 2 g; Cholesterol 5 mg; Sodium 55 mg
GOOD SOURCE OF Calcium, Copper, Iodine, Magnesium, Manganese, Phosphorus, Protein, Riboflavin, Vitamin D

BEFORE	AFTER
Sat. Fat 15g, Chol. 145mg	Sat. Fat 2.5g, Chol. 5mg
Fiber 3g, Sodium 105mg	Fiber 2g, Sodium 55mg

420 cal. | **180 cal.**

PUMPKIN PIE

1 recipe Better Basic Pie Crust (recipe follows)

One 15-ounce can solid-pack pure pumpkin (not pumpkin pie filling)

1 cup low-fat evaporated milk

4 large eggs

½ cup packed dark brown sugar

1 teaspoon ground cinnamon

½ teaspoon ground nutmeg

¼ teaspoon ground ginger

¼ teaspoon ground allspice

1 cup whipped cream, optional

This autumnal pie has all the classic appeal—silky, cinnamon-scented pumpkin custard cradled in a flaky pie crust—only it is so much better for you thanks to a smart whole-wheat pastry and the use of evaporated milk which gives the filling body and richness without the fat.

Preheat the oven to 350°F. Poke a few holes into the bottom of the crust with a fork.

In a large bowl, whisk together the pumpkin, evaporated milk, eggs, sugar, cinnamon, nutmeg, ginger, and allspice until well incorporated. Pour the filling into the pie shell. Bake until the filling is just set in the center, about 1 hour. Allow to cool completely. Serve topped with whipped cream, if desired.

Makes 8 servings

SERVING SIZE ⅛ pie
PER SERVING Calories 240; Total Fat 8 g (Sat Fat 4.5 g, Mono Fat 1.5 g, Poly Fat 0.3 g); Protein 8 g; Carb 35 g; Fiber 3 g; Cholesterol 125 mg; Sodium 140 mg
EXCELLENT SOURCE OF Vitamin A, Manganese
GOOD SOURCE OF Calcium, Fiber, Iron, Riboflavin, Phosphorus, Protein, Selenium, Vitamin K

BEFORE		AFTER	
440 cal.	Sat. Fat 15g, Chol. 140mg Fiber 2g, Sodium 330mg	Sat. Fat 4.5g, Chol. 125mg Fiber 3g, Sodium 140mg	**240 cal.**

BETTER BASIC PIE CRUST

½ cup all-purpose flour

½ cup whole-wheat pastry flour or whole-wheat flour

¼ teaspoon baking powder

1 teaspoon sugar

⅛ teaspoon salt

3 tablespoons cold unsalted butter, cut into small pieces

3 tablespoons Neufchâtel cheese (reduced-fat cream cheese)

3 tablespoons ice-cold water

Nonstick cooking spray

Yes, you can have a flaky pastry crust that's better for you. By using half whole-wheat pastry flour you get whole-grain goodness without sacrificing lightness, and by adding reduced-fat cream cheese you get tenderness with less butter. As with all pastry, the key to success is keeping it cold until you are ready to bake.

Place the flours, baking powder, sugar, and salt in a food processor and pulse until well combined. Add the butter and cream cheese and pulse until the mixture resembles a coarse meal. Add the cold water and pulse just until a dough is formed. Shape the dough into a 5-inch-wide disk. Wrap it tightly in plastic wrap and chill in the refrigerator for at least 1 hour and up to 2 days.

When ready to bake, spray a 9-inch pie plate with cooking spray. Lightly flour a work surface and roll the dough out to an 11-inch circle. Drape the dough over the rolling pin and transfer to the prepared pie plate. Press the dough lightly into the pie plate, tuck the edges under, and crimp them. Bake according to the pie recipe directions.

Makes one 9-inch pie crust

SERVING SIZE ⅛ pie crust
PER SERVING Calories 110; Total Fat 6 g (Sat Fat 3.5 g, Mono Fat 1.5 g, Poly Fat 0.3 g); Protein 2 g; Carb 12 g; Fiber 1 g; Cholesterol 15 mg; Sodium 70 mg
GOOD SOURCE OF Manganese, Selenium

	BEFORE	AFTER	
170 cal.	Sat. Fat 5g, Chol. 15mg Fiber .5g, Sodium 150mg	Sat. Fat 3.5g, Chol. 15mg Fiber 1g, Sodium 70mg	**110 cal.**

PECAN PIE

½ cup mashed cooked sweet potato (about ½ medium sweet potato)

½ cup dark brown sugar

½ cup dark brown corn syrup

⅓ cup fat-free evaporated milk

2 large eggs

1½ teaspoons vanilla extract

¼ teaspoon salt

1 recipe Better Basic Pie Crust (page 276)

1 large egg white

1½ cups pecan halves

1 cup whipped cream, optional

When I first tasted this pie I could hardly contain my excitement. I felt I had found the holy grail of pie-dom: making one of the world's most craved, high-calorie desserts lighter and, dare I say, even better. The secret ingredients are mashed sweet potato and evaporated milk, which let you use a lot less butter and corn syrup than usual. I like it even better than a typical recipe because while it is intoxicatingly sweet, it is not cloyingly so.

Preheat the oven to 350°F.

In a large bowl, whisk together the sweet potato, brown sugar, corn syrup, evaporated milk, eggs, vanilla, and salt until smooth.

Brush the edges of the pie crust with egg white and pour the filling over the crust. Scatter the pecans evenly over the top of the filling. Bake until the filling is just set in the center, 50 to 55 minutes. Cool completely and serve with whipped cream, if desired.

Makes 8 servings

SERVING SIZE ⅛ pie
PER SERVING Calories 390; Total Fat 20 g (Sat Fat 5 g, Mono Fat 9.5 g, Poly Fat 4.5 g); Protein 7 g; Carb 49 g; Fiber 3 g; Cholesterol 70 mg; Sodium 220 mg
EXCELLENT SOURCE OF Manganese, Selenium, Vitamin A
GOOD SOURCE OF Copper, Fiber, Magnesium, Molybdenum, Phosphorus, Protein, Riboflavin, Thiamin

BEFORE		AFTER	
	Sat. Fat 13g, Chol. 115mg	Sat. Fat 5g, Chol. 70mg	
670 cal.	Fiber 3g, Sodium 350mg	Fiber 3g, Sodium 220mg	390 cal.

PEACH COBBLER

FOR THE FILLING:

4 large ripe peaches or 4 cups unsweetened frozen sliced peaches, thawed

1 teaspoon fresh lemon juice

¼ teaspoon ground cinnamon

2 teaspoons cornstarch

Light brown sugar, to taste

FOR THE TOPPING:

½ cup all-purpose flour

⅓ cup whole-wheat pastry flour or whole-wheat flour

¼ cup granulated sugar

1 teaspoon baking powder

¼ teaspoon salt

¼ cup low-fat (1%) milk

1 tablespoon unsalted butter, melted

2 tablespoons canola oil

¼ teaspoon ground cinnamon

FOR SERVING:

1 recipe Vanilla Cream Topping (page 283), optional

One of the most glorious things about summer is fresh, ripe peaches—honey-sweet, juicy, and alluringly aromatic. Why bury that natural goodness in loads of goopy sugary stuff as many recipes do? This cobbler lets the fruit shine—with just a touch of lemon and cinnamon, and a crunchy, cakey topping to make it all the more decadent.

Preheat the oven to 400°F.

To make the filling, if using fresh peaches, bring a 4-quart pot of water to a boil and fill a large bowl with ice water. With a paring knife, slice through each peach skin from end to end, but leave the peach intact. Place the peaches in the boiling water for 30 seconds. Using a slotted spoon, transfer the peaches to the ice water for 30 seconds. Remove the skin from the peaches. Split the peaches in half, remove the pits, and slice each peach into 8 slices.

In a large bowl, toss together the sliced peaches, lemon juice, cinnamon, and cornstarch. Add the brown sugar, 1 teaspoon at a time, to taste depending on the sweetness of the fruit. Pour the peach

	BEFORE	AFTER	
330 cal.	Sat. Fat 6g, Chol. 25mg Fiber 1g, Sodium 240mg	Sat. Fat 1.5g, Chol. 5mg Fiber 3g, Sodium 180mg	**210 cal.**

mixture into an 8-inch square baking dish.

To make the topping, in a medium bowl, whisk together the flours, granulated sugar, baking powder, and salt. Add the milk, butter, and oil and stir to combine. Distribute spoonfuls of the batter over the peaches, leaving some patches uncovered. Sprinkle with the cinnamon. Bake until golden brown, 30 to 35 minutes. Serve with a dollop of Vanilla Cream Topping, if desired.

Makes 6 servings

SERVING SIZE ¾ cup
PER SERVING Calories 210; Total Fat 7 g (Sat Fat 1.5 g, Mono Fat 3.6 g, Poly Fat 1.6 g); Protein 3 g; Carb 34 g; Fiber 3 g; Cholesterol 5 mg; Sodium 180 mg
EXCELLENT SOURCE OF Manganese
GOOD SOURCE OF Fiber, Selenium, Vitamin C

APPLE CRISP

FOR THE TOPPING:

⅓ cup old-fashioned rolled oats

¼ cup all-purpose flour

¼ cup whole-wheat pastry flour or whole-wheat flour

¼ cup sliced almonds

2 tablespoons toasted wheat germ

¼ cup packed dark brown sugar

¾ teaspoon ground cinnamon

¼ teaspoon ground nutmeg

⅛ teaspoon salt

1 tablespoon cold unsalted butter, cut into pieces

2 tablespoons canola oil

1 to 2 tablespoons cold water

FOR THE FILLING:

3 large Rome or Empire apples (about 1½ pounds)

3 medium Golden Delicious apples (about 1 pound)

3 medium Granny Smith apples (about 1 pound)

¼ cup fresh lemon juice

3 tablespoons pure maple syrup

2 tablespoons all-purpose flour

FOR SERVING:

1 cup Vanilla Cream Topping (1½ recipes, page 283), optional

Just the aroma of this crisp baking is sure to give you a serious case of the warm fuzzies—but that's only a hint of the satisfying taste to come. Three kinds of apples give the warm-spiced filling a delicious complexity with soft, sweet, tart, and toothsome all mingling together. And the almonds, wheat germ, and oats in the brown sugar–kissed topping provide a hearty toasted crunch.

Preheat the oven to 375°F.

To make the topping, place the oats, flours, almonds, wheat germ, brown sugar, cinnamon, nutmeg, and salt in a food processor and process until well combined. Add the butter and oil and pulse until lumps form. Add the water 1 tablespoon at a time until the dough just holds together when you press it between your fingers. Transfer to a bowl and using your fingers, press the dough to create several pea-size lumps for texture. Chill until ready to use.

To make the filling, leaving the peels on, core and cut the apples into ¼-inch-thick wedges. Toss the wedges with the lemon juice and

continued on page 282

	BEFORE	AFTER	
470 cal.	Sat. Fat 12g, Chol. 45mg Fiber 7g, Sodium 80mg	Sat. Fat 1.5g, Chol. 5mg Fiber 7g, Sodium 40mg	**280 cal.**

continued from page 280

maple syrup until well coated. Sprinkle with the flour and toss until well combined. Spoon the apple mixture into a 3- to 3½-quart shallow baking dish and sprinkle the dough evenly over the top.

Bake in the middle of the oven until bubbling, the apples are tender, and the topping is golden brown, 45 to 50 minutes. Serve with the Vanilla Cream Topping, if desired.

Makes 8 servings

SERVING SIZE 1 cup
PER SERVING Calories 280; Total Fat 7 g (Sat Fat 1.5 g, Mono Fat 3.7 g, Poly Fat 1.8 g); Protein 4 g; Carb 53 g; Fiber 7 g; Cholesterol 5 mg; Sodium 40 mg
EXCELLENT SOURCE OF Fiber, Manganese, Phosphorus, Vitamin C
GOOD SOURCE OF Magnesium, Thiamin

VANILLA CREAM TOPPING

¼ cup heavy whipping cream
1 tablespoon confectioners' sugar
¼ cup plain Greek-style nonfat yogurt
½ teaspoon vanilla extract

The yogurt in this creamy vanilla whip gives it a delightfully subtle cultured tang, making it especially good at bringing out the sweet-tart complexity in fruit desserts. Dollop it on a heap of fresh berries or on your favorite fruit crisp, cobbler, or pie.

Using an electric mixer, whip the cream until it is thickened. Add the sugar and continue to whip until it forms soft peaks. Gently fold in the yogurt and vanilla. The cream will keep in the refrigerator, covered, for 2 days.

Makes 6 servings

SERVING SIZE 2 tablespoons
PER SERVING Calories 45; Total Fat 3.5 g (Sat Fat 2.5 g, Mono Fat 1.1 g, Poly Fat 0.1 g); Protein 1 g; Carb 2 g; Fiber 0 g; Cholesterol 15 mg; Sodium 5 mg

BEFORE	AFTER
60 cal. Sat. Fat 3.5g, Chol. 20mg, Fiber 0g, Sodium 5mg	Sat. Fat 2.5g, Chol. 15mg, Fiber 0g, Sodium 5mg **45 cal.**

RUSTIC PEAR TART

FOR THE CRUST:

- ½ cup whole-grain pastry flour or whole-wheat flour
- ½ cup all-purpose flour
- 2 teaspoons granulated sugar
- ⅛ teaspoon salt
- 4 tablespoons cold unsalted butter, cut into small pieces
- 2 tablespoons low-fat buttermilk
- 3 tablespoons ice water

FOR THE FILLING:

- 3 medium pears
- 1 tablespoon fresh lemon juice
- 1 tablespoon plus 1 teaspoon cornstarch
- 3 tablespoons light brown sugar
- ⅛ teaspoon ground cinnamon
- 1 teaspoon honey
- ¼ teaspoon boiling water

FOR SERVING:

- 1 recipe Vanilla Cream Topping (page 283), optional

This easy tart has the casual elegance of a French country farmhouse. Fresh ripe pears are simply piled into a round of tender pastry, the edges are folded over, and the tart is baked to golden-brown perfection, then glazed with honey. It's impressive but totally fuss-free—you don't even need a pie plate to make it.

To make the crust, put the flours, granulated sugar, and salt in a food processor and pulse to combine. Add the butter and pulse about 12 times, until the mixture resembles a coarse meal. In a small bowl, combine the buttermilk and ice water. Add to the food processor and pulse 3 to 5 times, just until a dough forms. Shape the dough into a flat disk, wrap it in wax paper, and chill at least 1 hour and up to 2 days.

Preheat the oven to 425°F. Line a baking sheet with parchment paper.

To make the filling, peel the pears, core them, and slice them into ¼-inch slices. In a large bowl, toss the pear slices with the lemon juice. Sprinkle the cornstarch, brown sugar, and cinnamon over the pears and toss until the pears are evenly coated.

	BEFORE	AFTER	
300 cal.	Sat. Fat 9g, Chol. 35mg Fiber 4g, Sodium 55mg	Sat. Fat 5g, Chol. 20mg Fiber 4g, Sodium 55mg	**220 cal.**

On a lightly floured surface, roll the chilled dough into a large 9-inch circle. Drape the dough over the rolling pin and transfer to the prepared baking sheet. If the dough breaks, patch the holes with your fingers.

Arrange the pears in a mound in the center on the dough, leaving a 2-inch border. Fold the border over the filling. It will only cover the pears partially and does not need to be even.

Bake for 15 minutes, then, keeping the tart in the oven all the while, reduce the heat to 350°F, and continue to bake until the pears are tender and the crust is golden brown, about 40 minutes.

In a small bowl, stir together the honey and boiling water. Brush the honey glaze all over the top of the fruit and crust. Transfer the tart to a plate and allow to cool slightly. Cut into 6 wedges and serve warm or at room temperature with the Vanilla Cream Topping, if desired.

Makes 6 servings

SERVING SIZE ⅙ tart
PER SERVING Calories 220; Total Fat 8 g (Sat Fat 5 g, Mono Fat 2 g, Poly Fat 0 g); Protein 3 g; Carb 36 g; Fiber 4 g; Cholesterol 20 mg; Sodium 55 mg
GOOD SOURCE OF Fiber, Thiamin

PHYLLO CHERRY TURNOVERS

3 tablespoons cornstarch

3 tablespoons fresh lemon juice

1 cup water

3 cups halved and pitted fresh or frozen (thawed) sweet cherries

⅓ cup sugar

8 sheets frozen phyllo dough, thawed

3 tablespoons canola oil

Here flaky layers of phyllo dough form delectable pocket pies, plump with sweet cherry filling. You get all of the taste and texture you crave without the dense, high-cal pastry and heavy dose of sugar to weigh you down. These are so good in every way, you can't help but grin when you eat one.

Place the cornstarch, lemon juice, water, and sugar in a saucepan and whisk until the cornstarch is dissolved. Add the cherries, turn the heat to medium high, and, stirring, bring to a boil. Reduce the heat to medium low and simmer until the cherries have softened and the mixture has thickened, 10 to 12 minutes. Remove from the heat and let cool completely.

Preheat the oven to 375°F.

Place 1 sheet of the phyllo on a clean, dry work surface and brush lightly with some of the oil. Layer another sheet on top.

Using a pizza cutter or sharp knife, cut the phyllo stack in half lengthwise so you have 2 long stacks. Spoon about ¼ cup of the cooled cherry filling onto one of the phyllo stacks about 2 inches from the top.

BEFORE	AFTER
480 cal. Sat. Fat 16g, Chol. 60mg Fiber 2g, Sodium 370mg	Sat. Fat 0.5g, Chol. 0mg Fiber 2g, Sodium 95mg **180 cal.**

Fold the top corner of the phyllo stack over the filling to form a triangle-shaped pocket. Continue to fold the triangle-shaped pocket down the strip of phyllo in a way that maintains the triangle shape so a turnover is formed. Repeat with another ¼ cup of filling and the second stack of phyllo, then brush outside of each triangle lightly with oil. Repeat with the remaining phyllo, filling, and oil.

Place the turnovers on a baking sheet. Bake until crisped and browned, about 20 minutes. Serve warm or at room temperature.

Makes 8 servings

SERVING SIZE 1 turnover
PER SERVING Calories 180; Total Fat 7 g (Sat Fat 0.5 g, Mono Fat 4.0 g, Poly Fat 1.7 g); Protein 2 g; Carb 31g; Fiber 2 g; Cholesterol 0 mg; Sodium 95 mg
GOOD SOURCE OF Vitamin C

CHERRY BERRY GELATIN DESSERT

½ cup fresh raspberries

½ cup fresh blackberries

½ cup fresh blueberries

½ cup sliced strawberries

1 cup unsweetened tart cherry juice

2½ packets unflavored gelatin

½ cup honey

2½ cups water

½ cup Vanilla Cream Topping (page 283), optional

These smile-inducing dessert cups are just like the familiar jiggly red gel, only these are made with real cherry juice, honey, and fresh berries, so they're free of artificial ingredients and packed with antioxidants and fresh taste.

In a medium bowl, gently toss together the berries .

Place the cherry juice, gelatin, and honey in a medium saucepan and bring to a simmer over medium heat. Cook, stirring, until the gelatin dissolves, about 3 minutes. Stir in the water.

Fill 6 parfait glasses or cups with ¾ cup each of the cherry-gelatin mixture and ¼ cup of the mixed berries. Refrigerate until set, about 6 hours. Serve topped with a dollop of Vanilla Cream Topping, if desired.

Makes 6 servings

SERVING SIZE 1 cup
PER SERVING Calories 140; Total Fat 0 g (Sat Fat 0 g, Mono Fat 0 g, Poly Fat 0 g); Protein 3 g; Carb 34 g; Fiber 2 g; Cholesterol 0 mg; Sodium 15 mg
EXCELLENT SOURCE OF Vitamin C
GOOD SOURCE OF Manganese

	BEFORE	AFTER	
160 cal.	Sat. Fat 0g, Chol. 0mg Fiber 0g, Sodium 90mg	Sat. Fat 0g, Chol. 0mg Fiber 2g, Sodium 15mg	140 cal.

CREAMY VANILLA AND ORANGE POPSICLES

1 cup vanilla frozen yogurt

¼ cup mandarin orange segments, packed in water, drained

¾ cup orange juice

Like yin and yang on a Popsicle stick, it's no wonder this perfectly balanced combo of rich, creamy vanilla and refreshing orange is such a universally favorite frozen dessert.

Allow the yogurt to soften at room temperature until it is pliable and easy to scoop. Spoon ¼ cup of the yogurt into each of four 4-ounce Popsicle molds or small paper cups, pressing down with a spoon or small spatula to release as many air bubbles from the yogurt as possible. Place in the freezer for 2 hours.

Remove from the freezer and place 2 or 3 mandarin orange segments on top of the yogurt in each mold. Top with 3 tablespoons orange juice, then insert Popsicle sticks and return to the freezer for at least 5 hours or overnight. When ready to eat, loosen the Popsicles from the molds by thawing at room temperature for 5 minutes or placing the mold very briefly in warm water.

Makes 4 servings

SERVING SIZE 1 Popsicle
PER SERVING Calories 100; Total Fat 2.5 g (Sat Fat 1.5 g, Mono Fat 0 g, Poly Fat 0 g); Protein 2 g; Carb 16 g; Fiber 0 g; Cholesterol 10 mg; Sodium 25 mg
EXCELLENT SOURCE OF Vitamin C

BEFORE		AFTER	
160 cal.	Sat. Fat 6g, Chol. 60mg Fiber 0g, Sodium 60mg	Sat. Fat 1.5g, Chol. 10mg Fiber 0g, Sodium 25mg	**100 cal.**

ANGELIC AMBROSIA

½ cup pecan halves

One 20-ounce can pineapple chunks, packed in juice, well drained

One 11-ounce can mandarin orange segments, packed in water or light syrup, well drained

1 cup halved and pitted fresh or frozen (thawed) sweet cherries

⅓ cup unsweetened shredded coconut

⅔ cup mini marshmallows

1 recipe Vanilla Cream Topping (page 283)

This is an earthly fruit salad made heavenly tasting and cloud light with a sweet creamy dressing, puffs of mini marshmallows, shredded coconut, and crunchy pecans.

Toast the pecans in a dry skillet over medium-high heat, stirring frequently, until fragrant, about 5 minutes. Allow to cool, then chop coarsely.

In a medium bowl, gently stir the pineapple, mandarin orange segments, cherries, coconut, marshmallows, and pecans to combine. Fold in the Vanilla Cream Topping.

Chill, covered, for at least 1 hour before serving.

Makes 6 servings

SERVING SIZE about 1 cup
PER SERVING Calories 230; Total Fat 11 g (Sat Fat 4 g, Mono Fat 4.5 g, Poly Fat 2 g); Protein 3 g; Carb 31 g; Fiber 4 g; Cholesterol 15 mg; Sodium 15 mg
EXCELLENT SOURCE OF Vitamin C
GOOD SOURCE OF Copper, Fiber, Manganese, Thiamin

BEFORE		AFTER	
410 cal.	Sat. Fat 12g, Chol. 40mg Fiber 4g, Sodium 40mg	Sat. Fat 4g, Chol. 15mg Fiber 4g, Sodium 15mg	230 cal.

MULLED CIDER–BAKED APPLES

4 medium baking apples, such as Rome, whole, unpeeled, and cored (1½ pounds)

2 cups apple cider

6 tablespoons pure maple syrup

3 whole cloves

Zest of ½ orange

Zest of ½ lemon

2 tablespoons fresh lemon juice

4 cinnamon sticks

One of my most treasured food traditions—one I have enjoyed since childhood—is apple picking in upstate New York. Every year, when the leaves are in full color and the air is crisp and cool, I head up for the day and return with bags and bags of apples in every variety imaginable, some for eating and some for cooking. This recipe is one of my annual favorites. I like to simmer the apples until they are so soft you can eat them with a spoon but their skin stays intact so they are beautiful to serve. A touch of citrus gives just the right brightness to the maple-spiced cider syrup that's drizzled on top.

Put the apples, standing upright, in the bottom of a large saucepan with a lid. Add the cider, maple syrup, cloves, orange and lemon zest, and lemon juice. Place a cinnamon stick in the center of each apple and bring to a simmer. Reduce the heat to low and continue to simmer, covered, until the apples are very tender but not falling apart, 15 to 20 minutes. Transfer the apples to a serving platter and keep warm, covered.

Increase the heat to medium high and boil the cider mixture, uncovered, stirring occasionally, until it is slightly syrupy and reduced to about 1 cup, about 15 minutes. Strain the spiced cider syrup through a fine-mesh strainer, if desired, then drizzle over and around the apples.

Makes 4 servings

SERVING 1 apple and ¼ cup sauce
PER SERVING Calories 260; Total Fat 0.5 g (Sat Fat 0 g, Mono Fat 0 g, Poly Fat 0.2 g); Protein 1 g; Carb 66 g; Fiber 6 g; Cholesterol 0 mg; Sodium 10 mg
EXCELLENT SOURCE OF Fiber, Manganese, Vitamin C
GOOD SOURCE OF Potassium

	BEFORE	AFTER	
270 cal.	Sat. Fat 3.5g, Chol. 15mg Fiber 6g, Sodium 5mg	Sat. Fat 0g, Chol. 0mg Fiber 6g, Sodium 10mg	**260 cal.**

DOUBLE CHOCOLATE AND
BANANA MILKSHAKE

1 pint chocolate frozen
  yogurt or light ice cream

2 cups nonfat milk

1 tablespoon unsweetened
  natural cocoa powder

2 very ripe bananas, cut into
  chunks and frozen

1½ cups ice

Frozen ripe bananas make this rich chocolate shake naturally sweet, thick, and frothy.

Place the yogurt, milk, cocoa, bananas, and ice in a blender and blend until smooth. Divide among four glasses and serve immediately.

Makes 4 servings

SERVING SIZE 1½ cups
PER SERVING Calories 210; Total Fat 3.5 g (Sat Fat 2 g, Mono Fat 0.9 g, Poly Fat 0.1 g); Protein 8 g; Carb 39 g; Fiber 4 g; Cholesterol 15 mg; Sodium 105 mg
EXCELLENT SOURCE OF Calcium, Iodine, Phosphorus, Riboflavin
GOOD SOURCE OF Fiber, Magnesium, Manganese, Potassium, Protein, Vitamin B6, Vitamin B12, Vitamin D

	BEFORE	AFTER	
430 cal.	Sat. Fat 10g, Chol. 45mg Fiber 1g, Sodium 150mg	Sat. Fat 2g, Chol. 15mg Fiber 4g, Sodium 105mg	**210 cal.**

DARK CHOCOLATE PRETZEL CLUSTERS

4 ounces any shape thick-style salted pretzels

6 ounces dark chocolate (60% to 70% cocoa solids), chopped

Chocolate with a salty crunch is all the rage now—even the mass market candy makers have caught on. But some of us are long-time devotees. Dark chocolate–covered pretzels have been a favorite of mine since childhood, so when I found myself with a bag of broken pretzels what else could I do but smother them in the best quality chocolate and turn them into a mouthwatering candy cluster.

Line a baking sheet with wax paper.

Put the pretzels into a sealable plastic bag and crush them with a rolling pin or mallet into about ¼-inch pieces. You should wind up with about 2 cups of pretzel pieces.

Place the chocolate in the top of a double boiler set over barely simmering water. Make sure the bottom of the pan does not touch the water. Melt the chocolate, stirring frequently, about 1 minute. Remove the pan from the heat. Add the pretzel pieces to the chocolate and stir until well coated.

continued on page 296

	BEFORE*	AFTER	
150 cal.	Sat. Fat 3g, Chol. 0mg Fiber 1g, Sodium 150mg	Sat. Fat 3g, Chol. 0mg Fiber 2g, Sodium 130mg	**110 cal.**

*compared a packaged chocolate pretzel candy

continued from page 294

Scoop heaping tablespoon-size stacks of the chocolate-covered pretzel pieces onto the prepared baking sheet. Place the baking sheet in the refrigerator and allow to cool and set, about 20 minutes. Store and serve at room temperature.

Makes 12 servings

SERVING SIZE 1 piece
PER SERVING Calories 110; Total Fat 5 g (Sat Fat 3 g, Mono Fat 0.1 g, Poly Fat 0.1 g); Protein 2 g; Carb 16 g; Fiber 2 g; Cholesterol 0 mg; Sodium 130 mg

PINEAPPLE UPSIDE-DOWN CAKE

2 tablespoons unsalted butter, softened

⅓ cup packed dark brown sugar

Six ½-inch-thick pineapple rings

1¼ cups all-purpose flour

¾ cup whole-wheat pastry flour

½ cup granulated sugar

1 teaspoon baking powder

½ teaspoon baking soda

½ cup water

½ cup low-fat buttermilk

⅓ cup canola oil

2 large eggs

1 large egg white

1 teaspoon vanilla extract

This dense, tender vanilla cake with its decadent, caramelized pineapple topping is sure to overturn the notion that you need 3 cups of sugar and 3 sticks of butter to make this delightfully retro dessert.

Preheat the oven to 350°F.

Spread the butter on the bottom of a 10-inch nonstick layer cake pan. Sprinkle the brown sugar evenly on top of the butter, then arrange the pineapple rings on top of the sugar in one layer.

In a medium bowl, whisk together the flours, granulated sugar, baking powder, and baking soda. In another medium bowl, whisk together the water, buttermilk, oil, eggs, egg white, and vanilla. Stir the wet ingredients into the dry ingredients, mixing until well combined. Pour the batter over the pineapples. Bake until the top is lightly browned and a wooden skewer inserted into the center of the cake comes out clean, 30 to 35 minutes. Allow to cool, then invert onto a plate to serve.

Makes 10 servings

SERVING SIZE 1 slice
PER SERVING Calories 280; Total Fat 11 g (Sat Fat 2.5, Mono Fat 5.8 g, Poly Fat 2.5 g); Protein 5g; Carb 41; Fiber 2 g; Cholesterol 50 mg; Sodium 150 mg
EXCELLENT SOURCE OF Manganese, Selenium, Vitamin C
GOOD SOURCE OF Folate, Protein, Riboflavin

	BEFORE	AFTER	
480 cal.	Sat. Fat 14g, Chol. 120mg Fiber 1g, Sodium 150mg	Sat. Fat 2.5g, Chol. 50mg Fiber 2g, Sodium 150mg	280 cal.

INDEX

Note: Page references in *italics* indicate photographs.

A

Almond(s)
Apple Crisp, 280–82, *281*
Cereal Party Mix, 71
Crispy French Toast Fingers, 26–28, *27*
Kitchen Sink Cookies, 258–59
Sole Almondine, 200–201
Three Bears Porridge, 32
Ambrosia, Angelic, 290
Apple(s)
Coffee Cake, 39–40
Crisp, 280–82, *281*
Mulled Cider–Baked, 291
and Spinach–Stuffed Pork Chops with Mustard Wine Sauce, 157
Waldorf Salad, 251
Apricot(s)
-Ginger Dipping Sauce, 87
Kitchen Sink Cookies, 258–59
Arugula
French Bread Pizza, *114*, 115
Avocado(s)
Cream, 70
Five-Layer Mexican Dip, 54–55
Green Goddess Dipping Sauce, 186
Spread, BLT with, *124*, 125

B

Bacon
BLT with Avocado Spread, *124*, 125
Stuffed Potato Skins with Avocado Cream, 68–69
Banana
and Double Chocolate Milkshake, *292*, 293
-Pecan Bread, 49
Pudding with Vanilla Wafers, *268*, 269–70
-Walnut Multigrain Pancakes, 37–38
Bean(s)
Autumn Vegetable Curry, 208–10, *209*
Baked, Stove-Top, *242*, 243
and Beef Tacos, Crispy, 133–34
Black, Chili, Smoky, *204*, 205
Chili, and Corn Bread Pie, 206–7
Cincinnati Turkey Chili, *176*, 177–78
Easy Cassoulet, 179–80, *181*
Five-Layer Mexican Dip, 54–55
Green, Casserole with Crispy Shallots, 226–28, *227*
Loaded Nachos, 74–75
Minestrone Soup, 109
Navy, Soup with Ham, 102, *103*
Roasted Red Pepper Hummus, *52*, 53
Three- , Salad, Sweet-and-Tangy, 252
Beef
and Bean Tacos, Crispy, 133–34
Braised Brisket with Carolina-Style BBQ Sauce, *144*, 145–46
Corned, Hash and Eggs, 18
Country Fried Steak with Gravy, 142–43
Hamburger Healthier, 135

Horseradish, Cheddar, and Caramelized Onion–Stuffed Burgers, 147–48, *149*
Lasagna, Better, 128–30, *129*
New Classic Meatloaf, 139–41, *140*
Open-Face Philly Cheese Steak Sandwich, 112–13
Shepherd's Pie, 131–33
Stew, Hearty, *136*, 137–38
Stuffed Cabbage with Sweet-and-Sour Tomato Sauce, 150–51
Swedish Meatballs, 80–81
Berry(ies). *See also* Blueberry(ies); Strawberry(ies)
Cherry Gelatin Dessert, 288
Pumpkin Bread with Cranberries, *44*, 45
Three Bears Porridge, 32
Blueberry(ies)
Cherry Berry Gelatin Dessert, 288
Maple Sauce, 29
Muffins, Better, *34*, 35–36
Bread(s). *See also* Tortilla(s)
Banana-Pecan, 49
Better Blueberry Muffins, *34*, 35–36
Corn, with Sweet Corn Kernels, 21
Crispy French Toast Fingers, 26–28, *27*
Crumbs, Whole-Wheat, Light-and-Crisp, 73
French, Pizza, *114*, 115
Garlic Breadsticks, *234*, 235
Honey Whole-Wheat Cinnamon Raisin, 46–48, *47*
Mango-Stuffed Challah French Toast, 25
Pudding, Double Chocolate, 272
Pumpernickel Croutons, 105
Pumpkin, with Cranberries, *44*, 45
Zucchini-Walnut, 42, *43*
Breakfast and brunch
Apple Coffee Cake, 39–40
Banana-Walnut Multigrain Pancakes, 37 38
Buttermilk Waffles, 30
Citrus Salad with Cherries, 33
Cookies, 41
Corned Beef Hash and Eggs, 18
Crispy French Toast Fingers, 26–28, *27*
Mango-Stuffed Challah French Toast, 25
Mushroom, Onion, and Gruyère Quiche with Oat Crust, 22, 23–24
Quiche Lorraine with Spinach, 19–20
Three Bears Porridge, 32
Broccoli
-Cheddar Soup, *94*, 95–96
and Cheese Calzones, 211
Hamburger Healthier, 135
Sesame Chicken with, 172–73
Stuffed Potato Skins with Avocado Cream, 68–69
Brownies, Dark Chocolate, *262*, 263
Buckwheat and Bow Ties (Kasha Varnishkas), 229
Burgers, Horseradish, Cheddar, and Caramelized Onion–Stuffed, 147–48, *149*
Buttermilk Waffles, 30

C

Cabbage. *See also* Sauerkraut
Colorful Cole Slaw, 244

Cabbage, continued
Pasta Salad with Garden Vegetables, 250
Shrimp Spring Rolls, 84–86, *85*
Stuffed, with Sweet-and-Sour Tomato Sauce, 150–51
Cakes
Coffee, Apple, 39–40
Little Devil's Food Cupcakes, 264–65
Pineapple Upside-Down, 297
Calzones, Broccoli and Cheese, 211
Canadian bacon
Stuffed Potato Skins with Avocado Cream, 68–69
Carrot(s)
Pasta Salad with Garden Vegetables, 250
-Raisin Salad with Pineapple, 245
Cassoulet, Easy, 179–80, *181*
Cauliflower
Autumn Vegetable Curry, 208–10, *209*
Shepherd's Pie, 131–33
Skillet Mac and Cheese, *212,* 213
Cereal Party Mix, 71
Cheese
Baked Jalapeño Poppers, 72
Better Beef Lasagna, 128–30, *129*
Blue, Dip, *76,* 78
Blue, Rustic Mashed Potatoes with, 238, *239*
and Broccoli Calzones, 211
Broccoli-Cheddar Soup, *94,* 95–96
Cheesy Pizza Dip, 62
Chicken Alfredo with Zucchini Ribbons, *160,* 161–62
Chicken Parmesan, 163
Corn and Cheddar Spoon Bread, 240–41
Eggplant Rollatini, 214–15
"Everything" Parmesan Crisps, *90,* 91
French Bread Pizza, *114,* 115
Garden Tuna Melt, 118
Grilled Turkey Reuben Sandwiches, 119
Herbed Squash Casserole, 224–25
Horseradish, Cheddar, and Caramelized Onion–
Stuffed Burgers, 147–48, *149*
Loaded Nachos, 74–75
Mac and, Skillet, *212,* 213
Mini Cheesecakes with Strawberries, 266, *267*
Mushroom, Onion, and Gruyère Quiche with Oat
Crust, *22,* 23–24
Open-Face Philly Cheese Steak Sandwich, 112–13
Pimiento, 89
Quiche Lorraine with Spinach, 19–20
Scalloped Potatoes au Gratin, *220,* 221–22
Stuffed Mushrooms, 82–83
Stuffed Potato Skins with Avocado Cream, 68–69
Triple Onion French Onion Soup, 106–8, *107*
Cheesecakes, Mini, with Strawberries, 266, *267*
Cherry(ies)
Angelic Ambrosia, 290
Berry Gelatin Dessert, 288
Citrus Salad with, 33
Kitchen Sink Cookies, 258–59
Turnovers, Phyllo, 286–87
Chicken
Alfredo with Zucchini Ribbons, *160,* 161–62
and Biscuit Pot Pie, 164–66, *165*

Broiled Buffalo Wings, *76,* 77
Dogs in Blankets, 88
Easy Cassoulet, 179–80, *181*
Fried Rice, Spicy, with Peanuts, 174, *175*
Honey-Crisp Oven-Fried, *170,* 171
Marsala, 167–68
Noodle Soup, Three-Generation, 110–11
Parmesan, 163
Salad, Herbed, 169
Sesame, with Broccoli, 172–73
Chili
Cincinnati Turkey, *176,* 177–78
Smoky Black Bean, *204,* 205
Chili-Garlic Dipping Sauce, Creamy, 195
Chili Tortilla Chips, 56
Chinese Corn and Crab Chowder, 97
Chocolate
Chunk Cookies, *256,* 257
Dark, Brownies, *262,* 263
Dark, Pretzel Clusters, 294–96, *295*
Double, and Banana Milkshake, *292,* 293
Double, Bread Pudding, 272
Kitchen Sink Cookies, 258–59
Little Devil's Food Cupcakes, 264–65
Pudding, Grandma's, 274
Chowder
Chinese Corn and Crab, 97
New! New England Clam, 100–101
Cincinnati Turkey Chili, *176,* 177–78
Cinnamon Raisin Bread, Honey Whole-Wheat, 46–48, *47*
Clam Chowder, New! New England, 100–101
Cobbler, Peach, 278–79
Codfish Stew with Fennel and Orange Essence, 198–99
Coffee Cake, Apple, 39–40
Cole Slaw, Colorful, 244
Cookies
Breakfast, 41
Chocolate Chunk, *256,* 257
Kitchen Sink, 258–59
Oatmeal-Raisin, Soft and Chewy, 271
Peanut Butter, 260, *261*
Corn
and Cheddar Spoon Bread, 240–41
and Crab Chowder, Chinese, 97
Creamed, 223
Five-Layer Mexican Dip, 54–55
Kernels, Sweet, Corn Bread with, 21
Corn Bread and Chili Bean Pie, 206–7
Corn Bread with Sweet Corn Kernels, 21
Cornmeal. *See also* **Polenta**
Banana-Walnut Multigrain Pancakes, 37–38
Chili Bean and Corn Bread Pie, 206–7
Corn and Cheddar Spoon Bread, 240–41
Corn Bread with Sweet Corn Kernels, 21
Country Fried Steak with Gravy, 142–43
Crab
Cakes, Crispy, 194
and Corn Chowder, Chinese, 97
Dip, Devilish, 67
Shellfish and Okra Gumbo, 190–91

Cranberries, Pumpkin Bread with, *44*, 45
Cream Topping, Vanilla, 283
Crisp, Apple, 280–82, *281*
Croquettes, Herbed Salmon, *192*, 193
Croutons, Pumpernickel, 105
Cupcakes, Little Devil's Food, 264–65
Curried Creamy Egg Salad Sandwich, 123
Curry, Autumn Vegetable, 208–10, *209*

D
Desserts. *See also* Cookies; Pudding
    Angelic Ambrosia, 290
    Apple Crisp, 280–82, *281*
    Cherry Berry Gelatin, *288*
    Creamy Vanilla and Orange Popsicles, 289
    Dark Chocolate Brownies, *262*, 263
    Dark Chocolate Pretzel Clusters, 294–96, *295*
    Double Chocolate and Banana Milkshake, *292*, 293
    Little Devil's Food Cupcakes, 264–65
    Mini Cheesecakes with Strawberries, 266, *267*
    Mulled Cider–Baked Apples, 291
    Peach Cobbler, 278–79
    Pecan Pie, 277
    Phyllo Cherry Turnovers, 286–87
    Pineapple Upside-Down Cake, 297
    Pumpkin Pie, 275
    Rustic Pear Tart, 284–85
    Vanilla Cream Topping, 283
Devil's Food Cupcakes, Little, 264–65
Dips
    Apricot-Ginger Dipping Sauce, 87
    Avocado Green Goddess Dipping Sauce, 186
    Blue Cheese, *76*, 78
    Cheesy Pizza, 62
    Creamy Chili-Garlic Dipping Sauce, 195
    Devilish Crab, 67
    Five-Layer Mexican, 54–55
    Honey-Mustard, 66
    Mustard, Creamy, with Chives, 197
    Roasted Red Pepper Hummus, *52*, 53
    Triple Onion, 60

E
Eggplant Rollatini, 214–15
Egg(s)
    Corned Beef Hash and, 18
    Peas, and Chives, Creamy Potato Salad with, 248, *249*
    Salad, Creamy Curried, Sandwich, 123

F
Fennel
    Colorful Cole Slaw, 244
    and Orange Essence, Codfish Stew with, 198–99
Fish. *See also* Shellfish
    Codfish Stew with Fennel and Orange Essence, 198–99
    Fingers, Favorite, 196
    Garden Tuna Melt, 118
    Herbed Salmon Croquettes, *192*, 193
    Sole Almondine, 200–201
French Toast, Mango-Stuffed Challah, 25

French Toast Fingers, Crispy, 26–28, *27*
Fruit. *See specific fruits*

G
Garlic
    Breadsticks, *234*, 235
    -Rosemary Braised Lamb Shank with Creamy Polenta, *154*, 155–56
Grains. *See also* Cornmeal; Oat(s); Rice
    Buckwheat and Bow Ties (Kasha Varnishkas), 229
    Creamy Shrimp and Grits, 187–88, *189*
Grapefruit
    Citrus Salad with Cherries, 33
Grapes
    Waldorf Salad, 251
Green Bean(s)
    Casserole with Crispy Shallots, 226–28, *227*
    Sweet-and-Tangy Three-Bean Salad, 252
Greens. *See also* Cabbage; Spinach
    Chopped Fixins Salad, 253
    French Bread Pizza, *114*, 115
    Southern-Style, 246–47
Grits and Shrimp, Creamy, 187–88, *189*
Gumbo, Shellfish and Okra, 190–91

H
Ham
    Navy Bean Soup with, 102, *103*
    Quiche Lorraine with Spinach, 19–20
Hamburger Healthier, 135
Hash, Corned Beef, and Eggs, 18
Hominy
    Pork and Tomatillo Posole, 152, *153*
Honey-Mustard Dip, 66
Honey Whole-Wheat Cinnamon Raisin Bread, 46–48, *47*
Horseradish, Cheddar, and Caramelized Onion–Stuffed
    Burgers, 147–48, *149*
Hummus, Roasted Red Pepper, *52*, 53

K-L
Kasha Varnishkas (Buckwheat and Bow Ties), 229
Lamb Shank, Garlic-Rosemary Braised, with Creamy
    Polenta, *154*, 155–56
Lasagna, Better Beef, 128–30, *129*
Legumes. *See also* Bean(s)
    Simply Perfect Split Pea Soup, 104
Lemon-Dill Pita Chips, 57

M
Mac and Cheese, Skillet, *212*, 213
Mango-Stuffed Challah French Toast, 25
Meat. *See* Beef; Lamb; Pork
Meatballs, Swedish, 80–81
Meatloaf, New Classic, 139–41, *140*
Milkshake, Double Chocolate and Banana, *292*, 293
Minestrone Soup, 109
Muffins, Better Blueberry, *34*, 35–36
Mushroom(s)
    Better Beef Lasagna, 128–30, *129*
    Chicken Marsala, 167–68

Mushroom(s), continued
Green Bean Casserole with Crispy Shallots, 226–28, *227*
New Classic Meatloaf, 139–41, *140*
Onion, and Gruyère Quiche with Oat Crust, *22*, 23–24
Soup, Cream of, 99
Stuffed, 82–83
Mustard
Dip, Creamy, with Chives, 197
-Honey Dip, 66

N
Nachos, Loaded, 74–75
Nuts. *See also* Almond(s); Pecan(s); Walnut(s)
Spicy Chicken Fried Rice with Peanuts, 174, *175*

O
Oat(s)
Apple Crisp, 280–82, *281*
Banana-Walnut Multigrain Pancakes, 37–38
Breakfast Cookies, 41
Crust, Mushroom, Onion, and Gruyère Quiche with, *22*, 23–24
Kitchen Sink Cookies, 258–59
Soft and Chewy Oatmeal-Raisin Cookies, 271
Three Bears Porridge, 32
Okra and Shellfish Gumbo, 190–91
Onion
Caramelized, Horseradish, and Cheddar–Stuffed Burgers, 147–48, *149*
Triple, Dip, 60
Triple, French Onion Soup, 106–8, *107*
Orange(s)
Angelic Ambrosia, 290
Citrus Salad with Cherries, 33
and Vanilla Popsicles, Creamy, 289

P
Pancakes
Banana-Walnut Multigrain, 37–38
Crispy Baked Zucchini-Potato, 236–37
Pasta and noodles
Better Beef Lasagna, 128–30, *129*
Buckwheat and Bow Ties (Kasha Varnishkas), 229
Chicken Alfredo with Zucchini Ribbons, *160*, 161–62
Cincinnati Turkey Chili, *176*, 177–78
Hamburger Healthier, 135
Pasta Salad with Garden Vegetables, 250
Skillet Mac and Cheese, *212*, 213
Three-Generation Chicken Noodle Soup, 110–11
Peach Cobbler, 278–79
Peanut Butter Cookies, 260, *261*
Peanuts, Spicy Chicken Fried Rice with, 174, *175*
Pear Tart, Rustic, 284–85
Peas, Eggs, and Chives, Creamy Potato Salad with, 248, *249*
Pecan(s)
Angelic Ambrosia, 290
-Banana Bread, 49
Pie, 277
Three Bears Porridge, 32

Pepper(s)
Baked Jalapeño Poppers, 72
Chili Bean and Corn Bread Pie, 206–7
Open-Face Philly Cheese Steak Sandwich, 112–13
Pimiento Cheese, 89
Roasted Red, Hummus, *52*, 53
Smoky Black Bean Chili, *204*, 205
Phyllo Cherry Turnovers, 286–87
Pie Crust, Better Basic, 276
Pies
Chili Bean and Corn Bread, 206–7
Pecan, 277
Pumpkin, 275
Pimiento Cheese, 89
Pineapple
Angelic Ambrosia, 290
Carrot-Raisin Salad with, 245
Upside-Down Cake, 297
Pita Chips, Lemon-Dill, 57
Pizza, French Bread, *114*, 115
Pizza Dip, Cheesy, 62
Pizza-Dough Dippers, Rosemary, 61
Polenta, Creamy, Garlic-Rosemary Braised Lamb Shank with, *154*, 155–56
Popcorn, Paper Bag, 79
Popsicles, Creamy Vanilla and Orange, 289
Pork. *See also* Bacon; Ham
Chipotle BBQ "Pulled," Sliders, 120–22, *121*
Chops, Apple and Spinach–Stuffed, with Mustard Wine Sauce, 157
Shellfish and Okra Gumbo, 190–91
and Tomatillo Posole, 152, *153*
Porridge, Three Bears, 32
Potato(es). *See also* Sweet Potato(es)
Chips, Smoked Paprika, 58, *59*
Corned Beef Hash and Eggs, 18
Mashed, Rustic, with Blue Cheese, 238, *239*
Mashed, Smooth and Creamy, 233
New! New England Clam Chowder, 100–101
Salad, Creamy, with Eggs, Peas, and Chives, 248, *249*
Scalloped, au Gratin, *220*, 221–22
Shepherd's Pie, 131–33
Skins, Stuffed, with Avocado Cream, 68–69
-Zucchini Pancakes, Crispy Baked, 236–37
Pot Pie, Chicken and Biscuit, 164–66, *165*
Poultry. *See* Chicken; Turkey
Pretzel Clusters, Dark Chocolate, 294–96, *295*
Pretzels, Sesame Whole-Wheat Soft, 64–65
Pudding
Banana, with Vanilla Wafers, *268*, 269–70
Bread, Double Chocolate, 272
Chocolate, Grandma's, 274
Rice, Rum-Raisin, 273
Pumpernickel Croutons, 105
Pumpkin
Bread with Cranberries, *44*, 45
Pie, 275

Q

Quiche
Lorraine with Spinach, 19–20
Mushroom, Onion, and Gruyère, with Oat
Crust, *22*, 23–24

R

Raisin(s)
Breakfast Cookies, 41
-Carrot Salad with Pineapple, 245
Cinnamon Bread, Honey Whole-Wheat, 46–48, *47*
-Oatmeal Cookies, Soft and Chewy, 271
-Rum Rice Pudding, 273
Recipes
15 fix factors, 13–15
nutrition facts and comparisons, 11–12
Rice
Butternut Squash Risotto, 216, *217*
Fried, Spicy Chicken, with Peanuts, 174, 175
Pudding, Rum-Raisin, 273
Risotto, Butternut Squash, 216, 217
Rosemary Pizza-Dough Dippers, 61
Rum-Raisin Rice Pudding, 273

S

Salads
Carrot-Raisin, with Pineapple, 245
Chopped Fixins, 253
Citrus, with Cherries, 33
Colorful Cole Slaw, 244
Herbed Chicken, 169
Pasta, with Garden Vegetables, 250
Potato, Creamy, with Eggs, Peas, and Chives, 248, *249*
Three-Bean, Sweet-and-Tangy, 252
Waldorf, 251
Salmon Croquettes, Herbed, *192*, 193
Sandwiches
BLT with Avocado Spread, *124*, 125
Chipotle BBQ "Pulled" Pork Sliders, 120–22, *121*
Curried Creamy Egg Salad, 123
French Bread Pizza, *114*, 115
Garden Tuna Melt, 118
Grilled Shrimp Po'Boy, 116–17
Grilled Turkey Reuben, 119
Philly Cheese Steak, Open-Face, 112–13
Sauces
Avocado Cream, 70
Blueberry Maple, 29
Chunky Strawberry Topping, 31
Dipping, Apricot-Ginger, 87
Dipping, Avocado Green Goddess, 186
Dipping, Creamy Chili-Garlic, 195
Marinara, Quick, 63
Vanilla Cream Topping, 283
Sauerkraut
Apple and Spinach–Stuffed Pork Chops with Mustard
Wine Sauce, 157
Grilled Turkey Reuben Sandwiches, 119

Sausages
Dogs in Blankets, 88
Easy Cassoulet, 179–80, *181*
Shellfish and Okra Gumbo, 190–91
Seafood. *See* Fish; Shellfish
Sesame Chicken with Broccoli, 172–73
Sesame Whole-Wheat Soft Pretzels, 64–65
Shallots, Crispy, Green Bean Casserole with, 226–28, *227*
Shellfish
Chinese Corn and Crab Chowder, 97
Creamy Shrimp and Grits, 187–88, *189*
Crispy Crab Cakes, 194
Devilish Crab Dip, 67
Grilled Shrimp Po'Boy, 116–17
New! New England Clam Chowder, 100–101
and Okra Gumbo, 190–91
Oven-Fried Shrimp, *184*, 185
Shrimp Spring Rolls, 84–86, *85*
Shepherd's Pie, 131–33
Shrimp
Grilled, Po'Boy, 116–17
and Grits, Creamy, 187–88, *189*
Oven-Fried, 184, 185
Shellfish and Okra Gumbo, 190–91
Spring Rolls, 84–86, *85*
Side dishes. *See also* Salads
Buckwheat and Bow Ties (Kasha Varnishkas), 229
Corn and Cheddar Spoon Bread, 240–41
Creamed Corn, 223
Crispy Baked Zucchini-Potato Pancakes, 236–37
Garlic Breadsticks, *234*, 235
Green Bean Casserole with Crispy Shallots, 226–28, *227*
Herbed Squash Casserole, 224–25
Rustic Mashed Potatoes with Blue Cheese, 238, *239*
Scalloped Potatoes au Gratin, *220*, 221–22
Smooth and Creamy Mashed Potatoes, 233
Southern-Style Greens, 246–47
Stove-Top Baked Beans, *242*, 243
Sweet Potato Casserole with Meringue
Topping, 230–32, *231*
Smoked Paprika Potato Chips, 58, *59*
Snacks and starters
Avocado Cream, 70
Baked Jalapeño Poppers, 72
Blue Cheese Dip, *76*, 78
Broiled Buffalo Wings, *76*, 77
Cereal Party Mix, 71
Cheesy Pizza Dip, 62
Chili Tortilla Chips, 56
Devilish Crab Dip, 67
Dogs in Blankets, 88
"Everything" Parmesan Crisps, *90*, 91
Five-Layer Mexican Dip, 54–55
Honey-Mustard Dip, 66
Lemon-Dill Pita Chips, 57
Loaded Nachos, 74–75
Paper Bag Popcorn, 79
Pimiento Cheese, 89
Roasted Red Pepper Hummus, *52*, 53
Rosemary Pizza-Dough Dippers, 61